Table of Contents

CW01500626

PRACTICAL PROJECTS FOR OFF-GRID SURVIVAL

Build Field-Tested Step-by-Step DIY Solutions
To Secure Food, Water, and Energy
So You Can Live Prepared and Free in any Situation

J.D. Wright

Published by Ayana Publishing Co.
ISBN (Paperback): 979-8-9991380-1-9 | ISBN (Hardcover): 979-8-9991380-0-2 | ISBN (ebook) 979-8-9991380-2-6

Disclaimer

The information in this book is provided for educational and entertainment purposes only. It does not constitute legal, financial, medical, or professional advice. The author and publisher make no warranties, express or implied, regarding the accuracy or completeness of the content and disclaim all liability for any loss or injury resulting from its use. Always consult qualified professionals before acting on any information herein.

Medical Notice

The publisher and author are not licensed medical providers. First-aid techniques, natural remedies, and procedures described are intended to support off-grid preparedness, not to replace professional care. In an emergency, seek qualified medical assistance immediately.

"From the Fire" Story Disclaimer

All "From the Fire: Stories That Still Burn" accounts are based on publicly available sources such as videos, blogs, and news articles. Individuals featured have not reviewed or endorsed this book.

Trademarks

All product names and trademarks remain the property of their respective owners and are used for identification purposes only. No affiliation or endorsement is implied.

Printed in the United States of America
10 9 8 7 6 5 4 3 2 1

To my family and friends–

Thank you for your unwavering support, encouragement, and belief in me and this new adventure. This book wouldn't exist without you or my dearest friend, Oliver.

THE BOOK'S JUST THE BEGINNING
Unlock Your Access to the Off-Grid Survival Companion

This book gives you the knowledge—now here's where you put it into action.

The Off-Grid Survival Companion is a secure, password-protected site for verified book buyers. Inside, you'll find:

- Printable checklists and visual guides

- Step-by-step project diagrams

- Troubleshooting tools and curated recommendations

- Bonus content not available anywhere else

To unlock it, turn to page 184 to scan the QR code and get your access code.

Once inside, you can explore, download, and come back anytime.

Found this book secondhand?
Visit the landing page to learn how to get access.

Let's build something that works—starting now.

INTRODUCTION:
THIS ISN'T ABOUT THE APOCALYPSE

That evening is like every other. Setting your alarm, you flip through your phone, head to bed, and expect the next day to be the same.

But early in the morning, it is obvious that something is off.

The power is out. No big deal—it happens, and you still have your phone. But when you check your phone, there's no signal. "Huh?" You turn on the faucet. Nothing. "What's going on?" You open the fridge, and it's already warming up.

"Oh no."

By noon, the news had spread that the grid was down, and no one knew when it would come back up.

Within days, grocery store shelves are empty, fuel stations are shut down, and the ATM no longer works. Neighbors begin to panic. Law enforcement becomes overwhelmed, and aid won't be here anytime soon. "What am I going to do?!" It sounds extreme, but these situations aren't just hypotheticals. They have happened before—and they'll happen again. Maybe next time to you.

Natural disasters can cause destruction and disruption that upend and end lives. In 2021, a historic winter storm hit Texas, debilitating the power grid and leaving millions without heat or running water for longer than expected. Desperate residents stood in mile-long lines for drinking water.

Many were shocked to learn that over 240 people died that winter. It's hard to fathom when you're removed from the situation and just seeing or hearing about it. Disease can also bring our way of life to a halt. The most recent crisis was in 2020 when the COVID-19 pandemic upended everyone's lives. Global supply chains were disrupted, store shelves emptied, food prices skyrocketed, and even necessities were difficult to find. Many who hadn't prepared were suddenly faced with scarcity and delays.

We're familiar with what disaster looks like and the consequences that can come from it. Yet when disaster isn't staring us in the face, we rarely think about what would happen. Most cities have only three days' worth of food. When the grid fails, survival doesn't depend on government aid—**it depends on you.**

Whether you want to get independence or just a backup plan, this book provides practical strategies to help you prepare at any level.

This guidebook is for anyone who wants to take back control, whether you are a prepper, exploring energy independence, or have children just starting to question the systems we all rely on. You might be rural, suburban, or even urban. Maybe you're just prepping for short-term outages or perhaps you're ready to unplug from the grid entirely. **Wherever you're starting from, this guide is built to meet you there.**

The Illusion of Stability: Disaster Reveals System Flaws

The conveniences of modern life have lulled us into complacency. We assume water will always flow from the tap, food will always be stocked at the store, and

Day 1
The power goes out.
You assume it will return soon.

Day 2
No water. Perishable food spoils.
Grocery shelves empty.

Day 3
Emergency services are stretched thin. Gas stations run dry.
PANIC SPREADS.

Day 4
Crime rises. Unprepared families begin to scavenge for essentials.

Day 7+
Government aid is delayed.

The unprepared struggle.
The prepared remained secure.
WHAT WILL YOUR STORY BE?

power will always be available at the flick of a switch. But what if it wasn't? Power grids fail, water systems become contaminated, and supply chains break down. What seems like an inconvenience at first can spiral into a full-scale crisis.

What You'll Learn in This Book

In the chapters ahead, you'll learn how to secure safe water, set up off-grid energy, grow and store food, stay warm, manage sanitation, communicate during disruptions, and protect your home when systems fail. You'll also explore how to scale your efforts building a lifestyle that fits your values, land, and budget.

But this book goes beyond just ideas. You'll find:

- Step-by-step breakdowns of DIY systems that are beginner-friendly and practical, without costly trial and error.
- Troubleshooting tips and backup strategies for when things don't go as planned—so you know what to do when a system breaks or fails.
- Adaptable for any climate, region, or land type—rural or urban, hot or cold, dry or humid.
- Printable checklists, build guides, and visual references to help you take action confidently, even if you're just getting started.
- Innovative planning tools to personalize your off-grid journey based on your land, household, and priorities.
- "From the Fire. Stories That Still Burn." Stories from everyday off-gridders— sharing what worked, what didn't, and what they wish they'd known.
- Each chapter includes QR codes linking to bonus tools, real-world examples, and printable resources in the Off-Grid Survival Companion.

Icons throughout the book help you find what you need, fast.

 STEP-BY-STEP PROJECT
DIY Instructions

 CHECKLIST
Build a System That's Safe

 FROM THE FIRE.
Stories That Still Burn.

These icons help you spot exactly what you need, right when you need it—whether you're reading cover to cover or flipping to a section in a moment of urgency.

Whether you're new to off-grid living or looking to improve the systems you already have, this guide meets you where you are offering clear next steps, climate-aware solutions, and practical strategies to help you move forward with confidence.

When the lights go out, will you be left in the dark? This book will show you how to secure your water, energy, and food before disaster strikes.

The Power of Self-Sufficiency

Off-grid survival and emergency preparedness are about freedom, not fear. They allow you to take control of your critical resources so you're not vulnerable when the system fails.

Some think that living off the grid requires giving up comfort or shutting yourself away from the world. Ultimately, living off the grid is more about having control than it is about giving things up.

- **Your electricity will stay on even if the grid goes down.**

- **Your water supply will continue even if there are issues with the city pipes.**

- **You will not have to worry about food security with bare grocery store shelves.**

Surprisingly, off-grid living is not limited to the rich or those who are deeply into survival skills. A lot of people begin by decreasing their dependence on public utilities while still enjoying the modern conveniences.

You don't need to overhaul your life overnight. The best off-grid setups grow in layers—one system, one skill at a time.

But to get there, you need to plan wisely and avoid the mistakes that sabotage too many off-grid journeys.

Family Dynamics and Off-Grid Planning

Whether you're planning for yourself or your whole family, going off-grid introduces a shift in routines, expectations, and even relationships. That's not a bad thing, but it does deserve some thought.

If you have a spouse, partner, or children, include them in your early conversations. Not everyone may be equally ready or excited. In fact, one of the most common reader questions we hear is:

What if my partner doesn't want to live off-grid? or
How do I include my kids without making them hate it?

Throughout this book, you'll find family-focused sidebars to help you:

- **Involve kids in food, water, and power systems in safe, empowering ways**
- **Navigate different comfort levels with prepping or off-grid lifestyle changes**
- **Adapt system designs with shared responsibilities in mind**

This book is designed to support your journey even if your household isn't 100% aligned yet. Start where you are, and invite your family into the process.

Avoiding Common Off-Grid Mistakes

Making the move to off-grid living is a significant shift in lifestyle. It provides a sense of freedom, but it also creates its own set of obstacles. Many novices often encounter major mistakes that lead to wasted resources, time, and money. Yet, these kinds of errors can be avoided with enough preparation.

Underestimating Power and Water Needs

One of the biggest mistakes new off-gridders make is failing to assess how much power and water they actually need. This is not fiction. These types of breakdowns have already happened—in big ways.

When your systems fail, it's not just inconvenient it can become dangerous quickly. The most innovative way to avoid those costly mistakes is to learn from the people who've experienced them.

FROM THE FIRE. STORIES THAT STILL BURN.
What They Did, What They'd Do Differently

Throughout this book, you'll hear directly from people who've done what you're working toward off-gridders, homesteaders, and everyday preppers who've learned by doing. These stories are pulled from real lives, not idealized examples, so you can see what worked, what didn't, and what they'd do differently.

You'll meet some of them more than once, as their experiences offer different lessons at different stages of the journey. These voices are here to keep the content grounded in reality and to remind you that no one builds it all at once.

FROM THE FIRE. STORIES THAT STILL BURN.
Regan and Kirsty's path to a reliable solar setup

After nine months of living off-grid, Regan and Kirsty Perry—the husband-and-wife team behind Rustic Spirits Homestead—discovered that even well-researched solar systems can fall short without real-world testing.

Early in their build, they installed solar gear in a full-sun area near the panels but underestimated how intense the summer heat would get. Their batteries and electronics began overheating, putting their entire system at risk. Their fix? A shade structure, better airflow, and plans for future upgrades like ventilation and insulation to protect system longevity.

They also miscalculated solar orientation. By aligning the array with their tiny home, slightly off true north, they created unexpected morning shadows. Combined with older solar panels that underperform in partial shade, this caused a noticeable energy loss. Eventually, they relocated the panels and adjusted the tilt angle seasonally to maximize efficiency.

 ————————————————————————

You might not make the same mistakes we made, but you can certainly learn the lessons we've learned. — Regan and Kirsty, Rustic Spirits Homestead.

————————————————————————

What They'd Do Differently: Stay flexible. Build systems that allow for adjustment as you learn more about your land, your seasons, and your energy needs. Planning for change made all the difference.

SCAN ME

Want to see what went wrong—and how they fixed it?
Watch Regan and Kirsty's full story: "We Seriously MISCALCULATED When We Set Up Our Off-Grid Solar System".

Planning for change made all the difference.

Their story is a powerful reminder that even well-planned systems need room to evolve. But not every off-grid journey begins with a detailed blueprint—or even a full budget.

 FROM THE FIRE. STORIES THAT STILL BURN.
Jay and Jen Didn't Build It All at Once—You Don't Have To Either

They didn't go off-grid with a considerable investment or a perfect plan. They started small—installing a few solar panels, gradually adding batteries, and learning as they went. With no formal background in solar, they built a DIY system for under $4,000 that powers their entire off-grid cabin in northern Michigan.

Over time, they upgraded their system with an inverter, charge controller, and tracking mount, optimizing for limited sunlight and harsh winters. Their choices reflected their budget, their land, and their lifestyle—and they avoided the trap of trying to do everything at once.

> *You don't need tens of thousands of dollars to live off-grid. We built this system ourselves, one step at a time, and it's been powering our cabin for over three years. —Jay, Off Grid with Jay and Jen.*

What They'd Do Differently: It's okay to grow into off-grid life. Starting small isn't a failure—it's freedom. By focusing on one need at a time, they avoided burnout and built a system that truly works for *them*. Their biggest win? Knowing they didn't have to have it all figured out on day one.

Jay and Jen's story reflects a different kind of wisdom—about pacing, priorities, and building freedom without needing perfection.

SCAN ME

Want to apply what you're learning right from the start?
Access printable tools, visuals, and checklists at the Off-Grid Survival Companion Site—designed to help you assess, plan, and take action.

From Hesitation to Momentum:
Your Off-Grid Journey Starts Here

Off-grid living isn't built in a day. It's built in moments of persistence—testing ideas, learning from mistakes, and adapting as you go. The stories you've just read prove that even seasoned off-gridders face challenges, but each problem solved brings them one step closer to freedom.

By picking up this book, you've already taken the first step toward a more independent and resilient life.

Now, it's time to take control.

CHAPTER 1: Mindset First, Tools Second – or You're Building on Sand

Living off-grid means adopting a way of life that prioritizes sustainability, resilience, and independence. In the modern world, where most people rely heavily on centralized utilities for water, electricity, food, and waste disposal, going off-grid offers an alternative path, one that provides not only self-sufficiency but also a deeper connection to the earth and the resources that sustain us.

What Is Off-Grid Living?

Simply put, off-grid life is about rejecting the conventional grid-based systems providing utilities and energy. Off-grid people or homes create their systems to satisfy these basic needs rather than depending on municipal power lines, water services, and food distribution networks. Install solar panels and wind turbines for electricity; gather and filter rainwater; grow and preserve food; use greywater or composting systems to control waste.

Off-Grid vs. Homesteading

Although the terms are sometimes used synonymously, homesteading and off-grid living differ in many ways. Homesteading typically focuses on long-term agricultural self-reliance: raising animals, growing crops, and developing permaculture systems to provide food year-round. Off-grid living, on the other hand, can be applied in various environments, urban, suburban, or rural and emphasizes independence from external utilities and survival readiness rather than solely relying on land-based food production. Both approaches share the goal of self-reliance but differ in their methods and focus.

Building a Resilient Off-Grid Setup, Phase by Phase

Transitioning off-grid isn't an all-at-once process. This phased approach helps you meet your most critical needs first, like food, water, and power, while giving you a path to grow your setup over time. Use the outline below to strengthen your off-grid survival system without overcomplicating it.

PHASE 1:	**PHASE 2:**	**PHASE 3:**
Build a Stable Foundation	**Strengthen Core Systems**	**Optimize for Self-Sufficiency**

Timeframe: 0–6 Months	**Timeframe:** 6–18 Months	**Timeframe:** 18+ Months
Install a basic solar setup, establish rainwater collection, and grow a small garden for short-term food resilience. Learn basic food preservation and emergency filtration.	Expand your solar power and battery storage, introduce greywater reuse, and plant hardy perennials or herbs that thrive in your climate. Add indoor or container growing options if conditions are harsh.	Ensure your essentials— energy, water, and food —run smoothly and reliably. Use this phase to fine-tune storage, diversify energy, and add redundancies that boost survival confidence.

Overcoming Early Off-Grid Challenges

Many underestimate the challenges of transitioning to off-grid living, including steep learning curves, unexpected system failures, and adjusting to life without traditional conveniences. Some struggle with information overload, decision paralysis, or financial miscalculations. However, with the right approach, these challenges can be managed.

When You're Not Doing This Alone

Not everyone may be equally excited—or ready—to shift into an off-grid mindset. That's normal. Whether you're navigating skepticism, fear, or different comfort levels, you don't need perfect alignment to start.

Here's how to move forward together:

- **Start with small wins. Involve kids in safe, hands-on tasks like filtering water or checking solar output.**

- **Respect different paces. Let family members engage at their level while you quietly build systems they benefit from.**

- **Make it part of life, not pressure. Off-grid routines work best when they feel empowering, not forced.**

Even if you're solo for now, design your systems to scale. When others are ready, they'll have a strong foundation to step into.

Already Off-Grid or Transitioning?

This book is structured with beginners in mind, but that doesn't mean you'll be bored if you're already living off-grid or actively transitioning.

Throughout each chapter, we include advanced upgrade suggestions, layered decision-making tools, and troubleshooting boxes that speak directly to experienced readers. If you've already tackled the basics, look for these callouts like the one to the right.

Every system in this book is designed to grow with you. Even experienced off-gridders can struggle when they try to do too much, too fast. Others have learned that the hard way.

Only Have $100? Start Here.

You don't need thousands of dollars to start building resilience. For under $100, you can buy:

- A rain barrel or water storage container
- A Sawyer Mini or LifeStraw water filter
- A basic USB solar charger

These three items give you immediate access to off-grid water and backup power—no land required.

Focused on emergency readiness first?

It's okay to address your most urgent needs while still building your foundation. The tools in this book are flexible—use what serves you now, and come back to the rest as you grow your systems.

 ## CHECKLIST
Conduct a Weekend Test

Over a single weekend, turn off your utilities and rely solely on your backup power, stored water, and pantry supplies. Use this checklist to build confidence and uncover weak points—before an actual emergency does it for you.

Start on a Friday evening:

☐ **Power Up:** Charge your solar generator and test any backup power sources (solar, gas, or battery bank).

- **Common issues:** Inverter not powering larger appliances, overloading circuits, or batteries draining faster than expected.

- **Quick fixes:** Unplug non-essentials, rotate devices, use low-wattage lighting only, and check connections.

☐ **Water Ready:** Ensure stored water is accessible (not frozen, appropriately sealed) and test at least one method of purification (boiling, carbon filter, gravity-fed, etc.).

- Don't rely on taste—run the whole purification process to evaluate speed, ease of use, and clarity.

- **Avoid Duplication:** This test does not replace full water setup planning in Chapter 2, but gives you a real-world check on your backup readiness.

☐ **Food Supply:** Use only shelf-stable emergency food from your pantry: canned goods, dehydrated meals, rice, beans, pasta, and nut butters.

- Try preparing meals with limited cooking tools (rocket stove, solar oven, etc.) if available.

- **Evaluate:** Are meals satisfying, nutritious, and realistic to prepare without grid power?

☐ **Grid Off:** Turn off your home's main breaker (or individual systems: HVAC, water heater, internet router).

- You do not need to call the utility company for a short shutoff, but you should notify household members for safety.

- Check if you can still flush a toilet. Do any "phantom loads" still draw power?

☐ **Document Everything:** Keep a running log (notebook or voice memo) of every success, failure, or frustration.

- **Prompt ideas:** "What did I wish I had right now?" "What surprised me?" "What drained power fastest?"

- Try journaling in periods to catch fatigue patterns or overlooked needs.

☐ **Evaluate:** At the end, list every system that fell short or wasn't covered.

- **Examples:** Water ran out on Day 2 → need more containers. Battery bank died overnight → need insulation or second unit. Cooking was too slow → need backup fuel or alternate method.

- **Action Step:** Mark priority fixes and check your next chapter for tools or worksheets that help fill the gap.

What you learn during a short test run can be eye-opening—but it's just the beginning. Trying to fix everything at once is one of the fastest ways to burn out.

It's easy to get excited and want to build everything at once, but even experienced off-gridders will tell you that pace matters. Trying to overhaul your entire setup overnight often backfires. That's precisely what happened to Jon and Emilie in their first year off-grid.

FROM THE FIRE. STORIES THAT STILL BURN.
The Ventilation Mistake That Could Have Cost Us

When Jon and Emilie James set out to build their off-grid cabin, they were determined to get everything just right. With full-time jobs and limited time on the land, they tried to make fast progress—closing in the roof, insulating the cabin, and protecting it from drafts.

But one well-intentioned decision nearly cost them everything.

They sealed off the ends of the roof trusses to keep warmth inside, unaware they were trapping moist air above the insulation. When viewers pointed out the risk, Jon got on the phone with an experienced builder who confirmed the mistake: the lack of airflow could cause severe mold and damp issues long-term.

They immediately tore it out and started again, installing proper ventilation, learning as they went.

> *A lot of these tools are ones we've never used before. We realized we had to slow down, set them up properly, and learn how to do it right.*
> —Jon James, Camp Out West

What They'd Do Differently: Don't rush just to make progress. Even well-meaning shortcuts can turn into expensive rebuilds. Slowing down to learn the right approach isn't wasted time—it's what protects the systems you're counting on.

SCAN ME

Curious how they caught the mistake in time?
Watch Jon and Emilie's real off-grid story, We Made a Mistake... Building a Life Off Grid with No Experience—what went wrong, how they fixed it, and the lesson that saved their cabin.

Escaping Analysis Paralysis

The overwhelming amount of information available on off-grid living can lead to endless research without action. Some struggle with choosing the best energy system, food storage method, or water filtration setup, delaying progress.

But knowledge alone won't get you off the grid—action will. When fear of failure leads to inaction, sometimes the only way forward is just to start.

 FROM THE FIRE. STORIES THAT STILL BURN.
He Built Too Big—Then Realized Smaller Was Smarter

When Curtis Stone first moved off-grid in the boreal climate of British Columbia, he designed a top-tier energy system—48 solar panels, 100 kWh of lithium batteries, and a powerful diesel generator. It worked beautifully. But later, he admitted the truth: he could've saved half the cost if he'd just started smaller.

Instead of gradually building his system, Curtis overplanned and overbuilt, spending nearly $100,000 upfront. His reasoning? He feared being underpowered and wanted to avoid running a generator. But years later, after seeing how much solar he wasted during shoulder seasons and how little fuel he actually used, he knew he could've started with a leaner setup and scaled later.

You can have this exact system for cheaper—just burn more fuel in the short term. —Curtis Stone, Off Grid with Curtis Stone

What He'd Do Differently: Start with a smaller solar array, a basic generator, and fewer batteries. Learn your real needs through use, not theory. Then upgrade from experience, not fear.

SCAN ME

What if you could cut your system cost in half—without losing reliability?
Watch Curtis share what he learned the hard way in What I'd Do Differently With My Off-Grid Power System on YouTube.

By now, you've seen that going off-grid is less about perfection and more about progress. You've explored what off-grid living really means, how to phase your systems for resilience, and how others overcame burnout, hesitation, or costly missteps. Whether you're planning, actively transitioning, or focused on emergency readiness, the next step is to begin building momentum. Start where you are—with what's possible right now. These quick-start projects are simple, effective entry points to help you move from idea to implementation.

THREE Quick Wins: DIY Projects to Build Confidence

1. Set Up Basic Emergency Power

Choose a small solar generator that fits your budget and energy needs (like charging lights, phones, or a fan). Pair it with a lithium-ion battery bank that can store at least 200–500Wh of energy. Position a lightweight solar panel (60–100W) in direct sun, connect everything per the manual, and test by powering a small device. You'll create a quiet, portable backup power source without a significant upfront investment.

2. Collect Your First Rainwater

Place a food-grade rain barrel (or clean trash can with a lid) under a downspout to catch runoff during the next storm. Use it for watering plants, flushing toilets, or washing tools. As you build confidence, expand by adding a spigot, leaf filter, and overflow outlet. For drinking water, plan to install a basic sediment and carbon filter, and purify with boiling or UV.

3. Try a Container Garden

Pick a sunny, south-facing area and use 5-gallon buckets or grow bags with drainage holes. Fill them with quality organic potting mix and start with beginner-friendly crops like herbs, lettuce, or cherry tomatoes. Water consistently and monitor for pests. Harvest regularly to encourage new growth and expand slowly, adding one or two containers at a time.

DON'T BUILD IT AND FORGET IT

Every system needs upkeep. Set simple monthly check-ins: wipe solar panels, test water filters, rotate pantry goods, and scan for wear or leaks.

For families or those just starting out: set a recurring reminder and keep tasks short—15 minutes is enough to build a habit and involve everyone without overwhelm.

In extreme climates: check for frozen pipes, overheating batteries, or mold.

For preppers: run system drills seasonally—redundancy only matters if it still works.

Avoiding Financial Surprises Off-Grid

Some struggle with information overload, decision paralysis, or financial miscalculations. Others underestimate how much daily life changes when the grid goes away. But with the right mindset and a few practical first steps, you can reduce overwhelm and start building real momentum. The checklist below will help you begin.

 FROM THE FIRE. STORIES THAT STILL BURN.
The True Cost of Living Off-Grid: Lessons from Our First Winter

Chris and Kristie encountered unforeseen difficulties in their first winter living off-grid that tested their financial planning and fortitude. Even with great preparation, they encountered unexpected costs for heating, insulation, and energy use. These shocks made clear the need to budget for seasonal fluctuations and the continuous expenses of maintaining an off-grid lifestyle.

What They'd Do Differently: Living off-grid is an ongoing commitment rather than a one-time outlay. They discovered how to create a flexible budget that accommodates unexpected costs and disperses money for seasonal needs. Their experience emphasizes the need for financial flexibility and lifelong learning to achieve a sustainable off-grid life.

SCAN ME

Think you've budgeted enough?
Discover the hidden costs they faced and how they adapted. Watch their full story: The True Cost Of Living Off Grid | Our First Winter Results, - Off-Grid with Chris and Kristie.

Avoiding Common Pitfalls in the Off-Grid Transition

It's easy to get distracted by gear lists or bogged down in conflicting advice, but that's rarely what holds people back. What derails most off-grid plans is a lack of clear vision. Without knowing what you're building toward—or why—it's hard to make decisions that truly support your lifestyle and goals. That's where the next step begins.

Start with a Clear Off-Grid Plan

Before you go further, clarify what you're building and why. Knowing your household's "why" helps you focus and define success for your off-grid lifestyle.

1. Clarify What Matters.

Start with the essentials—energy, water, food, and security—and build from there on what matters most to you and your family.

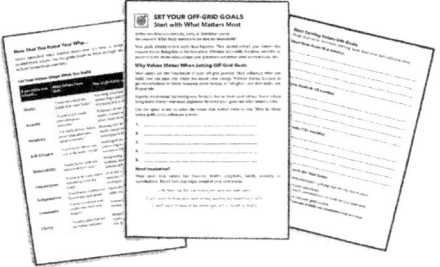

SCAN ME

Feeling scattered or unsure where to focus first?
Use this to cut through the noise. Scan to access the **Off-Grid Survival Companion**—with a printable version of the Off-Grid Goals Worksheet to help you align your values, clarify priorities, and map out your short-, mid-, and long-term milestones.

2. Monitoring Progress

Using basic scoring systems and checklists in this book to track the accomplishments you make. Ask yourself often what is working and modify your goals as necessary.

3. Building a Support Network

Join off-grid living-oriented local groups, internet forums, and communities. Share knowledge, tools, and experiences with like-minded people to grow personally and get support.

4. Legal Considerations and State Policies

Investigate your state's legal requirements for off-grid systems. Consult reliable internet resources for rules on water rights, solar panel installation guidelines, and composting rules.

You're not behind. You're exactly where you need to be.
And this book meets you there.

 ## CHECKLIST
Reduce Grid Dependence (Starting Now)

Use this checklist as a working tool to track your progress. Each category below is explored more deeply in its chapter, with step-by-step projects, visual tools, and troubleshooting guides to help you move forward with confidence. You can revisit and revise this checklist as your setup evolves—or download a printable version in the Off-Grid Survival Companion to update as you go. **Already tackled your first few systems?** Use this list to expand and strengthen your setup.

Water Independence *(Chapter 2)*

☐ Set up a rain barrel under a gutter downspout, or even a clean trash bin with a lid works.

☐ Store two weeks' worth of drinking water in sealed containers, kept in a cool, dark place away from direct sunlight and chemicals.

☐ Practice one method of purification—boiling, carbon filter, or gravity-fed—and test it using real water, not just a dry run.

Energy Reduction and Backup *(Chapter 3)*

☐ Swap one appliance for a low-power alternative (LED light, manual grinder).

☐ Buy or borrow a portable solar generator, test it on a phone or light, and charge it fully before storing it.

☐ Check cables and battery health every 30–60 days. Keep gear dry and out of direct sun or snow exposure.

Food Security and Preservation *(Chapter 5)*

☐ Grow one easy crop (lettuce, herbs, or green onions in a container).

☐ Track what your household eats in a week, and then build a shelf-stable backup that won't spoil in heat or humidity.

☐ Try freezing or dehydrating one food item you already use. Label and date it clearly.

Waste and Sanitation Management *(Chapter 6)*

☐ Research composting toilet options or try a DIY dry setup. Ventilate and manage odor with sawdust or peat.

☐ Create a basic emergency waste plan: bucket + liner + tight-fitting lid + clear disposal zone.

Essential Off-Grid Skills *(Chapters 4, 6, and 9)*

☐ Practice starting a fire without a lighter. Try one method: magnesium fire starter, ferro rod with tinder, or a 9V battery with steel wool.

☐ Cook one full meal without electricity (use a rocket stove, solar oven, grill, or no-cook option). Practice safe setup outdoors.

☐ Build a basic first aid kit and learn three emergency responses (cut, burn, and dehydration). Store in a cool, dry, and accessible place.

Adapt for Your Region *(Ongoing - look for callouts in each chapter)*

☐ Add one solution tailored to your climate, space, or legal limits (e.g., freeze-proof containers, rooftop solar, greywater bucket).

These early actions aren't just isolated tasks, they're the foundation of a larger system. As you make progress, your setup can evolve based on your needs, your goals, and your location. Off-grid living isn't one-size-fits-all. It grows with you.

Transitioning off-grid doesn't happen all at once, and it doesn't have to. Many successful off-gridders begin by taking small, manageable steps to reduce their reliance on utilities. For some, that means setting up a portable solar generator and collecting rainwater in basic barrels. Others might start with a raised bed garden or a month's supply of shelf-stable food. These early wins build momentum and confidence. Over time, you can layer in more advanced systems, like energy storage, greywater reuse, or backup heating based on your climate, land, and goals. The key isn't how much you do at once—it's that you keep moving forward, one wise decision at a time.

Changing with Different Lifestyles and Places

Whether small-scale or large-scale development, location defines the approach of off-grid living. Climate, local regulations, and space all help to shape people's systems of long-term sustainability.

Urban Off-Grid Living:

Rules and the space in the city might limit some decisions, but creativity can get beyond these constraints. Those who live in cities may rely on balcony gardens, neighborhood solar projects, and rainwater collecting systems designed for limited spaces. Local landowners, collaborative businesses, and bartering systems can help close gaps not readily under control right away.

Suburban Off-Grid Living:

Suburban homes sometimes feature room for medium-sized solar arrays, smaller animals like chickens, and bigger gardens. A suburban site also makes it simpler to incorporate off-grid elements, one solar panel, one rain barrel, or one raised bed at a time incrementally.

Rural Off-Grid Living:

People living in rural areas can grow most of their food, create water systems outside of municipal sources, and install rather large renewable energy systems. The trade-off is greater isolation; it requires more independence and a larger starting investment.

Whether your starting point is rural acreage, suburban lot, or an urban apartment, success depends on timing your advancement. The path Doug and Stacy travel is a striking illustration of what is achievable when one steps at a time, and one is committed to learning.

 FROM THE FIRE. STORIES THAT STILL BURN.
Doug and Stacy's 12-Year Off-Grid Life

Doug and Stacy are a powerful example of what's possible when you build one step at a time. Over a decade ago, they left behind urban life to pursue a simpler, self-sufficient lifestyle on 11 acres in Missouri. Doug built their 600-square-foot log cabin using traditional joinery techniques—without prior carpentry experience—and together they committed to living without public utilities.

In their first year, they focused on the essentials: collecting rainwater, heating with wood, growing vegetables and herbs, preserving food through fermentation and canning, and raising chickens for eggs and pest control. Each step brought more independence and confidence.

Their progress wasn't instant, but it was deliberate. They didn't try to build everything at once. Instead, they allowed each system to teach them something new. They adapted their setup over time, growing from basic resilience to long-term sustainability.

We didn't build it all overnight—we built it the old way.

What They'd Do Differently: Rushing invites burnout. Their slow-build approach helped them avoid overwhelm, master foundational systems, and stay aligned with their values. Doug and Stacy's story is a reminder that you don't need to get it all done fast—you just need to keep going.

SCAN ME

Curious what long-term off-grid living really looks like?
See how they built it—slowly, deliberately, and on their terms. Watch their full story: Off-Grid Living 12 Years Later

Adapting for Your Space and Climate

Off-grid living doesn't look the same in a suburban backyard as it does in a rural field. And what works in Arizona might fail in Minnesota.

That's why we've added space- and climate-specific tips throughout the book. Look for quick sidebars throughout each chapter. You'll also see QR codes linking to visual examples—like DIY container gardens in city garages or small-scale solar setups from rooftop to roadside.

SCAN ME

Take it a step further. Put your knowledge into action.
Scan the QR code for exclusive access to the **Off-Grid Survival Companion**—with printable checklists, guides, visual aids, and troubleshooting charts from the book, plus tools and product recommendations to help you adapt and build with confidence.

No matter your situation, the goal is to make progress from where you are now, not to chase someone else's version of off-grid.

From Mindset to Essentials:
The Next Step Toward Off-Grid Living

Building a self-sufficient life starts with the right mindset and a well-thought-out plan. Now that you've taken the first steps, put your knowledge into practice. Start small—set up a rain barrel, test a backup power source, or try a weekend off-grid challenge. The more you do, the more confident and prepared you'll become.

Your mindset is your most valuable survival tool.
Plan smart, adapt fast, and thrive.

CHAPTER 2:
Water Isn't Optional. It's Everything.

As we discussed earlier, when the Texas grid failed in 2021, not only were the lights out, but water also disappeared.

Pressure dropped, pipes froze, and the scramble started. Those who had collecting systems and stored water were safe, not just better off.

Until it doesn't, clean water seems assured. Drought, pollution, or infrastructure breakdowns can cut off supplies for several days or weeks.

Water is the system everything else depends on, whether your plans call for building emergency readiness, growing your systems, or going off-grid.

To be ready, not reactive, learn how to collect, clean, and store water. This chapter includes a helpful checklist to help you evaluate your site, negotiate regulations, and design a system fit for your way of life and surroundings.

Before the Tanks and Filters—Make a Plan

Before you begin designing your water system, it's essential to assess your environment, legal requirements, and long-term needs.

Summary of Off-Grid Water Systems:

The diagram shows a typical off-grid water system—from collection to filtration, storage, and optional greywater reuse. Not all parts are required, but each adds reliability based on your needs and environment.

WATER FLOW OVERVIEW

SOURCE OPTIONS

Rainwater   Surface Water   Well Water

FILTER AND PURIFY METHODS
Choose ONE based on conditions

BOIL   BLEACH   FILTER

WATER REUSE

GREYWATER TO GARDEN   STORE AFTER PURIFICATION   DRINK SAFELY

Planning? Don't Skip This.

Later in this chapter, you'll find a complete checklist to help you evaluate your land, understand legal requirements, and design a water system that's safe, sustainable, and tailored to your needs.

Collecting and Storing Rainwater for Off-Grid Use

Understanding Rainwater Harvesting

Rainwater collection is a sustainable approach to gathering and preserving water for home use, irrigation, and emergency readiness. Reducing reliance on municipal water sources helps this system be cost-effective and resilient over the long run.

Benefits of Environment and Practicality:

- Lessens demand on municipal and groundwater systems.

- Offers an autonomous, renewable water supply.

- It promotes sustainable irrigation and helps to reduce household water costs.

- Improves local watershed conditions by lowering stormwater runoff and soil erosion.

Even Rural Land Can Have Water Rules

Rainwater harvesting may seem like a no-brainer off-grid, but local rules still apply. Some states, counties, or land agreements restrict how much you can collect, where tanks go, or indoor use. Always check regulations before investing—off-grid doesn't mean unregulated.

- Offers a vital emergency water supply should municipal systems break down or a drought occur.

Legal Considerations and Regulations

Rainwater harvesting is legal in most U.S. states—but that doesn't mean it's always simple. Depending on your location, you may need permits, face limits on indoor or potable use, or follow rules about how much water you can store and where tanks can be placed.

Before you install anything, check both state laws and local enforcement policies. In some areas, you'll need to ask your county zoning office or health department about requirements for:

- Potable water use (drinking, cooking, bathing)

- Pressurized or gravity-fed systems

- Tank size, setbacks, or visibility restrictions

- Roof materials or approved surfaces

- Overflow management or erosion control

Even in rural zones, HOA rules or deed restrictions can block or limit rainwater collection, especially for visible tanks or systems connected to your home.

To help you get started, ask:

- "Do I need a permit to install a rainwater tank on this property?"

- "Are there any restrictions for using rainwater indoors or under pressure?"

- "Can I legally use a first-flush diverter or greywater for irrigation?"

- "Are there plumbing or sanitation codes I should be aware of?"

Rainwater Harvesting Laws by State

The map below offers a high-level summary of rainwater regulations across the U.S. While most states allow collection, specific policies vary widely. Some require permits, restrict storage size, or regulate how water is used.

Use the QR codes following to explore the most current tools, maps, and legal resources for your state.

Note: This information is based on public data as of early 2025. Always confirm requirements with local and state authorities before installing a system.

SCAN ME

Rainwater Harvesting Tool – U.S. Department of Energy
Estimate rainwater collection using your roof size and local rainfall.

Is It Legal to Collect Rainwater? – World Water Reserve
Check state-by-state legality with easy summaries and
helpful explanations.

State Regulations Map – Congress.gov
View official state legislature sites to verify the most current
legal details.

Even in states where rainwater harvesting is legal, enforcement and interpretation can be complicated. Just ask Mark Miller.

 ## FROM THE FIRE. STORIES THAT STILL BURN.
Legal Doesn't Always Mean Simple

Mark Miller chose to install a rainwater catchment system on the roof of his Utah car dealership with an eye toward conservation rather than merely cost savings. Reusing the water for vehicle washing would help him lessen his company's dependency on municipal water. But what first seemed to be a win-win soon ran against legal restrictions.

Utah law at the time banned anyone from gathering rainwater unless they possessed a valid water right, a regulation intended to safeguard downstream consumers depending on natural runoff. Until state officials showed up, Mark was unaware he was breaking the law. Though his intentions were good, he was advised to stop the system right away.

Mark was fortunately not giving up. Following months of negotiations, he was finally permitted to gather rainfall beneath Salt Lake City's current water rights.

Still, the encounter was eye-opening. Unexpected legal complexity accompanied what seemed to be a common-sense improvement.

What He'd Do Differently: The specifics count even if your state allows the collecting of rainwater. Permits, water rights, and even commercial vs. residential use, can alter what is permitted and not allowed. Before construction starts, always review municipal and state laws. *KSL News in Salt Lake City initially reported this story.*

Keep in mind Mark's story as we walk through how to set up your rainwater collection system from the very beginning.

Catch It. Store It. Use It.

Rainwater collection isn't just practical—it's flexible. Whether you're starting with a single barrel or planning a multi-tank setup, the steps below will help you design a system that fits your space and goals.

 STEP-BY-STEP PROJECT
How to Set Up a DIY Rainwater Collection System

This project outlines the essential steps to building an off-grid water supply, from simple collection barrels to fully pressurized systems.

Before You Begin

You now understand why water is among the first systems to fail and why your own supply counts. It is now time for planning. See local rainwater regulations, check your roof—it should be sloped, debris-free, and constructed of safe materials—and project how much water you might be able to collect. Specify your use as drinking, storage, or irrigation to help define the design and filtration requirements of your system.

Heads-Up
Don't Waste Space—or Invite Pests. Usable storage ends at the overflow pipe, not the tank's top—leave 10–12 inches for expansion to avoid spillage. And always cover your barrel with a lid or fine mesh to block sunlight and mosquitoes—uncovered tanks are a magnet for algae and bugs.

Skill Level: Beginner to Skilled

Basic barrels are beginner-friendly; complex setups may need skilled help.

Tools Required

- Budget-friendly swaps suggested.
- Drill with hole saw
- Hacksaw or PVC cutter
- Measuring tape and level
- Gutter sealant or silicone caulk
- Screws and wall brackets
- Shovel (if burying tank or trenching overflow)

Estimated Cost

$ - Laundry-to-Landscape Setup
$$ - Mid-Range System (shower/laundry, basic filtration)
$$$–$$$$ - Advanced Setup (pump, biofilter, multiple zones)

Estimated Time to Complete

2–4 hours: Basic single-barrel setup
1–2 days: Multi-barrel or storage tank system, depending on size, site prep, and filtration complexity

Materials List

- Prioritize food-safe, and weatherproof. Substitutes available.
- Food-grade rain barrels, IBC totes, or sealed water tanks
- Sloped gutters and downspouts
- First-flush diverter (floating ball)
- Leaf guards or inlet mesh screens
- Overflow pipe or drainage tubing
- Spigot or outlet valve
- Hose or PVC pipe (for connecting multiple containers)

DIY & Reuse Opportunities

- Reuse food-safe 55-gallon drums or IBC totes (often free or low-cost from farms or food service suppliers)
- Repurpose used gutters from building supply salvage yards or Habitat for Humanity ReStores
- Use fine mesh laundry bags or recycled window screens for cheap inlet filters
- Build tank platforms using pallets, cinder blocks, or leftover lumber

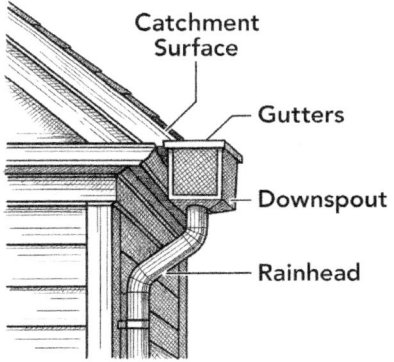

Catchment Surface
Gutters
Downspout
Rainhead

Step 1: Choose a Collection Surface

Start by choosing your collection surface—most off-gridders use a roof, shed, or greenhouse, though any clean, sloped metal surface works well. Choose one that's easy to access and clean. Avoid wooden shingles or pressure-treated materials, which can leach chemicals into your water.

To estimate how much rainwater you can collect, calculate the square footage of your collection area. As a general rule, one inch of rain on a 1,000-square-foot roof can yield around 600 gallons of water, so even small systems can add up quickly over time.

Adapt For Your Region: In hot climates, think about shaded or underground collecting tanks to cut evaporation. Insulate pipes and barrels or use flexible tubing in cold climates to stop freeze damage. Make sure lids in humid environments fit tightly to discourage mold and mosquitoes.

Step 2: Install or Update Gutter System

Install gutters along the lowest edge of the roof to effectively capture runoff if your building lacks them already. To guarantee a consistent flow of water, make sure they slope somewhat toward the downspout or collecting point. Add leaf guards or mesh filters that catch trash before it gets into your system to keep it clean and cut clogs.

Want to see how it all connects? The next page includes a full system diagram, showing how gutters, screens, downspouts, and your barrel or tank come together in a complete setup.

Step 3: Install a First-Flush Diverter (Floating Ball Style)

Before water flows into your storage container, you'll want to divert the first few gallons of runoff—this initial flow often carries dirt, pollen, bird droppings, and other debris from your roof.

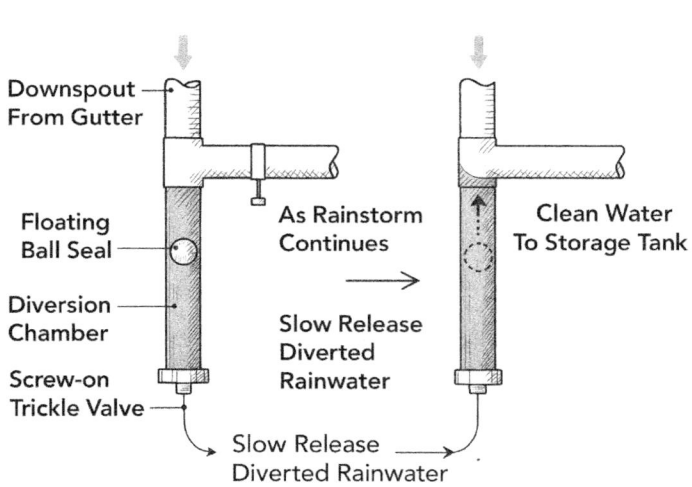

Downspout From Gutter

Floating Ball Seal

As Rainstorm Continues

Clean Water To Storage Tank

Diversion Chamber

Slow Release Diverted Rainwater

Screw-on Trickle Valve

Slow Release Diverted Rainwater

One easy and efficient fix is a floating ball first-flush diverter. A plastic ball inside floats upward and seals off the chamber once full as the pipe fills with dirty water, so it automatically guides cleaner water into your tank. Starting with this hands-off approach lowers maintenance and increases water quality right away.

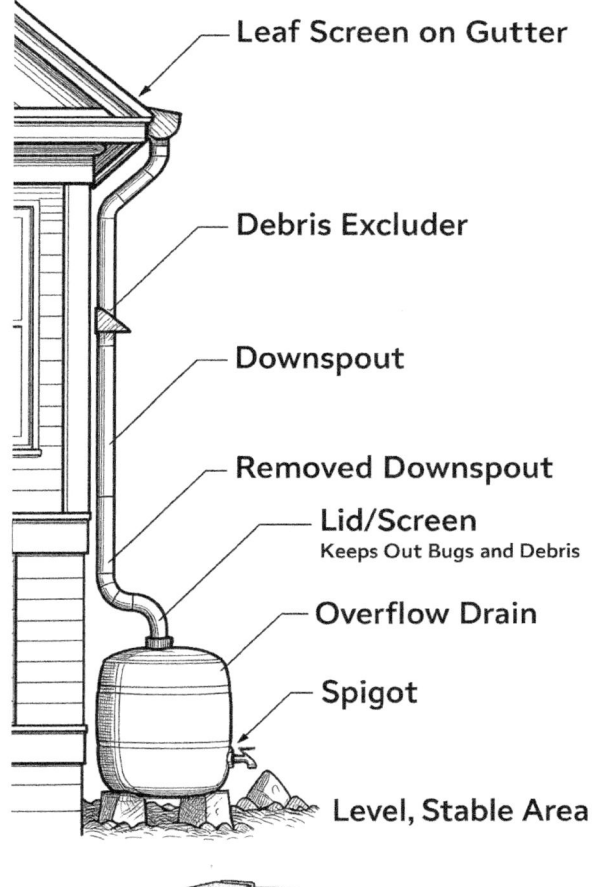

Leaf Screen on Gutter

Debris Excluder

Downspout

Removed Downspout

Lid/Screen
Keeps Out Bugs and Debris

Overflow Drain

Spigot

Level, Stable Area

Step 4: Set Up Your Water Storage

To gather your rainfall, pick sealed storage tanks, IBC totes, or food-grade barrels. The containers should be opaque and raised on a strong platform to prevent algae from spreading and allow gravity-driven water to flow.

To make accessing the water simple, add a spigot or outlet valve close to the tank's base. If you require more capacity, multiple containers may be coupled using hoses or PVC pipes.

Depending on your climate, site design, and long-term needs, you should also consider above-ground and underground storage when selecting between tanks.

Above-ground tanks are the most common choice for small to mid-sized off-grid systems due to easier setup and maintenance. Shown above: a storage tank with screened lid, overflow, and spigot. Water enters from a downspout or pump.

Underground tanks protect against heat and algae but require excavation and a pump to access stored water. They're ideal for hot climates and long-term use. Above, a buried tank with access hatch. Reduces heat and algae. Filled by downspout or pump.

Step 5: Anticipate safe drainage and overflow.

Install an overflow outlet near the top of your tank to stop water from pooling around your house or building. Send overflow into a gravel swale, garden bed, or secondary barrel. To channel water away from your foundation and lower erosion risk in heavy rain, use flexible tubing or PVC.

Step 6: Include Filtration

Whether you use the water for human consumption, cattle, or gardening, every rainwater system should incorporate at least rudimentary filtration. Install a screen or sediment filter at the inlet to block trash and prevent clogging.

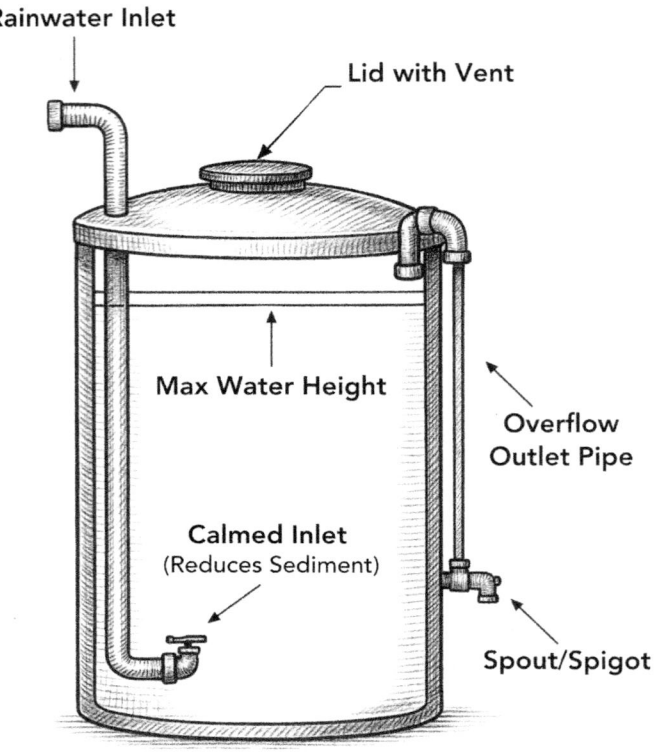

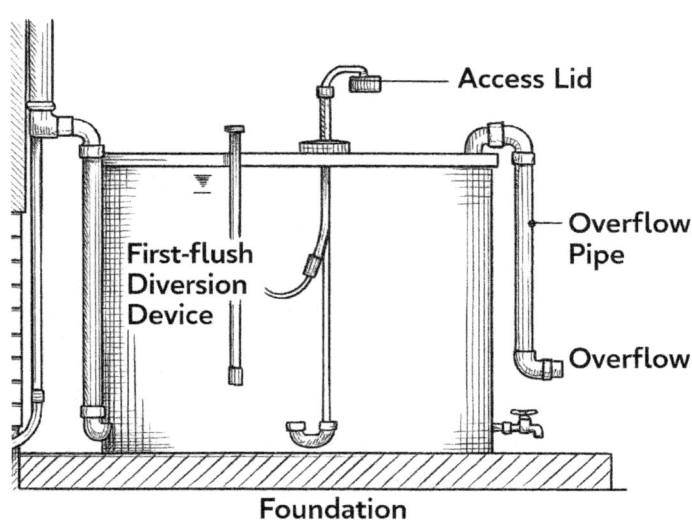

For potable or hygiene-related use, build in a multi-stage approach: use a combination of sediment filters, activated carbon, and purification methods like UV, boiling, or chemical treatment. Even if you're not planning to drink the water now, designing your system with future filtration or treatment upgrades in mind will save time, money, and unnecessary retrofitting later.

Step 7: Set Up Water Access

If you're sending water to another part of your home or yard, you can use a spigot, hand pump, or small 12V pump. Make sure the outlet is easy to reach and works with the hoses or containers you already have. Gravity-fed setups are the easiest and most reliable, especially off-grid.

Step 8: Maintain the System

Even the best rainwater system needs occasional maintenance. Clean gutters and screens often, especially in fall. Scrub tanks yearly and watch for algae or mosquitoes. In cold climates, drain or insulate before freezing.

SCAN ME

Want to See a Proven Fully Compliant Rainwater System?
This city-tested manual covers tank sizing, roof catchment design, and treatment options that meet safety codes and urban regulations.

Even with the right setup, one skipped step can take you out fast. Doug and Stacy learned that the hard way.

FROM THE FIRE. STORIES THAT STILL BURN.
Four Years Without Filtration—Then They Upgraded

When Doug and Stacy first moved to their off-grid homestead, they hauled water in jugs and five-gallon buckets for years before installing a rainwater collection system. Eventually, they built a 3,000-gallon gravity-fed setup that supplied their home without electricity.

For four years, they used sediment and carbon filters to remove visible particles and odors—but nothing to address bacteria or viruses. The water looked and tasted clean, but the risk was still there.

Then they added a Berkey system.

After learning more about airborne metals, pathogens, and off-grid water vulnerabilities, Doug decided it was time to take filtration seriously. He installed the Berkey as an extra layer—capable of removing viruses, heavy metals, and micro-contaminants. Their new system now delivers safe, drinkable water with zero electricity and maximum peace of mind.

You might be used to turning on a faucet and thinking it's all fine. But out here, you have to take every step seriously. You don't get a backup plan.

What They'd Do Differently: Add filtration from the start. Don't assume that because water is clear, it's clean. Even if you're not getting sick now, unfiltered systems carry long-term risks.

SCAN ME

How Safe Is Your Off-Grid Water?
Doug and Stacy share the upgrades they made after living off rainwater—and how they protect against hidden risks you can't taste or see.

Rainwater Collection Integrations

Solar Cells + Rainwater

Rooftop solar panels don't just generate electricity —they also make ideal rainwater collection surfaces. Their smooth, non-toxic surface funnels water efficiently into gutters while also shading storage tanks and powering small pumps or UV filters—an efficient solution for off-grid setups.

Vegetated Roof Rainwater Use

Rainwater systems fit green rooftops rather well. Acting as a pre-filter, plants and soil help to block debris before water gets to the storage tank. Then, in dry spells, stored rainwater can water the roof. High organic loads might require further maintenance and filtration.

Budgeting for a System of Rainwater Harvesting

The materials used and the system size determine the cost of establishing a rainwater collecting system. Strategic planning helps you start small and grow over time as your budget and needs allow.

System Type	Estimated Cost	Components Included
Basic (DIY)	$100–$500	Rain barrel, gutter modifications, mesh filter
Mid-Range	$500–$2,000	First-flush diverter, multiple barrels or small tank, pump system
Advanced	$2,000	Large underground cistern, full filtration, automated controls

Troubleshooting Common Issues in Rainwater Harvesting

Early proactive solutions for these common issues will help ensure a consistent and clean water supply for your off-grid living arrangement.

Problem	Possible Cause	Solution
Water smells bad	Algae or organic buildup in tank	Seal tanks, add UV light, clean often.
Low water	Clogged gutters or bad slope	Clear gutters, fix slope, remove clogs.
Water is cloudy	Sediment buildup	Add a pre-filter and clean tanks yearly.

Why Proper Water Storage Matters Most

Off-grid living and emergency planning depend critically on a long-term, drinkable water source. Still, just storing water is insufficient; the way you store it will affect its safety and use over time. Inappropriate storage can cause bacterial contamination, algae development, chemical leaching, and even water spoiling. Following best practices helps you to guarantee that your stored water stays safe, fresh, and easily accessible as needed.

Choosing the Right Storage Containers

Long-term water storage calls for different containers depending on their use. Some materials degrade over time or leach dangerous chemicals, compromising the quality of the water.

Storage Type	Benefits	Best For
Food-grade, BPA-free plastic	NSF-approved, lightweight, prevents leaching	General potable water storage
Stainless Steel	Durable, rustproof, leach-free	Permanent or buried storage
Glass (Small-Scale)	Safe and non-reactive, but heavy and fragile	Indoor emergency small reserves

How Often Should Stored Water Be Rotated?

Even correctly stored water should be rotated regularly to ensure freshness. The recommended rotation schedule depends on storage conditions and treatment methods. In general, aim to rotate untreated water every six months and treated or sealed water every 12 months, checking for signs of contamination before use.

DON'T SKIP THIS

Practice Fresh and Safe Stored Water. Mark containers with the storage date and schedule reminders to turn over often. Clean food-grade containers with a bleach solution first then refilled. Aerate water stored over 12 months by pouring between containers to improve taste. Toss it and clean the container before using if it smells, looks green, or has floating particles.

Treat Stored Water for Drinking

If stored water has been sitting for long periods, it's best to treat it before drinking. Even adequately stored water can develop a stale taste due to oxygen depletion. Use one of the following methods to ensure safety:

Option 1: Boiling

- Bring water to a rolling boil for at least 1 minute (or 3 minutes at higher altitudes).

- Let it cool before drinking.

Option 2: Chemical Treatment (Bleach Method)

- Use unscented household bleach (5–8% sodium hypochlorite).

- Add eight drops per gallon of clear water or 16 drops per gallon of cloudy water.

- Stir and let sit for at least 30 minutes before consuming.

Option 3: Filtration and Purification

Use activated carbon filters to remove odors and improve taste.

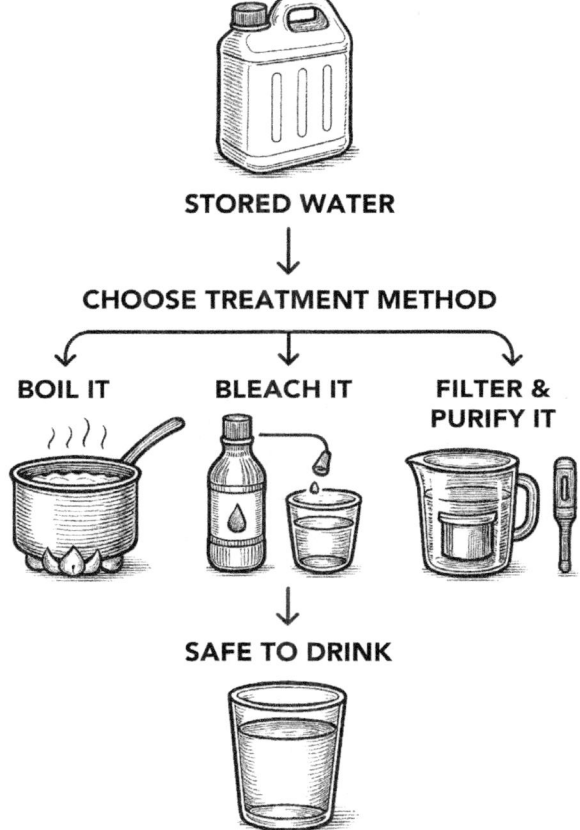

To kill bacteria and viruses, use a UV pen or gravity-fed purifier (e.g., Berkey, Sawyer, LifeStraw). For long-term use, consider reverse osmosis or ceramic filters.

Best Storage Locations for Long-Term Water Supplies

Where you store water is just as important as how you store it. Improper storage can lead to chemical leaching, bacterial growth, or freezing issues.

Follow these location guidelines:

Store water in cool, dark spaces like basements, insulated sheds, or underground cisterns. Avoid high-heat areas (attics, uninsulated garages) and keep away from chemicals.

Water storage is one of the most critical aspects of off-grid survival, but only when done correctly. Following best practices for selecting containers, preventing contamination, and rotating supplies ensures your stored water remains safe and drinkable for years to come.

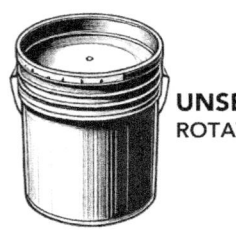

UNSEALED CONTAINERS
ROTATE EVERY 1-2 MONTHS

SEALED, TREATED WATER CONTAINERS
ROTATE EVERY 6-12 MONTHS

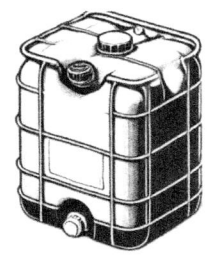

DISTILLED & AIRTIGHT STORAGE
LASTS 5+ YEARS

Flag This for Later

Stackable, space-saving containers will help you maximize indoor storage spaces and maintain visible, easily accessible, and organized emergency water storage.

Now that you know how to gather, preserve, and treat water for safe drinking, it's time to change gears. Greywater systems address a different issue: safely reusing water already in use—not storing it. Unlike rainwater or emergency reserves, greywater must travel fast and be carefully controlled.

SCAN ME

Take it a step further. Put your knowledge into action.
Scan the QR code for exclusive access to the **Off-Grid Survival Companion**—with printable checklists, guides, visual aids, and troubleshooting charts from the book, plus practical tools to help you adapt and build with confidence.

Understanding Greywater Reuse Systems

Greywater systems allow off-grid residents to repurpose wastewater from sinks, showers, and laundry for irrigation and other non-potable uses. Proper greywater management reduces water waste and increases sustainability when off-grid.

Practical Benefits of Greywater Reuse

- Reduces Water Waste: Reusing greywater can cut household water consumption by up to 50%.

- Supports Sustainable Irrigation: Provides a free, renewable water source for landscaping and gardens.

- Less Strain on Septic Systems: Reduces the amount of water entering septic tanks, prolonging their lifespan.

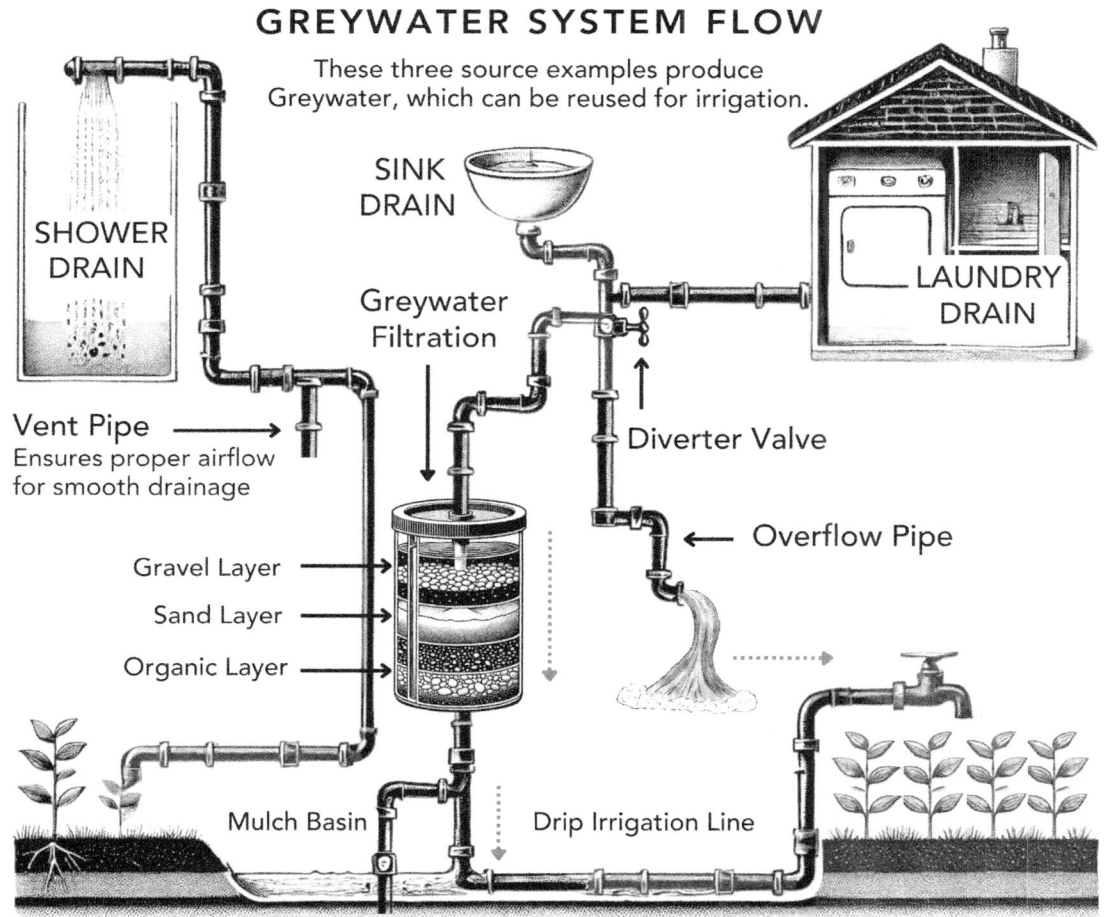

GREYWATER SYSTEM FLOW

These three source examples produce Greywater, which can be reused for irrigation.

SINK DRAIN

SHOWER DRAIN

LAUNDRY DRAIN

Greywater Filtration

Vent Pipe
Ensures proper airflow for smooth drainage

Diverter Valve

Overflow Pipe

Gravel Layer
Sand Layer
Organic Layer

Mulch Basin

Drip Irrigation Line

- Energy Savings: Reduces the need for pumping and treating municipal water supplies.

- Environmental Impact: Lessens the demand for freshwater resources and reduces pollution from wastewater discharge.

Choosing the Right Greywater System

Your ideal greywater system depends on what you're watering, how your home is plumbed, and how much elevation drop you have to work with.

- Gravity-fed systems are low-cost and ideal for sloped gardens, needing only a downhill outlet and basic plumbing.

- Pumped systems are better for flat land or when distributing greywater over long distances (e.g., to a lawn or garden beds). They require a small pump and more setup, but offer more flexibility.

No matter which system you choose:
- Install mesh screens at the source to catch hair, food, or debris.

- Use a simple biofilter (like a mulch basin or sand filter) to further purify water before it reaches plants.

- Avoid using greywater on edible crops unless it's delivered below the soil surface.

- Stick to biodegradable, non-toxic soaps and avoid bleach, salts, or boron-heavy detergents.

- Check your local laws—some states regulate greywater reuse, and codes may require certain safety features.

 STEP-BY-STEP PROJECT
How to Install a Greywater System

Greywater systems reuse lightly used water from sinks, showers, and laundry to irrigate non-edible plants. They reduce water waste, lower demand on your primary water source, and are especially useful in dry climates. Use the diagram on the left for a basic system layout.

Skill Level:
Beginner to Intermediate

Basic setups are beginner-friendly; pumps or multi-zone layouts require experience.

Estimated Time to Complete

2–4 hours: Basic greywater diverter with gravity-fed irrigation

Tools Required

Budget-friendly swaps suggested.
- Pipe cutter or hacksaw
- Wrench or pliers
- Shovel (for trenching lines)
- Screwdriver and mounting brackets
- Gloves and safety glasses
- Optional: drill for valve install

Estimated Cost

- **$** - Laundry-to-Landscape Setup
- **$$** - Mid-Range System (shower/laundry, basic filtration)
- **$$$–$$$$** - Advanced Setup (pump, biofilter, multiple zones)

Materials List

Prioritize food-safe, sustainable, and budget-friendly options
- 3-way diverter valve (rated for greywater)
- Flexible hose or PVC pipe (UV-stable and rated for non-potable water)
- Mesh trap or lint filter
- Optional: gravel and sand for biofilter
- Drip irrigation lines (subsurface is ideal)
- Mulch to cover irrigation lines
- Plant-safe, biodegradable detergents

DIY & Reuse Opportunities

- Repurpose old PVC or garden hose for non-pressurized lines (as long as they're not brittle or cracked)
- Reuse mesh strainers or laundry lint traps for filters
- Use reclaimed gravel or sand from landscaping stores or yard projects
- Use clean, chemical-free barrels or totes as surge tanks.

Before You Begin

Decide which greywater sources you'll use—showers, bathroom sinks, and laundry are the safest. Use the previous page's breakdown. Plan your layout for gravity flow; if the terrain is flat, you may need a pump. Check local regulations, as some areas require permits. Finally, map your irrigation zones based on plant type, soil depth, and available space.

Step 1: Identify Sources

Use water from sinks, showers, and laundry—never from toilets or kitchen sinks.

Step 2: Add a Diverter Valve

Install a three-way valve to send greywater to irrigation or your sewer/septic line.

GRAVEL LAYER

Step 3: Filter Debris

Use a mesh trap or lint catcher. Optional: Add a biofilter with gravel and sand.

SAND LAYER

ORGANIC LAYER
(OPTIONAL)

Step 4: Set Up Distribution

Use gravity-fed lines for slopes, pumps for flat areas, and bury drip lines under mulch to prevent pooling.

Step 5: Use Responsibly

Use plant-safe soaps. Only irrigate edibles with subsurface lines. Rotate zones to prevent pooling.

Don't Get Burned

Don't Cross the Streams. Greywater—from sinks, showers, or laundry—can be recycled for irrigation; blackwater from toilets is another matter entirely. It must be directed to a safe septic or composting system and carries dangerous germs. Never mix the two; this especially off-grid increases a significant health risk.

Maintenance and Safety

Clean filters regularly, monitor soil for salt buildup, and never reuse greywater from toilets or kitchen sinks. Use only biodegradable detergents, and check local regulations before setting up your system.

Water Purification Techniques

One cannot survive solely on a consistent water source. It has to be safe and clean for consumption. Rainwater, well water, surface water, and off-grid water supplies all contain different pollutants, including bacteria, viruses, heavy metals, and sediment. Knowing purifying techniques guarantees that your water stays safe and drinkable.

Understanding Water Contaminants

Before selecting a purification method, it's important to understand the types of contaminants commonly found in off-grid water sources:

- **Biological Contaminants**: Bacteria (E. coli, cholera), viruses (norovirus, hepatitis A), and parasites (Giardia, Cryptosporidium) that cause severe illness.

- **Chemical Contaminants**: Pesticides, herbicides, industrial chemicals, and heavy metals such as lead and arsenic.

- **Physical Contaminants include dirt**, sediment, rust, and organic matter that make the water cloudy and affect the taste.

- **Radiological Contaminants**: In certain regions, groundwater may contain radioactive elements like radon or uranium.

Essential Water Purification Methods

Different purification methods address different contaminants. The best approach is a combination of filtration and disinfection to ensure all threats are removed.

- **Sediment and Particle Filtration** removes dirt, sand, and rust using mesh screens, ceramic filters, or sand biofilters.

- **Activated Carbon Filtration**: Absorbs chlorine, pesticides, and VOCs, improving taste and odor.

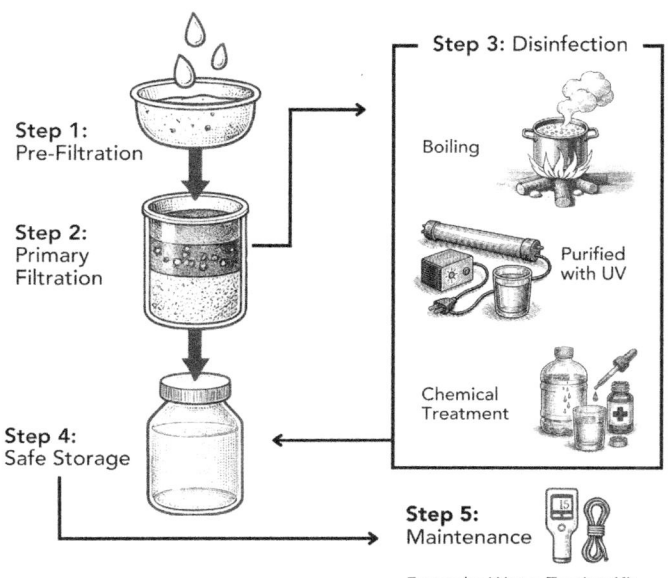

The visual shows how each stage of the layered purification system works together.

Purification Method	Removes Bacteria?	Removes Chemicals?	Removes Heavy Metals?	Best Use
Boiling	Yes	No	Yes	Emergency survival
Activated Carbon	No	Yes	No	Improving taste/odor
Reverse Osmosis	Yes	Yes	Yes	Full purification
UV Treatment	Yes	No	No	Backup disinfection

Advanced Filtration

- **Reverse Osmosis (RO) Systems:** Removes heavy metals and chemicals but requires pressurized water and wastes more water than it produces without recovery.

- **Solar Water Disinfection (SODIS):** Uses sunlight in clear bottles to kill bacteria and viruses. Low-cost, fuel-free method—ideal for emergencies or remote use.

SCAN ME

Are You Treating Your Water the Right Way?

See the CDC's Safe Water Guide for reliable tips on treating, storing, and managing drinking water in emergencies or off-grid settings.

 STEP-BY-STEP PROJECT
How to Build a Layered Water Purification System

No single method removes all contaminants. This layered system filters, disinfects, and stores water using simple materials.

Before You Begin

Know your water source—surface, rain, or well—and your end use (drinking, hygiene, or both). Plan for space, flow rate, and future needs. Filtration methods vary in speed and complexity. If storing water long-term or using it for others, check safety standards and local regulations.

Skill Level: Beginner to Skilled

Basic filtration and disinfection are beginner-friendly. Bio-sand systems or integrated UV setups require more planning and upkeep.

Estimated Cost

- **$** - Cloth + boiling or iodine
- **$$** - Inline filter + solar or UV
- **$$$–$$$$** - Layered filter + tank

Tools Required

- Scissors or knife
- Funnel (optional)
- Heat source
- Timer or watch
- Buckets or containers

Estimated Time to Complete

30–60 minutes: Basic setup
2–4 hours: DIY bio-sand system
1–2 days: Full setup with storage

Materials List

- Mesh screen, cloth, or coffee filters
- Activated carbon filter or DIY bio-sand filter materials
- Labels for treatment dates
- Disinfection method (iodine, chlorine, UV, SODIS, or boiling pot)
- Food-grade storage containers
- Water test strips (optional)

DIY & Reuse Opportunities

- Use recycled bottles or buckets for container-based filters
- Repurpose cloth or mesh for pre-filters
- Upcycle PET bottles for solar disinfection (SODIS)
- Use charcoal from fire pits for basic filtration layers

Step 1: Start with Pre-Filtration

- Use a mesh screen, coffee filter, or basic sediment filter to remove large particles like dirt, leaves, or sand.

- This protects your primary filter from clogging and extends its lifespan.

Step 2: Add a Primary Filtration Layer

Choose one of the following:

- Activated carbon filter – reduces chemicals, odors, and some pathogens.

- Bio-sand filter – a slower, natural method that removes bacteria and particulates.

Step 3: Use another Method

Even after filtering, some viruses or bacteria may remain.
Use one of these methods:

- Boiling – Bring water to a rolling boil for at least 1 minute (3+ min at high altitude).

- UV sterilization – Portable UV light pens or solar disinfection (SODIS) bottles can neutralize microbes.

- Chemical treatment – Add chlorine drops or iodine tablets (Use as directed).

Step 4: Store It Safely

- Once purified, transfer the water to clean, sealed, food-grade containers.

- Store in a cool, dark place to prevent bacterial regrowth.

- Rotate stored water every 6–12 months and label containers with treatment dates if long-term storage is needed.

Step 5: Maintain Your System

- Clean or replace filters regularly based on usage and manufacturer instructions.

- Stock backups: filters, drops, and essentials.

- Test your water periodically using DIY test strips or portable water testing kits.

Keep backup filters and a manual treatment method (like iodine tablets or a solar bottle) in your emergency kit or bug-out bag.

Climate & Setup Adaptations

- **Cold Climates:** Boiling and chemical treatment are more reliable than solar. Store filtered water in insulated containers.
- **Hot Climates:** Shade storage; SODIS needs 6+ hours of sun.
- **Remote Locations:** Use durable, low-maintenance, non-electric systems.

Emergency Water Purification Strategies

Alternative purification methods can provide safe drinking water in emergencies. Solar distillation uses the sun to evaporate and purify water, removing contaminants. Activated charcoal filtration helps remove chemicals and odors. Ceramic gravity-fed filters provide a slow but highly effective purification process without electricity.

Emergency Water Plans When You Have None:

Why You Need a Plan

Access to safe drinking water can disappear instantly in a survival situation. Whether it's a natural disaster, power grid failure, supply chain collapse, or a long-term off-grid emergency, knowing how to immediately source, purify, and store water is critical. Without water, dehydration sets in within 72 hours, and survival becomes nearly impossible.

Fast Response Reference

Crisis	Where to find water
No stored water?	Check home water heater, toilet tank (if untreated), ice.
No home sources?	Find flowing water (river, stream), purify before drinking.
No natural sources?	Harvest rainwater or extract moisture from air (emergency condensation method).

 ## CHECKLIST
How to Create an Emergency Water Plan

An emergency water plan ensures you have safe drinking water during outages or disruptions. These steps walk you through creating a simple, reliable backup using containers you likely already own.

Have you...

- ☐ Assessed your current water sources and supply?
- ☐ Shut down non-essential water use?
- ☐ Identified backup sources nearby (urban or wild)?
- ☐ Chosen a purification method suited to your situation?
- ☐ Stored purified water in safe, labeled containers?
- ☐ Rotated your stored water within the last 6–12 months?
- ☐ Locate emergency water sources
  - **Urban**: Water heater, toilet tank (if untreated), melted ice
  - **Wilderness**: Flowing streams, lakes, ponds, rain, dew, snow

- **Avoid**: Stagnant pools, runoff near roads, seawater without desalination

☐ Customize your plan - Adjust volume, storage, and purification methods based on household size, local climate, and water reliability. Consider extra layers if you're remote, preparing long-term, or planning for kids.

Quick Reference - Purification Methods

- Boil 1–3 min or bleach 8–16 drops/gal
- SODIS: 6+ hrs in full sun
- Portable Filter: Use as directed
- DIY Filter: Gravel, sand, and charcoal

✅ CHECKLIST
Build a Water System That's Safe and Compliant

Use this checklist to plan a reliable off-grid water system that meets both safety and legal requirements.

1. Confirm Legal Requirements & Restrictions

☐ Check your state's rainwater laws.

Contact your county zoning office to ask about:

☐ Permits for rainwater systems or wells

☐ Storage tank size/visibility limits

☐ Use of greywater or surface water

☐ Review your property deed and HOA documents for any restrictions—even in rural or non-traditional communities.

☐ Determine if your system needs to meet sanitation, filtration, or plumbing codes (especially for potable use).

2. Establish Your Primary Water Source

☐ Secure your main water source—well, rain, surface, or stored.

☐ If using a well, ensure it has proper filtration and a reliable backup pump.

Family Planning Tip

If you're planning with kids, elderly parents, or a mixed-readiness household, assign clear water roles. Kids can help monitor storage levels or refill solar stills. Make sure everyone knows which water is safe to drink, and which is reserved for hygiene or backup. Label containers clearly and test systems as a family so there are no surprises in a real emergency.

- [ ] Use gutters, a first-flush diverter, and closed storage for rainwater.
- [ ] If using surface water, treat and filter it.
- [ ] Store a minimum of two weeks' worth of emergency water for backup.

3. Choose and Secure Your Main Water Source

- [ ] **Well** - If using a well, confirm that it's permitted, has a safe yield, and is appropriately filtered with a backup pump.
- [ ] **Rainwater** - If using rainwater, install gutters, a first-flush diverter, and food-grade containers. Lift-up or pressurize storage if the flow is needed.
- [ ] **Surface Water** - If using surface water, implement a filtration and purification plan and check the legality of drawing from natural bodies.
- [ ] **Store Water** - If using stored water, maintain at least two weeks' worth of emergency water per person if using it as your backup emergency supply.

4. Install Proper Storage & Filtration Systems

- [ ] Use opaque, food-safe barrels or tanks to reduce algae and contamination.
- [ ] Install gravity-fed or pressure-based filtration depending on system size.
- [ ] Include multiple purification options: boiling, UV, chlorine/iodine, and carbon filters for flexibility.
- [ ] Plan for overflow to prevent erosion

5. Adapt to Climate and Terrain

- [ ] **In Dry Climates:** Use underground or shaded tanks to minimize evaporation and implement conservation strategies (mulch, drip irrigation).
- [ ] **In Cold Climates:** Insulate tanks and pipes, and consider snowmelt or solar-heated water tanks.
- [ ] **In Unpredictable Regions:** Diversify sources (rainwater, greywater, stored) and monitor seasonal yield trends.

If you rent or live in a small space, try stackable containers, folding rain catchers, or wheeled barrels. Some renters place IBC totes on balconies and use gravity-fed taps for non-potable uses. Focus on portable and modular water solutions.

6. Test and Maintain Your Water System

- ☐ Test water quality twice a year (for bacteria, heavy metals, and contaminants).

- ☐ Prevent algae and bacteria with yearly tank cleaning.

- ☐ Maintain backup filtration and purification supplies (extra filters, iodine, or chlorine tablets)

SCAN ME

Take it a step further. Put your knowledge into action.

Scan the QR code for exclusive access to the **Off-Grid Survival Companion**—with printable checklists, guides, visual aids, and troubleshooting charts from the book, plus practical tools to help you adapt and build with confidence.

Troubleshooting Off-Grid Water Systems:
Catch Problems Before They Spread

A water system failure can quickly become an emergency. Whether you use a well, rainwater, or greywater, problems can threaten your supply. Spotting and fixing issues early helps prevent small setbacks from turning into major crises. Below are the most common failures and how to fix them.

Rainwater Harvesting Problems and Solutions

Although rainwater collection is a great off-grid water source, low collection rates, clogs, and contamination can all compromise its usefulness.

Problem	Cause	Solution
Low Water Collection	Small catchment area, improper gutter slope	Adjust gutter angle, expand catchment surface, increase storage
Gutters and Filters Clogging	Leaves, dirt, debris in gutters and diverters	Install gutter guards, use fine-mesh pre-filters, clean monthly
Water Contamination	Animal droppings, algae, bacterial growth	Use diverter, UV/carbon filters, and peroxide/chlorine

Well System Problems and Fast Corrections

If you rely on a well, regular maintenance helps prevent pressure loss and water quality problems. Although deep repairs could require a specialist, these quick troubleshoots of basic issues can help.

Problem	Cause	Solution
Pump Not Working	Power failure, clogged intake	Reset circuit breaker, inspect pressure switch, clear intake
Low Water Pressure	Sediment buildup, clogged filter	Flush pipes, clean filters, check pressure tank
Discolored Water	Scale or worn well screen	Install a sediment filter, use iron-removal filtration

Greywater System Issues and Solutions

Greywater recycling reduces water waste, but odor buildup, clogging, and inefficient drainage are common problems.

Problem	Cause	Solution
Unpleasant Odors	Organic buildup, bacterial growth	Use enzyme treatment, aerate tank, flush with vinegar/peroxide
Clogging in Pipes/Filters	Soap scum, grease, hair blockage	Install grease trap, flush pipes monthly with hot water and baking soda
Greywater Not Draining	Soil saturation, filtration issues	Improve drain field with gravel/sand, check pump for blockages

 CHECKLIST
Maintain Your System, Prevent Failures

This checklist helps you avoid issues and maintain reliability.

Rainwater System Maintenance:

- [ ] Inspect and clean gutters, downspouts, and first-flush diverters every month at the very least.

- [ ] Check storage tanks for leaks, sediment buildup, and algae growth.

- [ ] Replace or clean water filters and screens every 6 months.

Additional Consideration: Install a mosquito-proof screen over all tank inlets to prevent infestations.

Well System Maintenance:

- ☐ Test water annually for bacteria, minerals, and contaminants.
- ☐ Inspect pump wiring and pressure switch connections every 6 months.
- ☐ Flush sediment from the system every year to maintain the flow rate.

Additional Consideration: Keep a manual pump or backup power source on hand in case of electrical failure.

Greywater System Maintenance:

- ☐ Clean grease traps and flush pipes with an enzyme solution every month.
- ☐ Check for drainage blockages and clear any debris from the system.
- ☐ Rotate greywater distribution areas to prevent soil oversaturation.

Additional Consideration: Use mulch basins to filter and disperse greywater more efficiently in garden zones.

SCAN ME

Not sure what to focus on now and what can wait?
Create a flexible water system using the checklists and graphics. With printable planning tools, diagrams, and troubleshooting guides from this chapter—along with extra help to keep things running—you have exclusive access to the **Off-Grid Survival Companion.**

Water Locked Down. Time to Level Up.

Now that you've secured your water supply, it's time to focus on powering your off-grid lifestyle. Just as a diversified water plan ensures sustainability, an innovative DIY energy system eliminates dependency on unstable infrastructure.

Without clean water, nothing else matters. Secure it first.

CHAPTER 3: TAKE CONTROL OF YOUR POWER – AND KEEP IT

Lighting Your Off-Grid Approach to Life

The modern power grid is fragile and prone to outages from severe weather, cyberattacks, economic instability, and rising costs, leaving grid-dependent households vulnerable. Generating your own electricity provides long-term security and control. This chapter covers three of the most practical DIY renewable energy solutions:

- **Solar Panels** – Scalable and widely adaptable.

- **Wind Turbines** – Ideal for areas with consistent wind.

- **Micro-Hydro Systems** – The most reliable for land with flowing water.

Each system has unique benefits and maintenance needs. This chapter provides step-by-step guidance for installation, troubleshooting, and optimizing efficiency to help you design a system that fits your location and energy demands.

Why Choose Solar Energy?

Solar power is one of the most affordable, accessible off-grid energy options. It provides electricity for lights, appliances, and battery storage with minimal maintenance. It works best in sunny climates—but modern systems also perform well in cloudy or seasonal conditions.

STEP-BY-STEP PROJECT
How to Set Up a Small-Scale Solar Setup

Set up a reliable solar system for lights, devices, and basic power—whether you're using a portable unit or building a fixed array.

Before You Begin

Select a sunny spot with the most daily exposure. Verify the input voltage and wattage capacity of any portable power station you use. Plan cable routes and securely mount panels for fixed configurations.

Skill Level: Beginner to Skilled

Plug-and-play is easy; custom setups need wiring know-how

Tools Required

- 100–200W monocrystalline solar panel
- Charge controller (PWM or MPPT)
- Deep-cycle battery or solar generator
- Pure sine wave inverter (for AC use)
- Outdoor DC wiring + connectors

Estimated Time to Complete

30–60 minutes: Portable kits
2–4 hours: Custom 100–200W system
1–2 days: Setup with battery + inverter

Estimated Cost

- **$** - Single panel + portable unit
- **$$** - Panel, controller, and battery
- **$$$–$$$$** - Inverter with storage

Materials List

- Mesh screen, cloth, or coffee filters
- Carbon or DIY bio-sand filter materials
- Labels for treatment dates
- Disinfection: iodine, chlorine, UV, SODIS, or boil
- Food-grade storage containers
- Water test strips (optional)

DIY & Reuse Opportunities

- Repurpose RV or boat batteries—test with a multimeter first
- Build panel stands from scrap lumber-angled frames using reclaimed wood.
- Find discounted kits or parts—check classifieds and surplus stores
- Use old extension cords or jumper cables—verify gauge and condition
- Mount controllers on salvaged wood
- Use totes or ammo cans for batteries

Step 1: Set Up the Solar Panel

Place your solar panel in full sunlight with no obstructions. For best performance, tilt it to match your latitude—steeper in winter, flatter in summer. Use a stable, raised surface or mount it to track the sun's path.

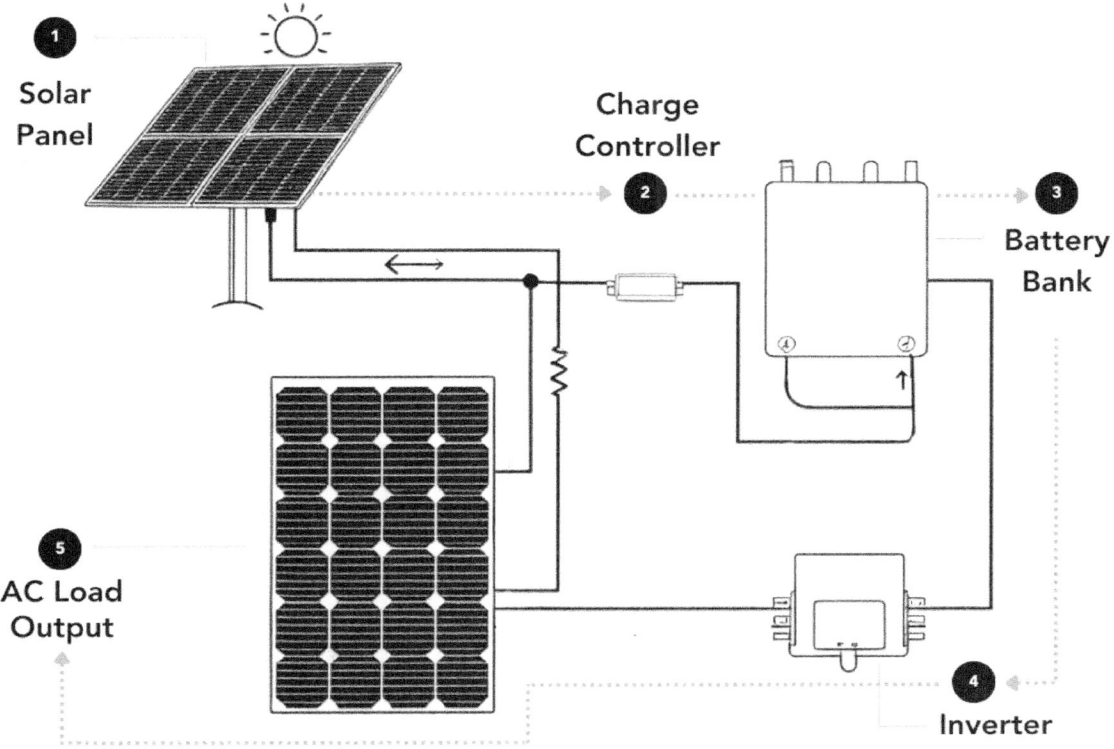

Step 2: Connect the Charge Controller

Wire the solar panel to a charge controller to prevent overcharging the batteries. With properly rated wire, match positive to positive and negative to negative for your configuration.

Step 3: Attach the Battery Bank

Attach the charge controller to a portable power station or battery bank. Use deep-cycle solar storage batteries, and make sure the polarity is correct and connections are tight.

Step 4: Add the Inverter (if needed)

Link a pure sine wave inverter to the battery bank if you intend to run AC appliances—such as a fan, blender, or lights. Should the wattage of your device match, it converts stored DC power to AC.

Step 5: Test and Power Devices

Once everything is connected, test your setup by plugging in small devices and checking for stable operation. Use a multimeter to verify voltage at key points—panel output, battery input, and inverter output.

Check battery levels regularly and reposition panels every season to maximize sun exposure and maintain consistent performance.

> **Beginner Mistake**
> Placing solar panels flat reduces efficiency, especially in winter.
> **The Fix:** Tilt panels based on your latitude. Steepen the angle in winter, flatten in summer. Seasonal adjustments can really improve power output.

Additional Consideration:

If your system isn't working as expected, check the solar troubleshooting chart to identify and fix common issues.

Apply These DIY Solutions for Solar Energy Issues

Even with a simple portable solar generator setup, issues can arise that impact performance. Here are some of the most common problems and their solutions: Check your solar setup weekly and adjust panel position as needed to keep it running reliably.

Larger fixed solar systems add complexity and require more troubleshooting. Below are issues specific to full off-grid setups.

1. Charge Controller Issues

Problem	Possible Cause	Solution
Charge controller does not turn on	Loose connections or incorrect voltage	Verify proper wiring, ensure battery voltage matches system voltage, check fuse
Overheating charge controller	High power load, poor ventilation	Relocate to a cooler, shaded area; check ventilation and heat dissipation
Display shows incorrect voltage	Faulty sensor or incorrect wire gauge	Use a multimeter to verify actual voltage; replace sensor if needed

2. Battery Bank Issues

Problem	Possible Cause	Solution
Batteries not holding charge	Battery sulfation or aging	Perform an equalization charge if using lead-acid, replace the old batteries
One battery drains faster than others	Unequal load distribution	Reconfigure wiring to balance loads evenly across all batteries
Batteries overcharging	Faulty charge controller settings	Adjust charge controller settings based on battery type and manufacturer recommendations

3. Inverter-Specific Problems

Problem	Possible Cause	Solution
Inverter not turning on	Low battery voltage or loose wiring	Check battery levels, ensure proper wiring connections
Inverter shuts off under load	Overload or incorrect sizing	Reduce load or upgrade to a higher-capacity inverter
Appliances buzz when using inverter	Modified sine wave may cause interference	Use pure sine wave for clean power

No Roof Access? Use a Solar Kit

Try a plug-and-play solar generator with a folding panel. Many renters use balcony setups or solar carts with wheeled panels. You can still run essentials—lights, fans, phone chargers, radios—without modifying the building.

4. Solar Panel Efficiency Loss

Problem	Possible Cause	Solution
System not producing expected power	Dirt, shading, or seasonal angle issues	Clean panels, remove shading, adjust tilt for seasonal sun changes
Power drops during peak sun hours	Overheating reduces panel efficiency	Improve airflow + reflect heat to boost efficiency
Voltage fluctuates randomly	Loose wiring or panel degradation	Inspect all connections and test individual panel outputs

FROM THE FIRE. STORIES THAT STILL BURN.
Powering a Cabin on a Budget

You first met Jay and Jen in the Introduction, where they shared how starting small helped them avoid burnout. Over time, they've kept layering in systems—and one of their biggest milestones was building a DIY solar setup to power their off-grid cabin.

Living in northern Michigan, they created a cost-effective and resilient solar system with thought for Beginning with seven AGM batteries and 400 watts of solar power, they subsequently enlarged their arrangement to include a 3,000-watt inverter. Now the system runs their basic needs: lighting, a refrigerator, laptops, and fans; this shows you how to create dependable off-grid power on a shoestring.

Jay emphasizes the importance of designing around your land and needs: full sun exposure, manageable loads, and flexible planning for seasonal changes. In winter, they occasionally rely on a solar generator—proof that having backup doesn't mean you failed, it means you planned smart.

We built our solar system ourselves, one step at a time, and it's been powering our cabin for over three years.—Jay

Their story is a reminder that with smart planning and hands-on learning, solar power can be both practical and accessible—even on a modest budget.

SCAN ME

 **Could You Build Your Off-Grid Power for Less?**
Jay and Jen walk through the exact solar setup they use to power their cabin—including what they bought, why it works in northern Michigan, and what they'd do differently. Watch their story: Simple Solar setup and our DIY solar shed.

But what if the sun isn't always reliable where you live? That's where wind energy can step in—as a powerful backup or supplemental source for your off-grid system.

Harness Wind Energy Off-Grid—Here's Why It Works

Wind turbines generate electricity from wind speeds above 10 mph, making them a valuable secondary power source for off-grid setups. Unlike solar, wind energy can be harnessed day and night, providing power during cloudy or stormy conditions. Best suited for coastal regions, open plains, and mountain ridges with steady winds. Properly installed turbines reduce reliance on batteries and generators by supplying direct energy to loads.

Thinking About Wind? First Consider These Pointers

For Families: Wind systems can run unattended once installed, but setup and maintenance involve heights and moving parts. Secure towers and involve older kids in safe, hands-on learning about off-grid energy.

For Preppers: Wind offers 24/7 power and resilience when solar is down. A well-anchored turbine can support critical loads like communications, freezers, or security systems—especially in prolonged outages.

For Different Regions: Wind power works best in coastal, open plains, or ridge areas with consistent wind above 10 mph. It's less effective in valleys, forests, or sheltered zones—always test conditions before committing.

STEP-BY-STEP PROJECT
How to Set Up a Wind Power System

Wind power delivers round-the-clock energy—even when the sun isn't shining. It can reduce battery strain, support essential loads, and scale alongside solar to boost energy independence over time.

Before You Begin:

Evaluate wind patterns at your location—steady winds above 10 miles per hour are ideal. Choose an open, sloped area free from trees or buildings. Anchor the tower securely and follow safety protocols when working at height.

Not ready for a tower? Try a rooftop kit or small DIY turbine to learn the basics.

Skill Level: Intermediate to Skilled

Wind systems require safe tower setup and understanding of wind load, voltage matching, and system grounding.

Estimated Cost

- **$** - DIY with salvaged parts
- **$$** - Kit w/ controller + battery
- **$$$–$$$$** - Full tower + inverter + bank

Estimated Time to Complete

2 to 3 hours: Basic turbine kit

2 to 4 days: Mounted tower system

2 to 3 weekends: Wind power setup

Materials List

- Wind turbine
  (400 watts or more recommended)
- Tower or mounting pole
- Guy wires and ground anchors
- Wind-compatible charge controller
- Deep-cycle battery bank
- Pure sine wave inverter

Tools Required

- Wrenches, socket set, and drill
- Ladder or scaffolding
- Wire strippers and multimeter
- Safety harness

DIY & Reuse Opportunities

- Repurpose treadmill motors or car alternators
- Make turbine blades from PVC pipe or scrap wood
- Use old TV towers or flagpoles as support structures
- Scavenge wire and hardware from deconstructed sheds or trailers
- Bike rims or hubs for blades
- Salvage junction boxes or enclosures for wiring

Step 1: Install the Wind Turbine

To access consistent wind, mount your turbine at least 30 feet above nearby obstacles. Choose an open area with average speeds above 10–12 mph and secure it using guy wires or a tilt-up tower.

Step 2: Connect the Generator

The spinning blades drive a generator that converts wind into DC electricity. Use weather-resistant wiring and ensure all hardware is firmly mounted.

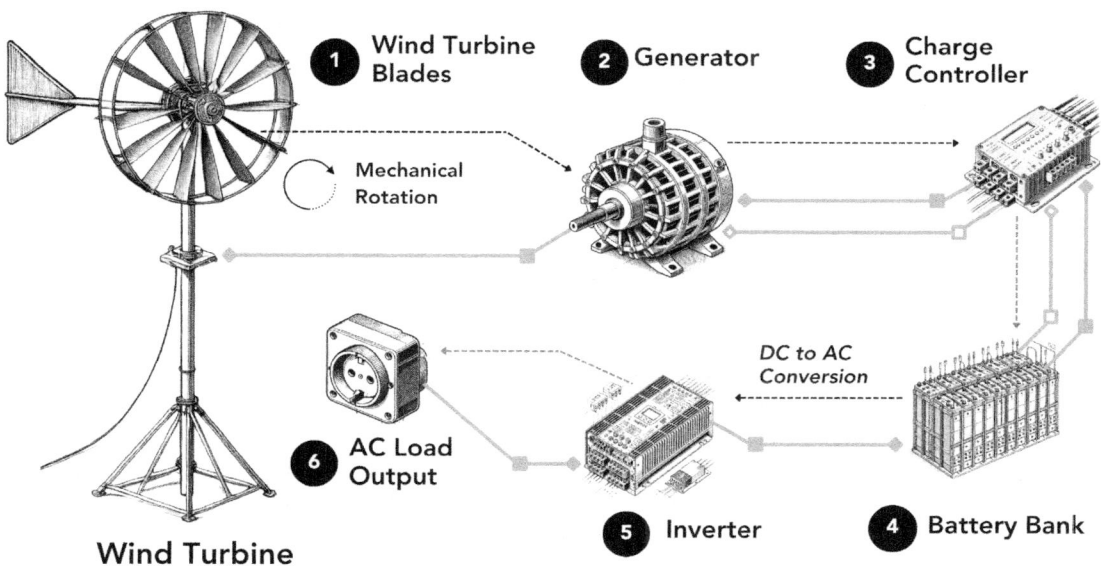

Wind Turbine

Step 3: Wire in the Charge Controller

Route the generator output through a charge controller to regulate voltage and prevent battery overcharging.

Step 4: Add a Battery Bank

Connect to deep-cycle batteries matched to your system voltage (12V, 24V, or 48V). The batteries store energy for when wind conditions drop.

Step 5: Install the Inverter

To power AC appliances, wire an inverter to the battery bank. It converts DC to household AC and should be properly sized for your energy load.

Step 6: Connect the AC Output and Test the System

Verify the power from the inverter using a multimeter or a device connected to the power supply. Monitor the output and inspect the turbine regularly.

Climate & Region Matter

Micro-hydro thrives in cool, wet regions with steady elevation—like the Pacific Northwest, Appalachia, British Columbia, or parts of New Zealand. Year-round flow is essential, especially through dry summers. In colder climates, protect your system from freezing with buried or insulated lines and regular winter flow checks.

Wind complements solar but requires consistent wind and regular maintenance.

Utilize These DIY Solutions for Challenges in Wind Energy

Wind energy isn't just set-it-and-forget-it. Even well-built systems need ongoing checks to stay efficient—especially in real-world, off-grid conditions. Whether you're noticing reduced output or unexpected noise, the chart below outlines common wind turbine issues, practical fixes, and how to stay ahead of problems with simple DIY upkeep. These aren't just technical tweaks—they're part of building a system that actually works for your land, weather, and energy needs.

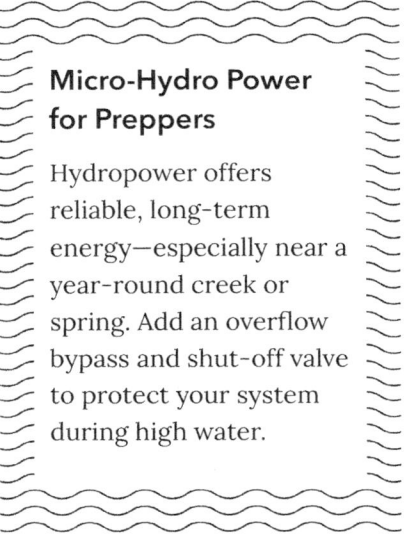

Micro-Hydro Power for Preppers

Hydropower offers reliable, long-term energy—especially near a year-round creek or spring. Add an overflow bypass and shut-off valve to protect your system during high water.

Problem	Possible Cause	Solution
Blades not spinning	Low wind or mechanical resistance	Check for obstructions, add lubrication, or raise tower height
Low power output	Poor turbine alignment	Adjust turbine to face main wind direction.
Excessive noise or wobble	Loose hardware or unbalanced blades	Tighten bolts and check for bent or damaged blades
Inconsistent output	Gusty wind or bad connections	Add guy wires, use quality wiring, check all terminals
System shuts down	Battery or Controller Overloaded	Check controller settings and battery levels

And if you've ever wondered whether adding wind is worth the effort, Mo's experience offers a powerful example of why diversifying your system can make all the difference—especially when solar falls short.

 FROM THE FIRE. STORIES THAT STILL BURN.
When the Sun Wasn't Enough, He Turned to the Wind

After setting up a solar system at his off-grid cabin, Mo noticed a familiar winter problem: not enough sunlight, not enough stored power. To stay energy-independent, he turned to a second source—wind.

In his video DIY Off-Grid Cabin Wind Turbine Install, Mo walks through how he added a wind turbine to supplement solar during cloudy or low-output days. He shares the full process, including tower height, turbine placement, and wiring setup. For him, it wasn't about building the perfect system—it was about adding smart layers that worked with his land and weather.

> *Solar's great, but it has its limits. The wind doesn't care if it's cloudy or snowing, and that's when I needed it most.—Mo*

His story is a reminder that energy independence isn't just about one source—it's about designing for your seasons, your location, and your needs.

⌐ SCAN ME

Can Wind Really Power an Off-Grid Cabin?
See how Mo installed a functional wind turbine system from start to finish, including parts, placement, and real-world performance in challenging conditions. Watch their story: DIY Off-Grid Cabin Wind Turbine Install.

Wind can thrive in open, gusty areas, but not every property has the ideal conditions. If you have consistent flowing water close by, you could already be seated on one of the most reliable off-grid power sources. Let us now discuss micro hydro.

Micro-Hydro: Why It's Worth It

Micro-hydro systems convert flowing water into electricity and offer one of the most consistent renewable power sources available. Unlike solar or wind, they operate 24/7 with minimal moving parts and little ongoing maintenance. This makes them ideal for locations with reliable, year-round water flow.

Family & Shared Use

Hydro systems need regular checks—get the whole household involved. Assign small tasks, label high-priority loads like fridges or pumps, and revisit your usage plan each season. Shared clarity prevents shared burnout.

Environmental Impact and Sustainability

A well-designed micro-hydro system minimizes ecological disruption by ensuring habitat conservation and reducing sediment buildup that could impact water quality. Regular maintenance is essential to prevent algae growth, debris blockages, and contamination, ensuring the system remains efficient and environmentally responsible. Periodic water quality checks further support long-term sustainability while protecting natural resources.

 STEP-BY-STEP PROJECT
How to Set Up a Micro-Hydro Power System

Before you begin: Check local laws first—water diversion isn't always legal, even on private land. Choose a reliable, year-round stream with good flow and vertical

Skill Level: Advanced

Requires plumbing, electrical wiring, and adapting to terrain. Ideal for those confident in DIY system design and safety.

Estimated Cost

- **$** - DIY turbine from salvaged parts
- **$$ - $$** – Prebuilt unit w/ plumbing
- **$$$–$$$$** - Full system: controller, battery, inverter, wiring

Estimated Time to Complete

2 to 4 hours: Small demo system
1 to 2 days: Basic stream turbine
3 to 4 weekends: Full penstock setup

Materials List

- Intake pipe with debris screen
- Penstock pipe (PVC or HDPE)
- Pelton-style micro-hydro turbine
- Hydro-compatible charge controller
- Battery bank
- Inverter
- Electrical wiring and connectors

Tools Required

- Shovel or trenching tool
- Drill and hole saw
- Pipe fittings and sealant
- Level and tape measure
- Multimeter

DIY & Reuse Opportunities

- Use leftover PVC for penstock
- Build housings from waterproof bins
- DIY turbines from spoons or alternators
- Repurpose farm wiring or anchors
- Reuse hose for intake line
- Salvage valves or fittings from old irrigation systems

drop. More water and more head mean more power. Place your intake safely, away from flood zones or unstable ground.

Step 1: Install the Water Intake Pipe

Place a screened intake pipe in a clean, flowing stream. Ensure the mesh is fully submerged and secured to prevent debris from entering. A settled, rock-lined area reduces clogging and sediment issues.

Step 2: Lay the Penstock Pipe

Run durable pipe (PVC, HDPE, or steel) downhill from the intake. Keep a steady slope to boost water pressure—more drop equals more power.

Step 3: Connect the Hydro Generator

Connect a hydro generator with an internal turbine at the bottom of the penstock. It converts the force of flowing water into DC electricity.

Step 4: Wire the Charge Controller

Route the electrical output through a charge controller to regulate voltage and protect your battery system from overcharging or spikes.

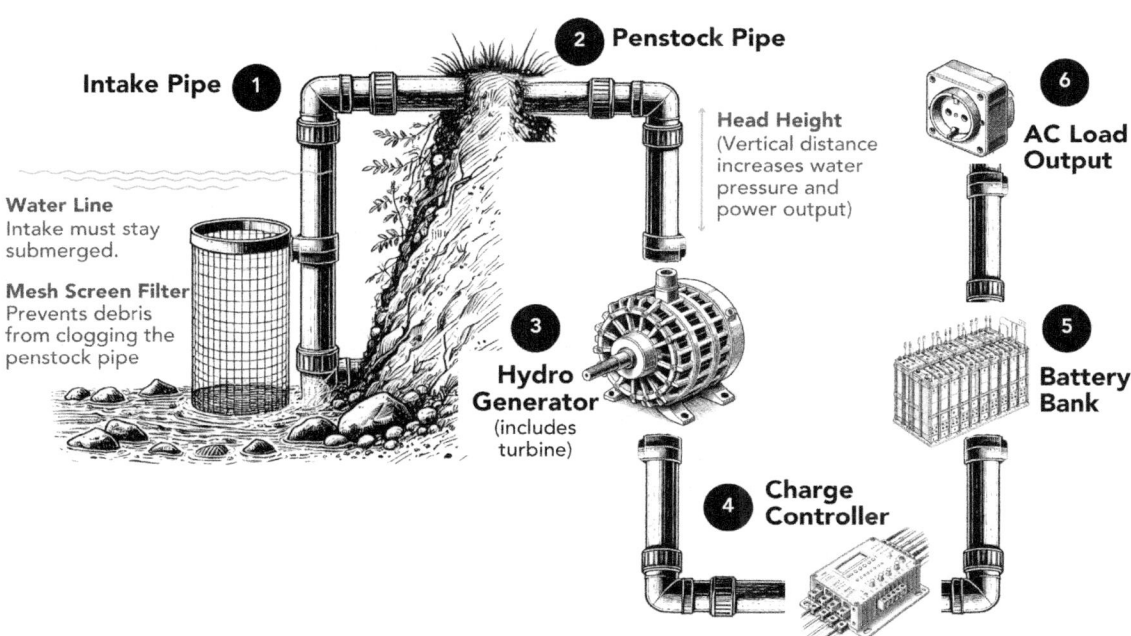

Step 5: Attach the Battery Bank

Connect to a deep-cycle battery bank (12V, 24V, or 48V, depending on system needs) to store power for use during low-flow conditions or at night.

Step 6: Add AC Output and Test Power

To power household appliances, wire an inverter to convert DC to AC, then test with a multimeter or plug in a device to confirm.

Not every off-grid site has the right terrain for hydro—but when it does, even modest systems can deliver outsized results. One couple learned this firsthand when they stopped chasing sun and started listening to the water already running through their land.

FROM THE FIRE. STORIES THAT STILL BURN.
A Humble Stream, a Steady Charge

For one off-grid couple featured in Backwoods Home Magazine, the key to year-round energy independence was hiding in plain sight—a small creek winding through their rural property. Tired of the limitations of solar in cloudy weather and the noise of generators, they looked to the flowing water for a quieter, more consistent solution.

They found an 80-foot drop along the creek—just enough vertical head for micro-hydro. With some DIY ingenuity, they fused 1,200 feet of 4-inch HDPE pipe to build a penstock, channeling water downhill to their turbine.

Setup Details:

- **Location**: U.S. homestead with year-round creek
- **Water Source**: Creek with ~80 ft head
- **Penstock**: 1,200 feet of 4-inch HDPE pipe
- **System Voltage**: 24V micro-hydro in workshop
- **Application**: 24V micro-hydro in workshop
- **Outcome**: Stable, quiet energy source without reliance on fuel or sun

What He'd Do Differently: Don't underestimate a small water source. At first, he thought the creek was too minor to power anything—but with the right drop and

DIY setup, it became their most consistent energy supply. His advice? Focus on site-specific potential, not size. Let your land teach you what works. Their setup didn't just deliver consistent power—it also reduced noise, fuel use, and system strain. - Backwoods Home Magazine – "A small creek provides plenty of power for this off-grid home"

And they're not alone. More off-gridders are discovering that sustainable systems don't just serve your needs—they protect the land that supports them. Let's take a closer look at how your energy choices impact both your environment and your long-term resilience.

Long-Term Efficiency and Sustainability Outcomes

A micro-hydro system can produce ~35 kWh/day—enough to run a home, well pump, and backup heat with minimal upkeep. It offers full off-grid power without fuel or frequent maintenance.

Micro-Hydro vs. Solar Energy. By leveraging micro-hydro energy, homeowners gain a year-round, low-maintenance power source for true energy independence.

Which System Fits Your Land? Every location has different strengths.

Go solar if... You have strong year-round sunlight and clear space

Go wind if... You have consistent wind above 10 mph and open exposure

Go hydro if... You have flowing water year-round with a decent elevation drop

Factor	Micro-Hydro	Solar
Reliability	24/7 power generation	Daytime-only production
Maintenance	Low	Moderate (cleaning, battery checks)
Upfront Cost	Medium to High	Medium
Best For	Flowing water sources	High-sunlight regions

Build Smart—No Matter Your Budget

One of the biggest concerns for those transitioning off-grid is the high cost of energy systems. Fortunately, you don't need to spend thousands upfront. Instead, you can start small and scale up. Below is a comparison of low-, medium-, and high-budget setups to help you choose the right starting point.

Category	Low-Cost Setup ($500 - $2,000)	Mid-Cost Setup ($5,000 - $15,000)	High-Cost Setup ($20,000+)
Energy Source	Small solar generator (Jackery 500W)	2-4 solar panels + battery bank	Full solar array (10+ panels) + wind/hydro backup
Storage	Portable lithium-ion battery	4-6 deep-cycle batteries	High-capacity lithium battery bank
Inverter	300W portable inverter	1,500W pure sine wave inverter	5,000W whole-home inverter
Backup System	None (manual energy rationing)	Gasoline generator	Hybrid system (solar + wind/hydro)
Cost Estimate	$500 - $2,000	$5,000 - $15,000	$20,000

" ⸺ 🔥 From the Fire ⸺

We don't even think about it anymore. It just works.
That's what off-grid power should feel like.

"

Why Go Hybrid? No Gaps in Power

No single energy source is 100% reliable. A solar-only setup may struggle on cloudy days, while wind turbines may fail on calm days. Combining multiple energy sources creates a resilient system that ensures continuous power.

Avoid Overspending on the Wrong Setup

Many people just starting out overspend on panels or inverters, ignoring storage and wiring. Even a modest, well-balanced $500 system—where every component is matched—can outperform a badly thought-out $1,500 system.

Hybrid System	Best For	Pros	Cons
Solar + Wind *Good all-season option for beginners*	Cloudy and windy regions	Power day and night	Wind turbines require maintenance
Solar + Hydro *High-output but site-dependent*	Areas with running water	Reliable 24/7 power	Requires access to flowing water
Wind + Battery Storage *Strong backup strategy in windy zones*	Wind and storm-prone	Stores excess wind power	Initial setup cost can be high

Which Hybrid System Fits Your Needs?

A hybrid approach minimizes downtime and maximizes energy availability.

Designing a Hybrid System

Hybrid systems work best when tailored to your site, energy needs, and climate. Start by identifying your primary source—usually solar—and then add a backup. Wind works well in cloudy, breezy regions; micro-hydro adds consistency if you have flowing water year-round.

Use compatible charge controllers and inverters that can handle multiple inputs. Some off-grid setups keep systems separate (e.g., solar and hydro) with a shared battery bank, while others use hybrid controllers. Just make sure your battery storage can handle your total power output to prevent overload or waste.

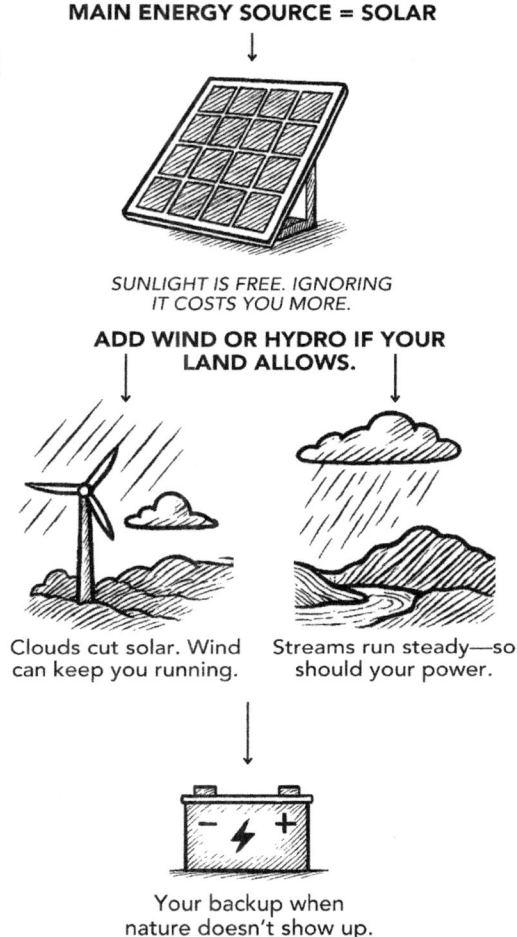

MAIN ENERGY SOURCE = SOLAR

SUNLIGHT IS FREE. IGNORING IT COSTS YOU MORE.

ADD WIND OR HYDRO IF YOUR LAND ALLOWS.

Clouds cut solar. Wind can keep you running.

Streams run steady—so should your power.

Your backup when nature doesn't show up.

Build around what nature gives you.
If you have wind, add a turbine. If you have access to a stream, prioritize hydro.

Let your land shape your system—it saves money and boosts reliability.

Battery Comparison Guide

Choosing the right battery makes your off-grid system reliable, efficient, and long-lasting, while helping you avoid costly failures or early replacements.

Which Battery Works for Your Setup?

Batteries are the core of any off-grid energy system, storing power for nighttime or low-output periods. While lithium-ion has a higher upfront cost, it offers long-term reliability and low maintenance.

Battery Type	Cost	Lifespan	Pros	Cons
Lead-Acid *Solid year-round*	$100-$300 per unit	3-5 years	Cheap, widely available	Short life, needs upkeep
Lithium-Ion *Best for low upkeep*	$500-$3K per unit	10-15 years	Long lifespan	Expensive upfront
Saltwater Batteries *Easy Find Beginner Pick*	$1,000+ per unit	10+ years	Non-toxic, sustainable	Higher initial cost, less efficient

Battery Maintenance and Longevity Guide

Batteries quietly power your off-grid life, but without proper care, they degrade quickly. Understanding key risks like overcharging, sulfation, and extreme temperature damage helps extend their life.

Maintain lead-acid batteries by checking electrolyte levels and cleaning terminals; keep lithium batteries within a stable temperature range. Ensure even charging across battery banks, insulate in cold climates, and ventilate in heat. If performance drops, check for hidden parasitic loads before blaming the batteries.

Battery Storage: Protect Your Power Supply

Beginner Mistake:
Extreme temperatures shorten battery life.
The Fix: Keep batteries indoors or in an insulated enclosure, especially during winter. Temperature control helps maintain performance and extend battery life.

Simple Battery Maintenance Schedule (clean + neutral)

Task	Prevents	Frequency
Check charge levels and voltage	Deep discharge damage	**Weekly**
Inspect and clean terminals	Corrosion, bad connections	**Monthly**
Balance charge cycles	Uneven battery wear	**Monthly**
Prevent sulfation buildup	Capacity loss, reduced efficiency	**Quarterly**
Monitor temperature exposure	Overheating, freezing issues	**Ongoing**
Check electrolyte levels (*lead-acid only*)	Drying out, battery failure	**Every 3 months**

Troubleshooting Common Battery Issues

Problem	Cause	Solution
Battery drains too fast	Overloading, parasitic drain, sulfation	Reduce loads, check wiring, equalize charge
Inconsistent charging	Uneven charge distribution	Balance charge cycles, inspect connections
Overheating	Overcharging, poor ventilation	Use a charge controller, improve ventilation
Won't hold charge	Sulfation, old battery	Equalize (lead-acid) or replace
Freezes in cold weather	Thickened electrolyte, capacity loss	Store in insulated area, use heating pad

Battery Protection in Extreme Conditions

Condition	Impact	Solution
Freezing (< 32°F / 0°C)	20-50% capacity loss, electrolyte freezing	Store indoors or use insulated enclosures
High Heat (> 85°F / 30°C)	Water loss (lead-acid), faster aging	Ventilate, use reflective barriers
Temperature Swings	Expands/contracts components, causing stress	Use thermal covers or battery insulation

Best Battery for Cold Climates: LiFePO4

- Performs efficiently in subzero temperatures (with heating elements).
- Longer lifespan than lead-acid batteries.

Emergency Backup Power and Grid Failures

Why You Need a Backup Power Plan

Even the best off-grid energy systems can fail due to extreme weather, mechanical issues, or seasonal changes. Having a backup power strategy ensures you remain self-sufficient. A backup generator is essential, but consider wood gasification for a sustainable alternative.

Backup Power Options

Backup Source	Pros	Cons
Gasoline Generator	Affordable, widely available	Noisy, requires fuel
Wood Gasification	Uses renewable fuel (wood)	Requires DIY setup
Manual Energy Sources (Hand Crank, Bicycle Generators)	No fuel needed	Low energy output

Extreme Weather Energy Security

Off-grid living means preparing for nature's unpredictability. While a well-designed system functions under normal conditions, hurricanes, snowstorms, wildfires, or flooding can disrupt energy production. Resilient off-gridders plan for redundancy to ensure power remains available during extreme events.

Preparing for Extreme Weather

- **High winds** – Use hurricane-rated mounts; lower turbines before storms.
- **Wildfires** – Clear ash from panels; use fire-resistant battery enclosures.
- **Flooding** – Raise up battery banks and inverters; use weatherproof enclosures.
- **Extended cloud cover** – Hybrid systems ensure power when the sun is low.
- **Storm-prone areas**– Flexible panels resist wind better than rigid ones.

Winter Energy Adjustments

Use steep tilts, coatings, or manual clearing to prevent snow buildup. Insulate batteries and use generators when solar underperforms. Lubricate wind turbines to prevent ice damage.

Wind Protection for Solar Panels

- Use racking rated for 140+ mph winds.
- Ground-mount panels if the rooftop is exposed.
- Adjust the tilt brackets to deflect strong winds.
- Remove portable panels before storms.

Flood Protection for Energy Systems

- Raise batteries at least 2 feet off the ground.

- Use waterproof, ventilated enclosures.

- Choose sealed AGM or lithium batteries for flood resistance.

- Install a Battery Management System (BMS) to regulate temperature and prevent over-discharge.

Protect Your Setup
Where you place your gear and how you shield it can make it last longer and work better in bad weather.

Winter Energy Security

Protecting parts helps, but prepping for full weather threats is key. Use the chart below to spot risks and plan ahead.

Extreme Weather Prep: Quick Reference Chart

Weather Threat	Key Risks	Off-Grid Protection Strategies
Snow & Ice	Frozen pipes, power loss, hypothermia	Insulate lines, use passive heat, and store essentials in warm spaces.
Heatwave or Drought	Water shortage, food spoilage, overheating	Use thermal mass, conserve water, and plant drought-tolerant food sources.
Heavy Rain or Flooding	Contaminated water, damage, isolation	Lift-up gear, divert water, and weatherproof electrical systems.
Hurricane or Windstorm	Structural failure, panel damage, debris	Reinforce structures, anchor energy systems, and clear nearby hazards.
Wildfire or Smoke	Air hazards, structure loss, fast evacuation	Create defensible space, filter air, and stage emergency gear.
Tornado or Extreme Wind	Destruction, flying debris, power outages	Prepare a safe room, secure outdoor items, and keep backup systems charged.
Electromagnetic Pulse (EMP)	Electronics failure, long-term grid down	Shield electronics, use manual tools, and protect solar controls.
Multi-Event Scenario	Stacked disruptions, supply loss, evacuation	Build in redundancy, train across systems, and prep evacuation options.

Winter Weather Recap: Practical Tips to Reinforce Readiness

Tilt panels to shed snow, use de-icing spray to prevent turbine freeze-up, insulate batteries or add heating pads, and combine wind with solar for reliable winter power.

Zoning Considerations and Avoiding Legal Pitfalls

Not all states allow off-grid energy production without restrictions. Some local governments require permits for wind turbines, hydro systems, or battery banks.

Key Legal Considerations

Energy Source	Common Restrictions	How to Stay Legal
Solar Panels	Roof-mounted may require HOA approval	Install ground-based panels if needed
Wind Turbines	Height and noise restrictions	Check local zoning laws before installation
Micro-Hydro	Water rights may apply	Obtain a permit if required by local laws

Check local energy laws before going off-grid.

SCAN ME

Take it a step further. Put your knowledge into action.
Exclusive access to the Off-Grid Survival Companion—with printable checklists, guides, visual aids, and troubleshooting charts from the book, plus practical tools to help you adapt and build with confidence.

Community Energy Sharing and Barter Networks

While energy independence is the goal, some off-grid communities choose to share energy or trade power for goods and services. This provides emergency redundancy and can reduce costs by pooling infrastructure.

Ways to Share Energy in Off-Grid Communities

In off-grid communities, neighbors can support each other through micro-grids that share solar, wind, or hydro power. During shortages, battery swaps allow for trading or renting stored energy. Some even trade excess power for food, labor, or repair help, creating a flexible, mutual support system. We'll dive deeper into how to set up a community network and barter system in **Chapter 8: Without Communication, Even Strong Systems Fail**.

Pros: Sharing energy can lower individual setup costs by pooling infrastructure. It also offers backup during system failures and supports local barter economies by allowing the trade of excess power for food, labor, or services.

Cons: It requires trust and clear agreements to avoid conflict. Some states restrict or prohibit shared energy use. Availability also varies with weather and demand, making it less reliable than fully independent systems. Check local regulations and establish clear agreements to avoid disputes.

When systems are shared, trust becomes the true power source.

Energy can be measured in watts, but resilience is measured in relationships. Whether swapping stored power or pitching in during a storm, community networks only work when people know—and show up—for each other.

Which brings us to a story that captures this spirit in action.

 # FROM THE FIRE. STORIES THAT STILL BURN.
The Power of Barter—and Relationships

Jonathan and Kylene Jones, known as The Provident Preppers, are seasoned preparedness educators who believe bartering is more than just a post-collapse skill—it's a timeless way to meet real needs while building stronger communities.

During a 90-day no-shopping challenge, their family relied entirely on food storage, garden harvests, and bartering. When cravings for fresh food hit, their children stepped up—hauling nearly 19,000 pounds of hay for a neighbor in exchange for Subway, pizza, and Chinese takeout. It wasn't just a lesson in sweat equity. It was a reminder that even without specialized skills, the willingness to work can still put food on the table.

But what really made their barter efforts successful? Trust. They knew their neighbors and understood their wants and needs. When a pig-raising friend shared their love for Nutella, the Jones family quietly stocked extra jars, knowing it could one day translate to pork on their table.

Their story underscores a vital point: the best bartering doesn't happen with strangers—it happens with people you already know and care about. And sometimes, the most valuable "currency" isn't goods at all. It's relationships, reliability, and a spirit of generosity.

> *We found that it wasn't always an equal exchange... Sometimes others were just blessing our lives because they could. And we did the same.*

What They'd Do Different:

Jonathan and Kylene say if they could go back, they'd start building their barter circle sooner. Getting to know neighbors, learning what matters to them, and quietly stocking tradable goods—like extra jars of Nutella—paid off when it mattered most. Their advice? Don't wait for a crisis to start connecting. Invest early in renewable resources you can share—like energy, labor, or homegrown food—and focus on being someone others trust enough to trade with.

⌐ SCAN ME

Curious what real-life preparedness looks like—beyond the basics?

Visit theprovidentprepper.org for practical guides, real stories, and family-tested strategies to help you build resilience, relationships, and readiness—before you need them.

✓ CHECKLIST
Final Checklist for Off-Grid Energy Success

- ☐ **Start small and expand gradually.** Begin with a manageable system to reduce upfront costs and gain hands-on experience before scaling up.

- ☐ **Use battery storage for long-term security.** Reliable battery banks ensure energy is available when the sun isn't shining or the wind isn't blowing.

- ☐ **Have a backup for power failures.** Keep a secondary energy source—like a generator or portable solar kit—for emergencies or maintenance downtime.

☐ **Confirm local energy laws before installing systems.** Check state and local regulations to avoid fines, restrictions, or unexpected legal roadblocks.

☐ **Explore energy sharing for added sustainability.** In community settings, trading or pooling power can cut costs, build trust, and create stronger local networks.

SCAN ME

Not sure which energy system fits your setup?
Use the tools and comparison guides to choose what works for your climate, space, and budget. You have Exclusive access to the **Off-Grid Survival Companion**—with printable planning worksheets, setup visuals, and decision tools from this chapter, plus bonus content to help you make informed choices and design a system you can trust.

Powering What Matters Most

With a reliable energy system in place, you're not just keeping the lights on—you're building stability, independence, and peace of mind. Off-grid living demands more than just generating power; it requires using it wisely, storing it securely, and adapting it to real-world conditions.

Survival isn't just about having energy—it's about making it last, no matter what comes next.

CHAPTER 4:
SHELTER IS YOUR FREEDOM – BUILD IT TO WITHSTAND ANYTHING

Selecting the Perfect Location

One cannot stress enough the importance of choosing a suitable spot for your off-grid haven. Your choice of land will affect your access to water, your ability to generate electricity, and your vulnerability during severe storms. A poorly selected site may expose you to legal constraints, forcing expensive changes, resource shortages, or flooding.

Still, the ideal location prepares you for resilience over the long term. Whether your intended site is a survival retreat or a permanent home, a well-selected location means less work, less risk, and more time focusing on self-reliance.

5 Key Factors for Survival Land Selection

No land is perfect, but some properties come with built-in survival risks. Whether you're buying your first off-grid property or evaluating land you've inherited, it's critical to assess key features that will impact your water access, energy potential, and long-term resilience. Some issues can be worked around with time and money—others can sabotage your entire setup. Use this list to spot smart advantages and avoid costly mistakes before you commit.

1. **Water Access**: Look for a year-round well, spring, or reliable rainwater source.
   Red Flag: Avoid sites with only seasonal streams or drought-prone conditions.

2. **Sun and Wind**: Prioritize south-facing land for solar potential and natural windbreaks for shelter.
   Red Flag: Deep shade or excessive wind exposure can limit energy production.

3. **Elevation and Drainage**: Choose land that's slightly sloped with natural runoff control.
   Red Flag: Flood zones or erosion-prone hills can compromise long-term safety.

4. **Soil and Vegetation**: Seek stable soil for building and native plants that offer food or usable materials.
   Red Flag: Sandy, unstable soil or areas at risk for landslides should raise concern.

5. **Legal Restrictions**: Favor off-grid-friendly zoning with no HOA limitations.
   Red Flag: Watch out for places that ban rainwater collection or require excessive permits for simple upgrades.

When assessing land for long-term off-grid survival, it's often easier to understand the impact of these factors by seeing them in action. The illustrations on the next page contrast ideal versus problematic survival land, highlighting the visible cues that often signal deeper advantages—or hidden threats. Use these visuals as a quick reference when evaluating properties in person or online.

What Kind of Land Will Keep You Alive?

Survival doesn't start with gear—it starts with ground. The land you choose will either support your systems or sabotage them. It's not just about owning property —it's about securing a foundation that lets you live, grow, and adapt without being dependent on unreliable infrastructure. The right site gives you stability, security, and options. The wrong one becomes a daily battle.

- **If your land can't provide water, you'll be hauling it**—or rationing it—at the cost of your health, time, and energy.

-

Best Land for Off-Grid Living vs. Worst Land for Off-Grid Living

- **If your location is too exposed, high winds, storms, and wildfires** can destroy your shelter and supplies in a single season.

- **If the soil can't hold weight or grow food,** you'll spend twice as much reinforcing and importing what should've come naturally.

- **If the land isolates you from community, materials, or emergency help,** even small issues can escalate fast.

Choosing wisely at the start isn't a luxury—it's a survival strategy.

Environmental Risks That Can Make or Break Off-Grid Living

Different climates pose different survival challenges, and many first-time off-gridders underestimate their impact. Ignoring climate factors is a mistake you can't afford to make.

Cold: Requires passive solar design, strong insulation, and efficient heating.

Hot: Seek natural shade and earth-sheltered structures to stay cool.

Dry Regions: Without deep wells or rainwater collection, water scarcity becomes a major risk.

STEP-BY-STEP PROJECTS
Hands-On Tests to Uncover Land Issues Early

Before You Begin: Take the time to physically evaluate the land. These quick DIY tests don't require special tools—just your senses, a little time, and a willingness to dig in. What you discover now could save you thousands later.

Skill Level: Beginner

No specialized knowledge required

Estimated Cost

$ – Typically under $20

Estimated Time to Complete

30 minutes: Active Setup
24–48 hours: Observation

DIY & Reuse Opportunities

• Repurpose old tarps or plastic packaging
• Reuse clean glass jars

Materials List

• Clear plastic tarp or plastic sheet (approximately 6'x6')
• Stakes or heavy rocks
• Mason jar (1-quart size)
• Clean water
• Notebook and pen

Tools Required

• Shovel or garden spade
• Measuring tape
• Timer (smartphone works fine)

Step 1: Soil Squeeze Test

Purpose: Verify soil drainage quality beyond visual inspection.

• Dig a hole 12 inches deep and wide in your build/garden area.

• Fill the hole with water, let it drain completely, then refill.

• Record how long the second fill takes to drain completely.

No drainage within eight hours points to major problems; professional advice advised. Evaluate your soil drainage results using the chart below to decide whether your site requires modifications—or a second review.

Drainage Speed	Interpretation	Recommended Action
Fast (<1 hour)	Sandy/gravelly; good drainage, poor nutrients	Plan soil amendments for gardening
Moderate (1–4 hours)	Ideal soil condition	Minimal adjustments needed
Slow (>4 hours)	Heavy clay/compaction; potential drainage issues	Consider drainage improvements or alternate site

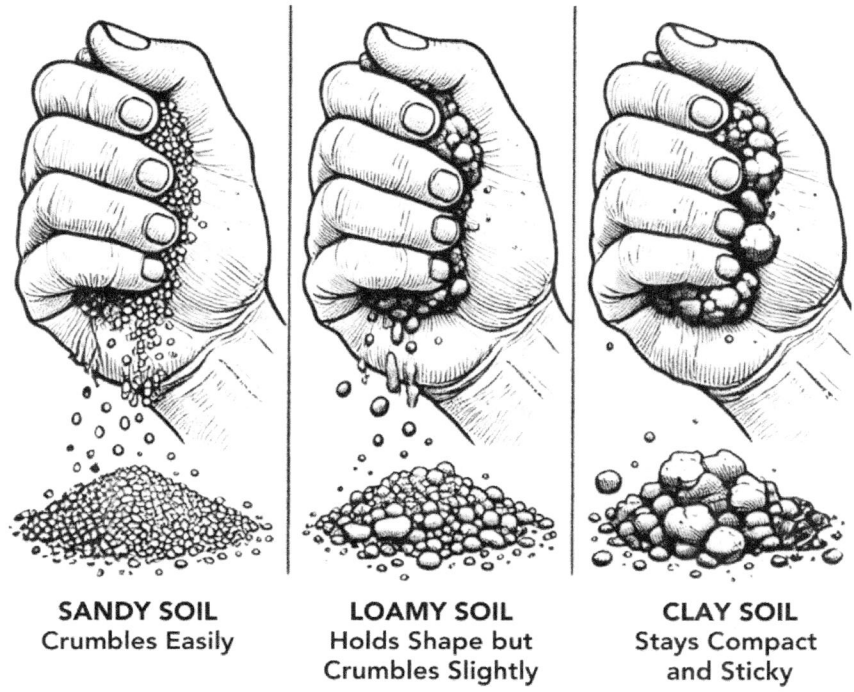

SANDY SOIL
Crumbles Easily

LOAMY SOIL
Holds Shape but
Crumbles Slightly

CLAY SOIL
Stays Compact
and Sticky

Now that you've tested drainage, it's time to dig deeper—literally.

Step 2: Soil Composition Test

Purpose: Accurately identify your soil type.

1. Collect and clear a soil sample from debris/stones.

2. Half-fill a mason jar with soil, add water to near the top, and shake vigorously.

3. Let sit undisturbed for 24 hours; clearly observe layers:

• Bottom: Sand > Middle: Silt > Top: Clay

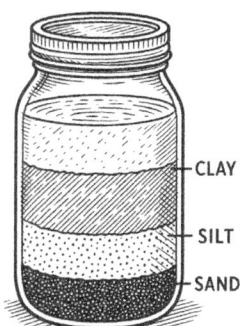

Ideal: 40% sand, 40% silt, 20% clay.

Composition Concern	Recommended Action
Excess clay (>20%)	Add sand, compost, organic matter
Excess sand (>40%)	Add compost, organic matter, clay
Slow (>4 hours)	Consider drainage improvements or alternate site

Step 3: Moisture and Condensation Test

Purpose: Uncover hidden moisture and drainage issues.

1. Lay a plastic tarp directly onto the soil in the proposed development area.

2. Secure tarp edges; leave for 24–48 hours.

3. Observe the tarp underside for condensation.

Condensation Level	Interpretation	Recommended Action
Significant condensation	High moisture content	Plan drainage, raised structures, waterproofing
Little/no condensation	Good drainage, minimal concerns	Proceed with confidence

Troubleshooting Guide

Issue	Possible Cause	Solution
Unclear soil layers	Poor mixing, excess soil	Repeat test with vigorous shaking; less soil
No drainage in test	Severe compaction/ heavy clay	Professional analysis or alternate site
Extreme tarp condensation	High water table/ flood risk	Investigate further or lifted-up structures

Sunlight Exposure Test

Purpose: Identify the best areas on your land for solar gain to optimize panel placement, heating strategies, and passive energy efficiency.

Use a shadow stick or solar tracking app to observe how light moves across the land. See the visual guide below for two simple methods to test sun exposure and plan the solar panel placement.

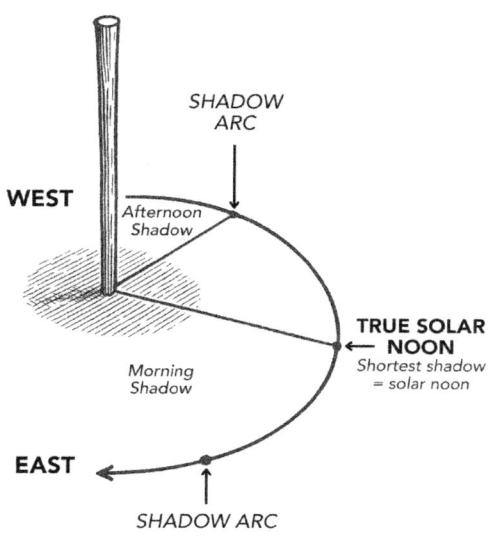

Manual Sunlight Tracking: Shadow Stick Method

Place a straight stick upright in the ground. Mark the tip of its shadow every 15–30 minutes. The shortest shadow marks true solar noon, and the arc shows your sunlight window.

Use string or stones to mark the arc and revisit it later to compare seasonal changes.

Solar App Tracking: Your solar guide in your pocket

Use a solar app to visualize real-time sunlight angles and exposure trends. This helps you fine-tune panel placement for better performance year-round.

Apps like Sun Surveyor, Sun Seeker, or PV Solar Forecast can help you get started.

Wind Exposure Test

Purpose: Identify prevailing wind direction and intensity to determine if natural windbreaks or shelter reinforcements are needed.

Tie a ribbon or surveyor's tape to a sturdy post in your proposed build area. Observe its movement over 1-2 days in varying conditions. Track direction and strength, then note if gusts are constant, seasonal, or terrain-driven. Use this data to guide building orientation, place windbreaks, or anchor key structures more securely.

Legal Landmines to Avoid

A beautiful piece of land is useless if off-grid living isn't legal. Many projects fail due to a lack of research before buying.

Common Legal Challenges to Watch For:

1. **Zoning and Permits:** Some areas restrict composting toilets, off-grid power, or water systems.

   - **Before you invest,** research your county's building codes and zoning ordinances—especially for alternative sanitation, solar setups, or graywater reuse. A quick call to your local planning office can save you from costly violations later.

   - **Example Misstep:** A couple in Missouri installed a DIY composting toilet without realizing their county required a permitted septic alternative. They were fined and forced to remove it within 30 days, delaying their move-in by months and racking up unplanned costs.

2. **Rainwater Collection Laws:** Certain states limit or ban rainwater storage.

   - **Check your state laws early**—some allow only rooftop collection, while others require permits or set volume limits. Use tools like the DOE Rainwater Harvesting Tool and World Water Reserve's Legal Map to plan your system legally and effectively.

   - **Example Misstep:** A solo off-gridder in Utah installed four 300-gallon tanks to collect rainwater—only to learn post-inspection that state law capped unregistered systems at two 100-gallon containers. He had to drain and dismantle part of his system to comply.

3. **Property Taxes and Fees:** Even rural land can have hidden costs that make self-sufficiency harder.

   - **Look beyond the purchase price.** Confirm your property's classification, check for any agricultural exemptions, and understand how adding infrastructure (like solar or a tiny home) might affect taxes. Call your assessor's office to ask about off-grid-related fees or reassessments.

   - **Example Misstep:** A family in upstate New York bought raw land, assuming taxes would stay low. After building a small cabin and installing solar, their

land was reclassified from "vacant rural" to "residential with improvements"
—tripling their annual property taxes overnight.

To avoid these costly surprises, use the checklist below to verify key legal and
logistical details before buying off-grid land.

CHECKLIST
What to Verify Before Buying Off-Grid Land

Check off each item as you verify the land meets the criteria:

Zoning & Land Use

☐ Off-grid dwellings are allowed on this property

☐ Solar panels and composting toilets are permitted

☐ No minimum dwelling size that restricts small structures

☐ Property is outside HOA control, or HOA permits off-grid setups

Water Rights & Collection

☐ Rainwater harvesting is legal in this location

☐ Well drilling is allowed and does not require excessive permitting

☐ Water rights transfer with the land deed

☐ No municipal service requirements for water/sewer

Housing Designation Flexibility

☐ Rainwater harvesting is legal in this location

☐ RVs, tiny homes, or mobile structures are allowed for full-time living

☐ Temporary or seasonal dwelling permits are available if needed

☐ Building codes don't require foundations or grid-tied utilities

☐ No limitations on staying full-time on unimproved land

Survival Retreat Priorities

Not everyone buying off-grid land is planning to live there full-time. For some, the
goal is a survival retreat—land that can serve as a fallback location during grid

failure, societal unrest, or natural disasters. If that's your purpose, selecting land that's both secure and legally flexible becomes even more critical.

☐ **The land is secluded but still accessible in emergencies**

☐ **Terrain offers natural cover or defense (woods, hills, barriers)**

☐ **Property has two water sources (well, stream, or rain catchment)**

☐ **Zoning laws do not restrict off-grid systems or survival measures**

Beginner Tips

- Start with an A-frame or earthbag shelter—both are cost-effective and forgiving.
- Use salvaged windows or doors to cut costs without sacrificing insulation.
- Focus on sealing and durability before worrying about advanced upgrades.

Whether you're building a full-time off-grid homestead or a fallback retreat, your shelter is your first line of defense. The next section covers how to construct a survival-ready, insulated structure that protects against the elements and minimizes energy loss, no matter how rough conditions get.

Build a Survival Off-Grid Shelter

Before you pick up a single tool, your site decisions matter. That's why earlier you tested the land for drainage, moisture, sunlight, and wind using simple tools like a ribbon, tarp, and shadow stick.

Now it's time to take that insight and translate it into a structure that's sturdy, insulated, and adapted to your specific climate and terrain. This section walks you through a flexible build process—with visuals of different structures and foundations to help you choose what fits your land, skills, and goals.

Designing for Passive Solar Gain

This layout harnesses natural sunlight, proper ventilation, and locally sourced materials to maintain a comfortable indoor climate all year—using passive solar design and thermal mass to cut energy bills and reduce the need for external heating or cooling.

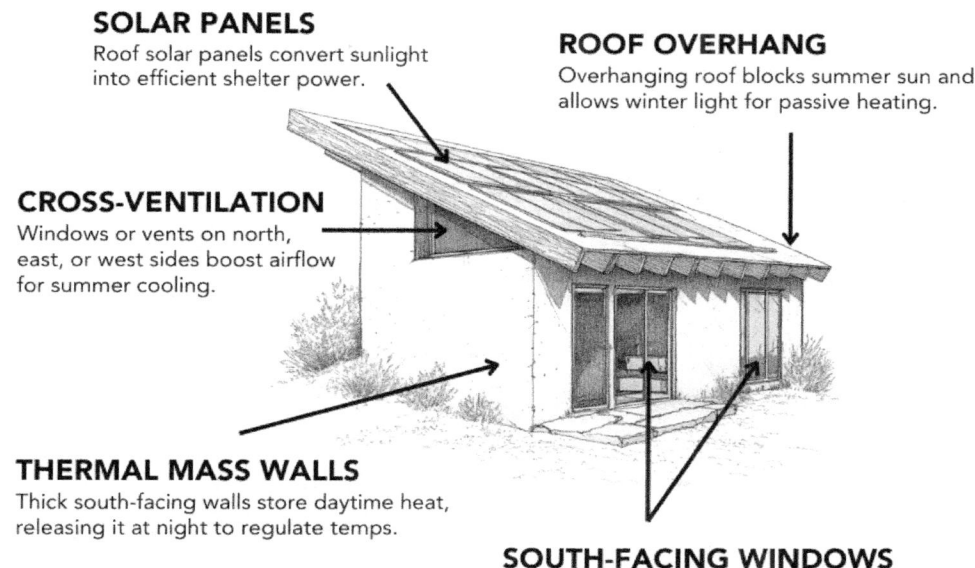

SOLAR PANELS
Roof solar panels convert sunlight into efficient shelter power.

ROOF OVERHANG
Overhanging roof blocks summer sun and allows winter light for passive heating.

CROSS-VENTILATION
Windows or vents on north, east, or west sides boost airflow for summer cooling.

THERMAL MASS WALLS
Thick south-facing walls store daytime heat, releasing it at night to regulate temps.

SOUTH-FACING WINDOWS
South-facing windows capture winter sun for natural heat.

Off-Grid Starts Where You Are

You don't need land to start building resilience. Many off-gridders begin by retrofitting a garage, basement, or shed—using the same insulation and weatherproofing strategies outlined in this chapter. Use what you have:

- Insulate to reduce energy loss, weatherproof for year-round use, and start small before expanding.
- Even a converted shed or finished basement can become a safe, self-reliant fallback space.

What to Choose First—and Why It Matters

You might think the foundation comes first—but in off-grid building, it's smarter to start with the structure. Your shelter choice determines the weight you need to support, the materials you'll use, and how your space interacts with the land. Only then can you confidently match it to the right foundation based on terrain, drainage, and weather risks. Think of it like this: **Form follows function.** Choose the shelter that fits your climate, budget, and needs—**then** pair it with a foundation that will keep it stable, dry, and long-lasting.

Shelter Adaptations That Actually Work
Build for your people, your region, and your risks.

What to Expect

- **Earthbag + A-frame shelters:** Fast, sturdy, and bug-out ready.
- **Reinforce small shelters:** Add solar, supply caches, or water barrels.
- **Choose fire- and flood-resistant materials:** Ideal for disaster-prone zones
- **Plan for layered defense:** Focus on safety, smart sealing, and backup storage.

Who You're Protecting

- **Multi-use space:** Bunks, lofts, or fold-away storage add flexibility in shelters.
- **Safety-first airflow:** Ventilation without hazards for kids or pets.
- **Durability matters:** Choose finishes that hold up to rough, repeated use.
- **Quiet corners:** Even in small spaces, low-stimulation zones ease stress and support sleep.

For families, resilience isn't just structure —it's comfort, safety, and flexibility. A well-designed space supports daily life, not just emergencies.

Where You Live

- **Cold climates:** Thick insulation, south-facing walls, steep-pitched roof
- **Hot regions:** Shade, reflective roofing, cross-ventilation
- **Humid areas:** Breathable, mold-resistant materials like hempcrete, wool, plaster
- **High-wind zones:** Hurricane ties, braced joints, compact framing
- **Flood-prone sites:** Raised foundation, gravel swale or drainage zone
- **Fire-risk areas:** Metal roof, ember-safe vents, fire-rate

Before investing in heating or cooling, design your shelter to need less energy in the first place. — Michael E. Reynolds, Architect of Earthship Homes.

STEP-BY-STEP PLAN
DIY Off-Grid Shelter Build

This streamlined step-by-step guide ensures your shelter is durable, well-insulated, and energy-efficient.

Skill Level:

Beginner: Earthbag or A-frame build
Intermediate: Post-and-beam + insulation
Advanced: SIPs or hybrid designs with structural reinforcements

Tools Required

- Tape measure, chalk line, square
- Hand or circular saw
- Hammer, drill, fasteners
- Knife, staple gun
- Shovel or post-hole digger

Estimated Cost
$ – Earthbag or fully salvaged builds
$$ - A-frame with salvaged windows
$$$-$$$$ – Full cabin or SIP structure with new insulation and roofing

Estimated Time to Complete

1 to 3 days: A-frame or earthbag structure
3–7 days: Post-and-beam with insulation
7–14 days: SIP or hybrid with upgrades

Materials List

Structure style matters—see materials and images below.

- Framing & Roofing: Lumber, SIPs, metal or reflective panels
- Insulation & Sealing: Straw, wool, foam, vapor wraps
- Openings: Solid doors, thermal windows, shutters
- Materials List Extras: Ties, gravel, drainage for flood/wind zones

DIY & Reuse Opportunities

- Reclaim framing lumber, barn wood, or shed materials
- Salvage insulation panels, windows, and doors from reuse centers
- Build foundations from gravel, pallets, or packed earth
- Use clay, straw, and sand to mix natural earthen plasters or renders
- Repurpose metal roofing from old sheds or barns

Before You Begin:

You've already explored how to research land and navigate legal challenges—feel free to reference those sections as needed. Before moving forward, take time to assess your land's specific conditions, including soil, drainage, and sun/wind exposure. Think ahead to systems you may want later—like solar, water catchment, or a root cellar—and review local building codes that could affect your foundation type, structure size, or materials. With that in mind, you're ready for the setup for choosing a shelter style that fits your land and lifestyle.

Step 1: Choose the Right Shelter Style for Your Land

Use the Guides Below To Compare Structure Options. Match Each Style to Your Site Conditions, Climate, and Skill Level.

Option 1: A-Frame Cabin

Best for: Snowy regions, steep terrain, fast builds

Great for rugged sites and cold climates, the A-frame is quick to build, naturally sheds snow and rain, and uses fewer materials than most framed cabins. It's ideal if you want a durable, efficient shelter with minimal complexity.

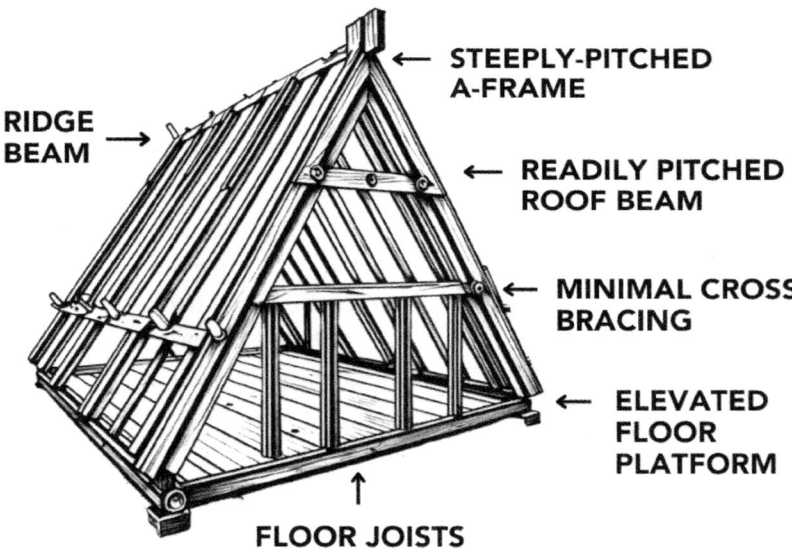

Top 3 Reasons to Choose A-Frame

1. **Strong Yet Simple:** The triangular shape distributes weight evenly, creating a sturdy structure with fewer materials. Ideal for DIY builders on a budget, this design doesn't require advanced framing skills or specialty tools.

2. **Great for Harsh Weather:** A-frame roofs naturally shed snow and rain, preventing buildup and leaks. This makes them a smart choice in cold or wet climates where maintenance access is limited and weatherproofing is critical.

3. **Heat-Holding Shape:** With less interior volume and steep angled walls, A-frames retain warmth efficiently. For anyone relying on passive solar, wood stoves, or minimal energy inputs, this design helps conserve heat and reduce fuel use.

Option 2: Earthbag Shelter

Best for: Dry climates, fire-prone zones, natural builds

Earthbags offer serious strength and insulation using low-cost, natural materials. They perform especially well on hot days and cold nights. A bit labor-intensive, but ideal if you want long-lasting protection and a low-impact footprint.

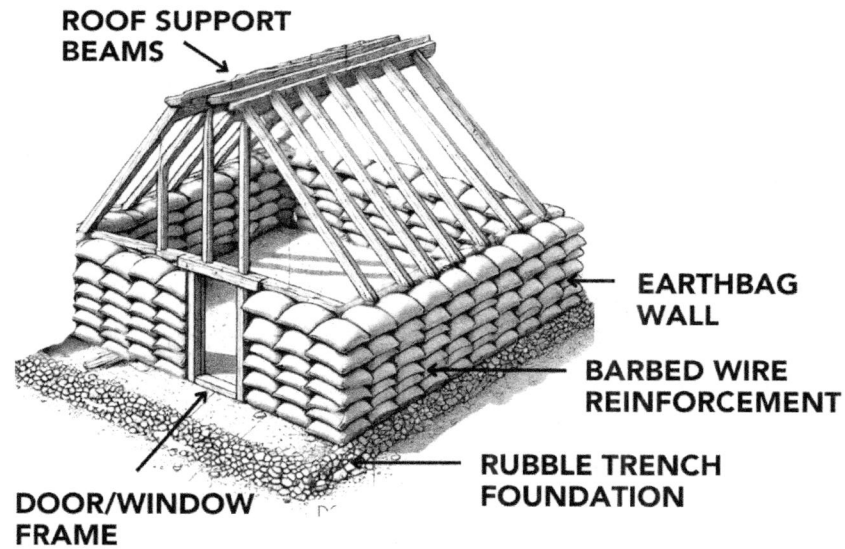

Top 3 Reasons to Choose Earthbag

1. **Tough in Any Climate:** Earthbag homes resist fire, floods, earthquakes, and extreme weather. They're ideal for harsh environments and long-term durability, with minimal maintenance required once built.

2. **DIY-Friendly:** No power tools or complex skills needed—just dirt, bags, barbed wire, and determination. Earthbag building is accessible for beginners and budget-conscious DIYers.

3. **Great for Emergencies:** Quick to build with on-site or local materials, earthbags offer a fast, low-cost shelter option after disasters or when supply chains are unreliable.

Option 3: SIP-Panel Cabin

Best for: Cold climates, fast builds, and lasting energy savings.

SIPs offer quick assembly with built-in insulation and airtightness—perfect if you're racing the seasons. They cost more upfront, but drastically reduce heating needs and speed up the build for solo or first-time off-gridders.

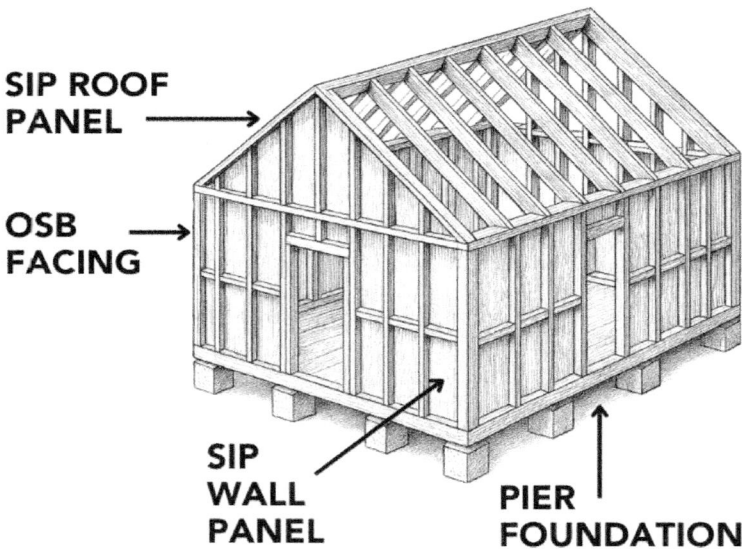

SIP ROOF PANEL

OSB FACING

SIP WALL PANEL

PIER FOUNDATION

Top 3 Reasons to Choose SIPs

1. **Energy-Efficient:** High-performance insulation is built right in, reducing heat loss in winter and cooling loss in summer—ideal for off-grid systems with limited energy.

2. **Quick to Build:** Large, prefabricated panels lock together fast with fewer seams and less labor, helping you get weather-tight quickly—even with limited help or short build windows.

3. **Tough in Harsh Conditions:** SIPs form a strong, rigid shell that handles high winds, heavy snow, and rough weather far better than standard stick-framing.

OPTION 4: Post-and-Beam Structure

Best for: Larger layouts, long-term homes, modular builds

Post-and-beam gives you strength and flexibility—great for lofts, open interiors, or expanding over time. It takes more skill and planning, but it's a smart choice if you're building a legacy structure to grow with you.

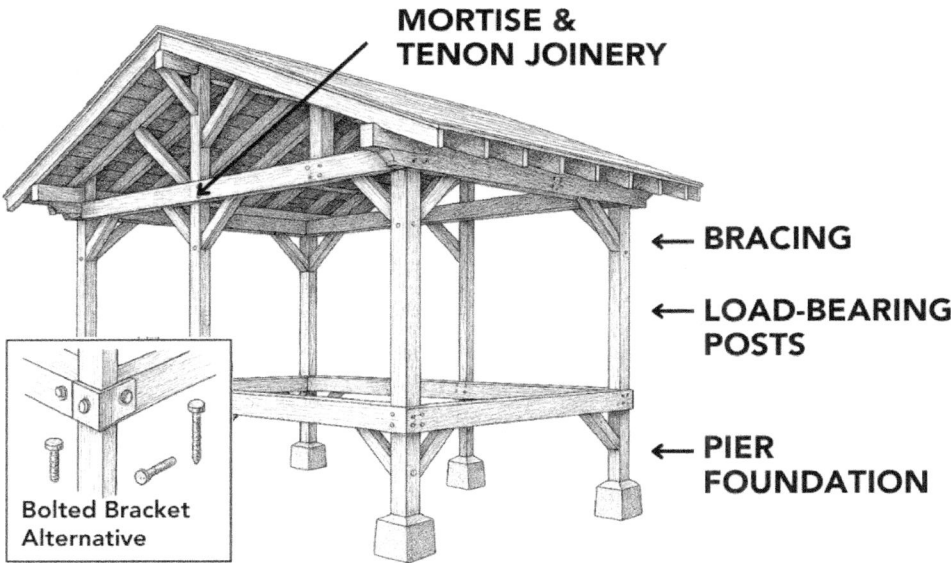

Top 3 Reasons to Choose Post & Beam?

1. **Long-Lasting Strength:** Post and beam frames use large timbers that hold up to storms, snow, and shifting terrain, making them a solid choice for permanent, legacy structures in rural or exposed locations.

2. **Open Interior Space:** With fewer load-bearing walls, this style gives you flexible floor plans that adapt easily to evolving needs—ideal for growing families, multipurpose rooms, or passive solar layouts.

3. **Off-Grid Friendly:** Can be built on piers, slabs, or stilts—perfect for uneven ground, flood-prone areas, or remote sites where heavy machinery isn't available or practical.

SCAN ME

 **Need help making your decision?**
Access the Shelter & Foundation Tools in the Off-Grid Survival Companion—complete with printable charts and smart prompts to help you plan confidently for your land, climate, and build style.

Match Your Foundation to the Structure and Site

You might think the foundation comes first—but in off-grid building, it's better to start with the structure. The shelter you choose determines how much weight your foundation needs to carry, how high it needs to sit above ground, and how to plan for moisture, frost, or expansion.

Once you've picked your structure style, use this section to find the right foundation based on your **terrain, drainage, climate, and skill level.**

Your Shelter-to-Foundation Fit Plan

- **Weight:** Can the foundation support the materials you plan to use?

- **Height:** Do you need elevation for airflow, flood protection, or terrain?

- **Conditions:** What challenges does your land pose—frost heave, water runoff, or unstable slope?

Once you know what your structure demands, choosing the right base becomes much easier.

Planning a Natural Build?

If you're considering earthbag, cob, or another natural wall system, a rubble trench foundation may be a better fit. It's made using compacted gravel and drainage pipe instead of concrete and is often used in off-grid natural building projects. You won't find full details here, but it's worth exploring through trusted natural building resources or training guides.

Step 2: Pick a Shelter That Fits Your Land

A good foundation does more than hold your shelter up—it protects it from shifting, sinking, flooding, and frost over time. Whether you're building on a slope, in a flood zone, or on rocky soil, your foundation should respond to the land beneath it. Use the options below to find the one that best supports your structure, both physically and practically.

Option 1: Pier Foundation

Best for: Uneven terrain, forested plots, flexible framing

Piers keep your structure level while lifting it off the ground—great for sloped sites or anywhere digging a full slab isn't practical. They're quick to install and pair well with A-frames, tiny homes, and post-and-beam builds. Make sure they are all frost-rated and securely anchored.

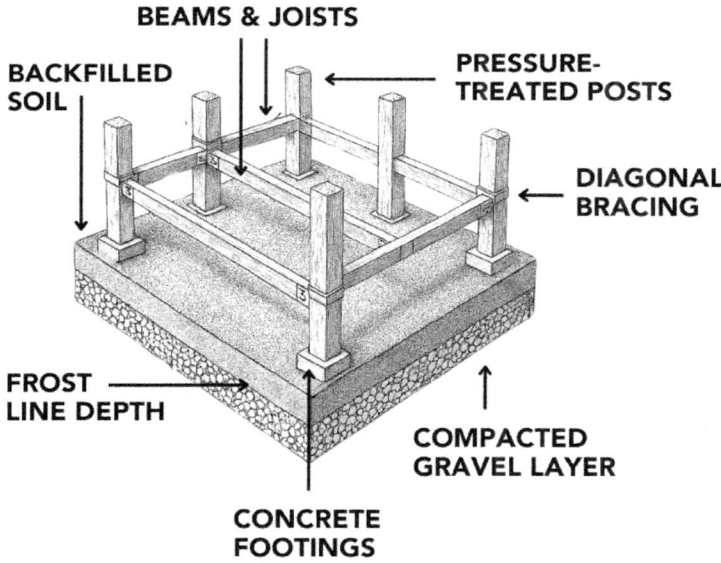

Top 3 Reasons to Choose a Pier Foundation

1. **Quick, Low-Cost Setup:** No excavation, concrete trucks, or complex footings—just basic tools and simple materials. Ideal for remote builds and fast DIY starts.

2. **Handles Rough Terrain:** It is ideal for slopes, rocky areas, or uneven land where other foundations struggle. It offers flexibility without heavy equipment or major grading.

3. **Keeps You Off the Ground:** Raised floors improve airflow, deter pests, and reduce flood risk—especially useful in damp climates or storm-prone zones.

Option 2: Stilt Foundation

Best for: Flood zones, tropical climates, high-humidity regions

Stilts raise the shelter above ground level for protection from standing water, humidity, or critters. They're common in coastal and wetland areas, and they work best when they are reinforced against high winds or shifting soils.

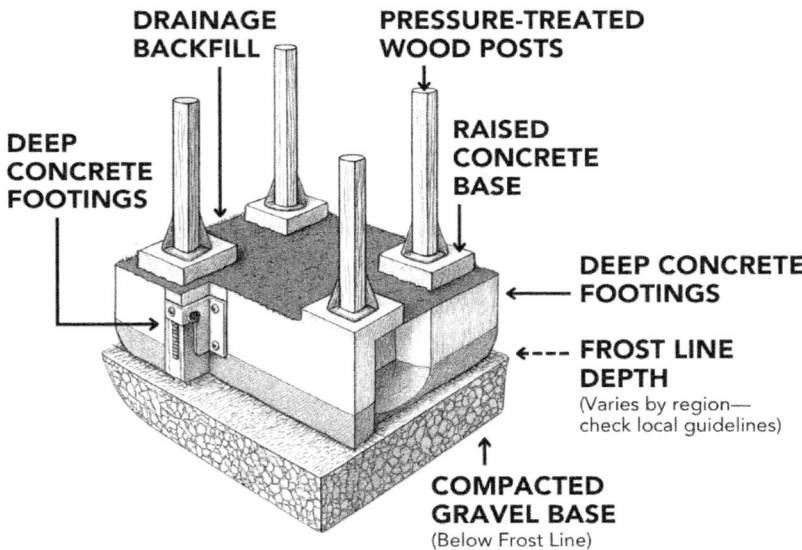

Top 3 Reasons to Choose a Stilt Foundation

1. **Protects Against Water:** It raises your build above floods, snowmelt, or soggy ground. This is essential for coastal, low-lying, or seasonal flood zones where ground-level structures risk costly damage.

2. **Better for Hot Climates:** Natural airflow beneath helps cool your shelter passively. This passive cooling reduces reliance on fans or AC—key when running limited off-grid power systems.

3. **Stays Strong in Shifting Terrain:** When braced, stilts are great on slopes, sand, or erosion-prone areas. Properly anchored stilts offer long-term stability where traditional foundations can crack or sink over time.

They're especially well-suited to A-frames, small cabins, or post-and-beam builds that need an elevated base with strong load-bearing support.

Option 3: Concrete Slab

Best for: Flat land, high-load builds, permanent cabins

Slabs offer a stable, long-lasting base—ideal if you're building in a dry, level area and want strong support for heavy walls or SIP panels. They're more labor- and tool-intensive and require planning for plumbing or conduits before the pour.

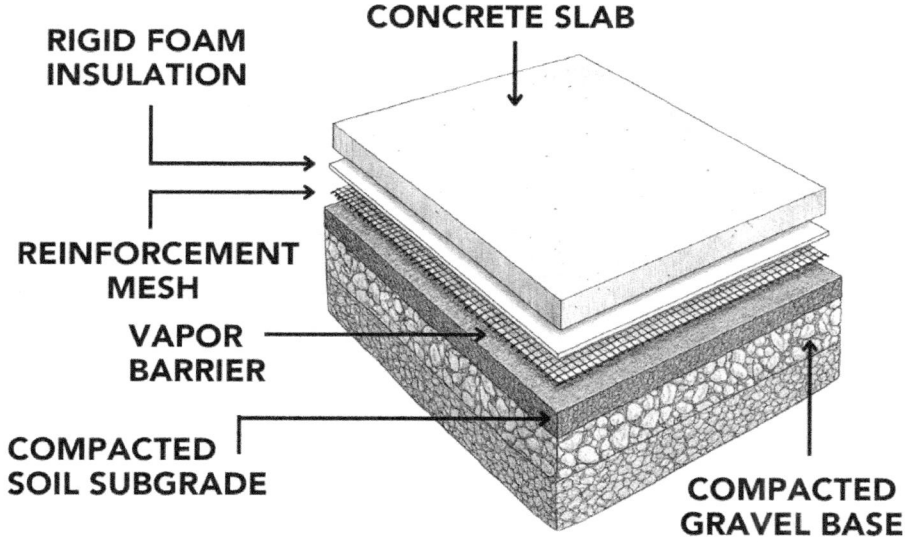

Top 3 Reasons to Choose a Slab Foundation

1. **Affordable and Durable:** A slab foundation offers a strong, permanent base with minimal materials and labor—great for off-gridders seeking a simple, cost-effective solution that won't rot or shift over time.

2. **Low-Maintenance for Stable Climates:** Ideal in dry or temperate areas, slab builds avoid moisture buildup, rodent issues, or crawlspace repairs—making them especially practical in regions without severe ground movement or frost.

3. **Built-In Thermal Mass:** Concrete absorbs daytime heat and slowly releases it at night, helping stabilize interior temperatures. When paired with passive solar design, this can reduce your energy load and keep your shelter more comfortable year-round.

Step 3: Insulate and Reinforce for Your Climate

Once framed, make your shelter livable with innovative insulation and reinforcements for year-round safety and comfort in your environment.

COLD CLIMATE: STRAW BALES
Straw bales trap heat and block cold, making them ideal for colder climates.

Pick Insulation That Works Where You Live

EFFICIENT: RIGID FOAM (SIPS)
Rigid foam in SIPs cuts heat loss and keeps temps steady—great for efficient builds.

Your choice about insulation directly affects your comfort, energy use, and resource needs over time. Match the material to your region and build goals.

MODERATE: HEMPCRETE
Hempcrete suits moderate zones with breathable, year-round comfort.

HUMID: HEMPCRETE
Hempcrete suits moderate zones with breathable, year-round comfort.

Reinforce for Local Hazards

Off-grid builds face real weather threats. Reinforce your shelter now to avoid major damage later.

- **High Wind Zones** → Use hurricane ties, reinforced joints, and cross-bracing.

- **Heavy Snow Areas** →A steep roof sheds snow and protects your frame.

- **Flood-Prone Locations** → Raise your shelter above ground and use water-resistant materials at all exposure points.

⌐SCAN ME

 **Starting with a cabin, trailer, or shed?**
Access the Shelter Essentials, if your not starting from scratch guide in the Off-Grid Survival Companion—complete with a practical guide and printable checklist to help you evaluate, adapt, and upgrade an existing shelter for off-grid living.

 # FROM THE FIRE. STORIES THAT STILL BURN.
Beating the Elements in Remote Alaska

Dennis and Amy, the couple behind Holdfast Alaska, live entirely off-grid in one of the most remote and weather-intense regions of the state. When they designed their homestead, they knew the structure had to withstand brutal winters, deep snow, and violent winds. Every decision they made—down to the roof angle and wall materials—was focused on survival and long-term resilience. **They used:**

- Thick insulation and strategic wall placement to minimize heat loss.

- Bermed earth walls on the windward side for natural thermal mass.

- A steeply pitched metal roof sheds snow and prevents collapse.

- Reinforced joints and smart anchoring to handle high winds.

We built our cabin to take a beating. The wind here will rip the roof off if you're not smart about design. - Dennis, New York Post, Jan 2025

Their shelter not only endured -30°F temperatures and multi-day blizzards but also efficiently used firewood throughout the season. While neighboring cabins suffered wind and snow damage, Dennis and Amy's foresight and reinforcement strategies kept them safe, secure, and off-grid without unnecessary resource loss.

⌐SCAN ME

 **Could your shelter handle a storm like this?**
See how this off-grid couple in Alaska prepared for their first major winter storm—and what they learned about reinforcing their cabin in real time. "Homesteading in Alaska | Preparing for our First Storm of Winter"

✅ QUICK CHECKLIST
Off-Grid Shelter Essentials

Run through this quick list before sealing up your structure.

Location Matters More Than Materials

- [ ] Choose sloped ground for drainage and natural windbreaks for protection.
- [ ] Prioritize water access first—insulation won't help if you run out of water.

Design for Efficiency

- [ ] Use passive solar principles to capture heat in winter and reduce heating needs.
- [ ] Small, compact designs retain heat better—avoid unnecessary space.

Choose Insulation Based on Climate

- [ ] **Cold Climates** – Thick insulation like straw bale or SIP panels.
- [ ] **Hot Climates** – Reflective roofing, earth-sheltered walls, cross-ventilation.
- [ ] **Humid Climates** – Mold-resistant insulation such as wool or hempcrete.

Build for Durability

- [ ] In high wind zones, use reinforced framing and hurricane ties.
- [ ] In heavy snow areas, ensure a steep roof for proper drainage.
- [ ] In flood-prone regions, raise the foundation and use waterproof materials.

Weatherproofing Your Living Space

A single storm can significantly test your off-grid home's resilience. A roof that leaks, pipes that freeze, or wind damage that compromises structural integrity can turn an off-grid retreat into a survival nightmare.

Whether you're preparing for long-term off-grid living or securing a survival retreat, weatherproofing ensures that your shelter stands strong against the elements, retains heat, blocks moisture, and prevents costly repairs.

Identifying Your Shelter's Weak Points

Before reinforcing your shelter, identify the most common failure points where heat loss, moisture intrusion, or structural wear could occur.

Vulnerability	Potential Issue	Solution
Roof and Gutters	Leaks, ice dams, poor drainage	Use metal roofing, proper pitch, and gutter mesh guards.
Windows and Doors	Drafts, energy loss	Weather stripping, caulking, storm windows, and reinforced doors.
Foundation and Walls	Water intrusion, cold floors, structural cracking	Seal foundation, install underfloor insulation, use breathable vapor barriers in humid areas.

Conduct a "Smoke Test" for drafts by holding an incense stick near windows and doors. If the smoke wafts, seal those gaps immediately.

A single weak point in your home's defenses can make off-grid living much harder when extreme weather hits. — Ethan, Off-Grid Survivalist

 STEP-BY-STEP PROJECT
Survival-Driven Weatherproofing Techniques

Reinforce the most vulnerable areas of your shelter—the roof, windows, foundation, and walls—to build resilience. These small upgrades drastically improve your odds in extreme conditions.

Before You Begin

These techniques are designed to work with most off-grid shelters—whether you've built from scratch or adapted a shed or prefab. Start with your structure's weak points and build up over time. Each upgrade strengthens your protection against wind, water, and extreme weather.

Step 1: Reinforce the Roof

• Install a metal roof for long-term strength, fire safety, and storm protection.

- Ensure a steep pitch to shed snow and prevent water pooling.

- Add ice guards near entryways to prevent snow and ice buildup.

- In hot climates, apply a solar-reflective coating to reduce indoor heat.

Step 2: Seal Windows and Doors

- Apply high-quality weather stripping around all frames.

- Use silicone caulk to fill cracks and gaps.

- Install storm windows or double-pane glass for insulation.

- Reinforce doors with solid wood or insulated steel.

- Add external shutters to protect against wind and flying debris.

Step 3: Protect the Foundation

- Seal with rubberized waterproof coatings to block water intrusion.

- Lay a vapor barrier beneath the flooring to control moisture.

- Use gravel beds and French drains to direct runoff away from the structure.

Step 4: Apply Protective Coatings and Wraps

- Use natural oil-based or eco-friendly sealants to prevent wood rot.

- Apply a waterproof house wrap that allows vapor to escape but blocks rain.

- Reapply exterior coatings every 3–5 years to maintain effectiveness.

Even the best weatherproofing degrades over time. To prevent leaks and structural weakening, reapply exterior sealants every 3–5 years.

 FROM THE FIRE. STORIES THAT STILL BURN.
Storms Struck Hard, but They Reinforced Smarter

A couple living off-grid in remote Alaska endured a devastating 75-mph winter storm that put their home to the ultimate test. Despite years of preparation, the storm revealed structural vulnerabilities they hadn't anticipated. After the storm, they quickly reinforced their buildings and adjusted their approach, sharing the hard-earned lessons that could help others avoid similar risks.

What They'd Do Differently:

- **Reinforce Early:** Don't wait for damage to force upgrades—fortify rooflines, joints, and high-wind surfaces before extreme weather hits.

- **Run Worst-Case Drills:** They now practice storm prep scenarios as part of seasonal maintenance, not just in response.

- **Don't Do It Alone:** Reaching out to other local off-gridders gave them ideas and proven tactics they hadn't considered—something they now do regularly.

Even the best upgrades fade over time. Below, use the Weatherproofing Inspection Tool to identify typical points of failure before they become more serious. From minor drafts to early indicators of water damage, these easy inspections will enable you to identify issues early on and maintain the strength of your shelter through all the seasons.

Preppers' Adaptation

Expanding a Survival Retreat

A survival retreat should be durable, low-maintenance, and easy to expand. Focus on modular upgrades over permanent infrastructure to stay flexible and self-reliant.

For a scalable survival retreat:
- Use collapsible rain catchment for fast setup and breakdown.
- Install portable solar generators rather than full solar arrays
- Build underground storage caches instead of a large root cellar
- Use expandable shed-style buildings that can serve multiple purposes

---

SCAN ME

Take it a step further. Put your knowledge into action.
Exclusive access to the Off-Grid Survival Companion—with printable checklists, guides, visual aids, and troubleshooting charts from the book, plus practical tools to help you adapt and build with confidence.

✅ CHECKLIST
Spot Small Problems Before They Grow

Roof & Overhangs

☐ Do you see signs of water staining or soft wood after storms?

☐ Is snow or water pooling instead of shedding cleanly?

☐ Are overhangs or attachments braced against strong wind?

Windows & Doors

☐ Can you feel air leaks or shifting temperatures around frames?

☐ Are caulk lines cracked or weather stripping peeling away?

☐ Do windows rattle or flex during strong wind gusts?

Foundation & Flooring

☐ Is there any dampness or condensation near the floor?

☐ Have you installed a vapor barrier or drainage layer?

☐ Are there signs of mold, rot, or insect damage near the base?

Exterior & Walls

☐ Has your exterior sealant worn off or flaked in places?

☐ Are there new gaps, cracks, or warping along the walls?

☐ Has it been more than 3–5 years since your last protective coating?

Even with a solid shelter and regular upkeep, unexpected conditions can reveal weak spots you didn't know were there.

SCAN ME

Stuck between options or unsure where to start?
Use diagrams and checklists to plan a shelter that fits your land, climate, and resources. Go to the **Off-Grid Survival Companion**— with printable references, step-by-step build guides, and practical tools from this chapter, plus content to help you take action and avoid costly mistakes.

Building Lasting Shelter

Covering your head with a roof marks only the start. The true value of off-grid shelter is found in its protection, adaptability, and support of daily life. Every improvement strengthens your setup, whether you're weatherproofing a do-it-yourself project, insulating a prefab, or strengthening a cabin. Work from what counts most—safety, stability, and comfort—then expand.

A good shelter is the basis that allows you room to relax, plan, and flourish—not only about staying dry or warm.

CHAPTER 5:
YOUR FOOD SUPPLY IS YOUR LIFELINE

Emergency Food Storage and Preservation

Understanding Off-Grid Food Security

Food security is essential for off-grid living. Without a steady supply, self-sufficiency is impossible. Grocery stores stock only a few days' worth of food, and in a crisis, shelves empty within hours. The key to resilience is a layered food storage system with short-, mid, and long-term reserves.

A lack of preparation can lead to food shortages during emergencies, economic instability, or natural disasters. By learning to store, preserve, and produce food off-grid, you can ensure long-term sustainability in any situation.

 _____

Growing your own food is like printing your own money. —Ron Finley, TED Talk: "A Guerilla Gardener in South Central LA" (2013)

_____

Shelf-Stable Foods and Storage Conditions

Food Type	Ideal Storage Conditions	Estimated Shelf Life	Storage Tips
Grains (Rice, Wheat, Oats, Cornmeal)	Cool, dry, airtight (Mylar bags + oxygen absorbers)	10-30 years	Store in airtight containers to prevent pests.
Canned Goods (Vegetables, Meats, Soups)	Pantry, 50-70°F	2-5 years	Rotate using FIFO (First In First Out) method; avoid dented cans.
Root Vegetables (Potatoes, Onions, Carrots, Beets)	Root cellar, 32-50°F, high humidity	3-12 months	Avoid storing onions and potatoes together.
Dehydrated Foods (Fruits, Vegetables, Meats)	Cool, dark, airtight	1-5 years	Store in vacuum-sealed containers or Mylar bags.
Freeze-Dried Foods (Complete Meals, Dairy, Proteins)	Cool, dry, airtight	25+ years	Best for long-term storage; keep in sealed packages.
Legumes and Beans	Cool, dry, airtight (Mylar bags + oxygen absorbers)	10-30 years	Protect from moisture and pests with proper sealing.
Flour and Baking Supplies	Cool, dry, airtight	6 months - 2 years	Store whole grains and grind as needed for longer shelf life.
Honey, Salt, Sugar	Any dry location, sealed	Indefinite	Keep moisture-free; never refrigerate honey.
Fermented Foods (Sauerkraut, Kimchi, Vinegar)	Pantry, 50-70°F	1-5 years	Store in glass jars away from direct sunlight.

Now that you know how long different foods last and how to store them properly, it's time to build a starter plan you can actually follow. The next step breaks it down into manageable, realistic actions—so you can start stocking up without guesswork or overwhelm.

STEP-BY-STEP PROJECT
How to Set Up a Beginner Food Storage Starter Plan

Creating a 30-day emergency food supply is one of the most effective ways to build resilience—whether you're preparing for job loss, natural disasters, or power grid instability. This plan helps you get started with shelf-stable essentials that are easy to find, store, and use.

Before You Begin:

Start with shelf-stable foods your household actually eats. Focus on calorie-dense basics, simple meals, and gradual stockpiling you can afford and rotate.

Skill Level: Beginner

Perfect for those just starting food storage. No prior experience needed—just a practical mindset and a bit of pantry space.

Tools Required

- Permanent markers and labels
- Food-grade buckets or airtight bins
- Optional: Mylar bags & oxygen absorbers
- Optional: Vacuum sealer or can sealer
- Basic measuring tools

Estimated Cost

$ – Pantry-only staples, reused containers
$$ - New containers, Mylar, more variety
$$$ – Full kit meals, comfort, upgrades

Estimated Time to Complete

1–2 hours (initial setup): Purchase, label, and store your core food supply
15–30 min/month: Review inventory, rotate items, and replace used or expired.

Materials List

- Staples: Rice (20 lbs), canned beans (10 cans), oats (10 lbs)
- Proteins/Fats: Peanut butter (2 jars), powdered milk (5 lbs), oil
- Seasonings: Salt, herbs, spices
- Morale Boosters: Tea, hard candy, instant cocoa, bouillon cubes
- Optional Extras: Canned vegetables, instant soup, noodles or rice, shelf-stable tortillas, canned fruit, granola bars, jerky, and canned chili

DIY & Reuse Opportunities

- Repurpose 2-liter soda bottles or juice jugs for grains or dry staples
- Store dry goods in glass jars with sealing lids to stay visibly fresh.
- Use clean restaurant-grade food bins from local suppliers
- Build a rotating shelf system from scrap wood
- Use chalkboard or repurposed file labels for tracking

Step 1: Set a 30-Day Goal

Estimate 2,000 calories per adult per day, adjusting for kids, diet needs, and activity. A 30-day supply builds resilience during outages, job loss, or supply disruptions.

Step 2: Choose 5 Survival Staples

Focus on versatile, affordable foods that cover basic energy and nutrients:

- Rice (20 lbs) – Base for meals, 30+ year shelf life.

- Canned Beans (10 cans) – Protein source, 2-5 year shelf life.

- Peanut Butter (2 jars) – High-calorie, 2-year shelf life.

- Powdered Milk (5 lbs) – Nutrient boost, 20-year shelf life.

- Oats (10 lbs) – Quick energy, 10+ year shelf life.

Step 3: Add Salt, Spices & Extras

Don't forget basic seasonings, oil, and shelf-stable comfort foods like tea or chocolate. These improve morale and prevent "food fatigue."

Step 4: Choose the Right Storage Containers

Use food-grade buckets, Mylar bags with oxygen absorbers, or vacuum-sealed containers. Keep storage cool, dark, and dry to extend shelf life.

Step 5: Label, Track & Rotate

Label all items with purchase or expiration dates. Use the FIFO (First In, First Out) method to rotate older stock every 6–12 months.

Step 6: Build Meals Around Your Staples

Create a few simple recipes (rice + beans, oatmeal + powdered milk, peanut butter + oats) to ensure your supply is actually usable in a crisis.

Step 7: Expand in Phases (As Budget Allows)

As your food storage grows, it helps to think in

Family & Real Life Tip

Let your kids or partner help pick "emergency snacks." Small rituals like familiar breakfasts or hot cocoa during a storm can ease stress. Involve your household in rotation days so it becomes a normal habit—not a panic plan.

budget-based phases. Start with essentials, then build toward long-term variety and convenience:

PHASE 1:
Build a 30-Day Core Supply

Timeframe: 0–6 Months

Budget: $50–$100

- Stock pantry staples: rice, oats, beans, peanut butter
- Add salt, oil, powdered milk, and shelf-stable snacks
- Use buckets, jars, or reused containers
- Focus on calories, shelf life, and low-cost meals

PHASE 2:
Add Variety and Comfort

Timeframe: 6–12 Months

Budget: Around $200

- Include freeze-dried veggies, powdered eggs, honey
- Add cocoa, tea, broth cubes, and seasoning blends
- Build out simple, morale-boosting recipes
- Improve organization and rotate with FIFO tracking

PHASE 3:
Scale for Long-Term Storage

Timeframe: 12-18 Months

Budget: $500+

- Invest in bulk grains, MREs, and freeze-dried meals
- Use Mylar bags, oxygen absorbers, and storage bins
- Layer your systems: pantry, long-term, grab-and-go
- Plan for power outages, interruptions, and redundancy

Stockpile or Grow—Where Will You Start?

There's no single "right" way to build food security off-grid. Some people feel better knowing their pantry is packed and ready for anything. Others find confidence in learning to grow and preserve what they eat. The truth is—both paths work. And you don't have to pick just one.

The Stockpiler's Strategy

Some off-grid families start by filling shelves. They want the reassurance that if something happens—a storm, job loss, supply chain hiccup—they don't have to scramble. Their pantry becomes a safety net: lined with canned goods, Mylar-packed rice and beans, powdered milk, and freeze-dried meals. Everything is labeled, calorie-counted, and rotated using FIFO. It's not about fear—it's about not being caught off guard.

For many, this is how they take back control. It's fast, doesn't require land or experience—and that's what makes it doable.

The Grow-and-Store Approach

Others lean into learning by doing. They start small—maybe with a few containers of herbs or tomatoes—and build from there. Over time, their meals include more they've preserved themselves: fermented veggies, home-dried apples, canned soups. Their backup plan is a blend of seed trays, foraging books, and barter swaps with neighbors. It takes time—but with each season, their system becomes more adaptable, more local, more their own.

For them, food security means self-reliance—not just storage. It's about growing a skillset they can trust, even if supply chains break down or budgets tighten.

Which Strategy Is Right for You?

You don't have to choose just one. Stockpiling brings immediate peace of mind. Growing and preserving offers long-term renewal. Many off-grid households start with what's manageable now, and evolve over time—layering security with skills.

Essential Storage Methods: Do's and Don'ts

To maintain a reliable off-grid food supply, proper storage is major. The table below highlights essential best practices and common mistakes to avoid:

Do This	Don't Do This
Store food in 50-70°F, dark, dry conditions	Storing in garages/attics (temperature swings)
Mylar bags + oxygen absorbers for grains and legumes	Not using oxygen absorbers (mold, pests)
Rotate stock regularly (FIFO method)	Ignoring expiration dates
Use airtight containers to block moisture	Storing grains in non-sealed containers
Track inventory and set bulk restock reminders.	Relying solely on frozen foods (power outages)

Always label and date stored food to track freshness, prevent waste, and rotate supplies effectively.

Following correct storage methods and avoiding common mistakes will help you build a self-reliant food system with long-term security and sustainability.

> **Emergency Food Storage Mistakes to Avoid**
>
> **Beginner Mistake:** Storing food in areas with fluctuating temperatures or near heat sources reduces shelf life.
>
> **Fix:** Store dry goods in cool, dark areas with stable temperatures, using airtight containers to prevent moisture, pests, and spoilage.

Dehydrating Food for Off-Grid Storage

Dehydration is a simple, low-tech method that removes moisture to prevent bacteria and mold. It's reliable, doesn't require refrigeration, and when done properly, dried foods can last from six months to several years—making it a smart choice for long-term food security.

When you live off-grid, every bit of food matters. Dehydration turns short-lived produce into a long-term asset. – Off-Grid Survivalist.

Choosing the Right Dehydration Method for Preparedness

Method	Best For	Pros and Considerations
Sun Drying	Fruits, herbs, some vegetables	Requires hot, dry climate (85°F+), low humidity; use mesh screens for protection.
Electric Dehydrator	Fruits, vegetables, meats, herbs	Precise temperature control (95-160°F), but requires electricity.
Oven Drying	Fruits, some vegetables, herbs	Uses a low oven temp (130-160°F); energy-intensive, requires monitoring.
Solar Dehydrator	Fruits, vegetables, meats	Passive solar heat, enclosed for protection and efficiency, ideal for off-grid survival.

Why Dehydration is Key to Emergency Food Storage

- No power needed – Sun and solar drying use zero electricity.

- Lightweight storage – Compact and easy to carry in emergencies.

- Long shelf life – Lasts 6 months to years when appropriately sealed.

- Minimal gear – Drying racks, mesh, and sun often suffice.

Store dehydrated foods in airtight glass jars, Mylar bags with oxygen absorbers, or vacuum-sealed pouches to maximize shelf life.

Long-Term Emergency Food Supplies

A long-term food supply is key to true off-grid self-sufficiency. It requires specialized preservation methods to stay fresh and safe. Tools like Mylar bags, oxygen absorbers, and airtight containers can extend shelf life for decades while guarding against spoilage, pests, and contamination.

Kid-Friendly Survival Food Tips

Survival food isn't just fuel—it's also comfort. These shelf-stable picks help keep kids calm, fed, and reassured off-grid or during emergencies.

Picky-Eater Pantry Wins:
- Fruit – Applesauce, raisins, dried mango, fruit leather
- Trail Mix – Oats, pretzels, seeds, chocolate chips
- Comfort Meals – Mac & cheese, ramen, cocoa
- Breakfasts – Oatmeal, powdered milk, pancake mix
- Snacks – Crackers, peanut butter, granola bars
- Treats – Chocolate, gum, small toys

Tips for Feeding Kids Off-Grid:
- Prep "emergency meal days" that feel familiar
- Let kids help track and rotate food
- Store essentials in containers they can open and recognize
- Include comfort items to ease stress—small treats go a long way.

Bonus Idea: Include a small notebook or printable to let kids track their own food stash. It makes survival feel like a game—not a crisis.

Low-Cost Food Storage

Building a Survival Food Supply for Under $200

A secure food reserve doesn't require much—smart planning can build one for under $200.

- Bulk Buys – 50 lbs rice ($25), 25 lbs beans ($20), 10 lbs oats ($10), 5 lbs salt ($5).

- Low-Cost Storage – Use $5 food-grade buckets or repurposed jars.

- Thrift Finds – Canning jars cost $0.50–$1 at second-hand stores.

- DIY Meals – Dehydrate leftovers and vacuum seal for storage.

- Reuse Containers – Soda bottles for water, coffee cans for dry goods.

Key Food Storage Methods and Materials

Long-term food storage relies on airtight sealing to block moisture, pests, and oxygen. Without it, even preserved foods degrade fast. Mylar bags, oxygen absorbers, and sealed containers protect nutrition, texture, and taste. Below are visuals to see how to properly store dry goods using Mylar bags:

Step 1:
Fill Mylar Bag with Grains, Beans, or Dry Goods

Step 2:
Insert an Oxygen Absorber to Prevent Spoilage

Step 3:
Seal the Mylar Bag with a Heat Sealer or Iron

Step 4:
Store Sealed Bags in a Food-Grade Bucket for Protection

Step 5:
Label Bucket with Date & Contents for Easy Rotation

Best Practices for Storage and Common Mistakes to Avoid

Mistake	Why It's a Problem	Quick Fix
Storing food in attic/garage	Temp swings cut shelf life	Store food in 50-70°F, dark, dry conditions.
Skipping oxygen absorbers	Pests ruin dry goods	Use Mylar bags + oxygen absorbers for grains.
No humidity control	Moisture = to mold/rust	Store in airtight bins with silica gel.
Not rotating stock	Food expires before use	Follow FIFO (First In, First Out).
Relying on frozen food	Outages spoil perishables	Store a mix of dehydrated, freeze-dried, and canned foods.

Food Rotation and Storage Planning:
Rotation Schedules to Prevent Spoilage and Waste

Even long-shelf-life foods need regular rotation to stay fresh, preserve nutrients, and avoid waste. Over time, packaging degrades and nutrients fade, so a rotation system keeps your emergency stock reliable.

 ## STEP-BY-STEP PROJECT
Creating a Food Inventory & Rotation Plan

Even a well-stocked pantry can fail you if you don't know what's in it. This step-by-step helps you build a simple, low-maintenance system to track what you have, use what you store, and avoid waste.

Before You Begin:

A survival food system isn't just about stockpiling—it's about keeping it usable. Without a simple inventory and rotation plan, it's easy to forget what you have, let food expire, or miss gaps in your supply. This system helps you stay in control, even during uncertain times.

Skill Level: Beginner

No tech skills needed.
Use paper, a whiteboard, or a spreadsheet—just stay consistent.

Tools Required

- Clipboard, binder, or notebook
- OR a whiteboard or spreadsheet
- Markers, pens, or dry erase
- Optional: colored labels or tape

Estimated Cost

Free - Use notebooks, folders, or digital tools you already have
$ – For label supplies, dry erase boards, or printed tracking sheets

Estimated Time to Complete

1–2 hours (initial setup): Set up your tracking system and label storage areas
15–30 minutes per month: Check inventory, rotate stock, and update log

Materials List

- Printable or digital inventory log
- Storage bins or shelf space (already in use)
- Labels or tape for visual organization
- Calendar or reminder app for rotation check-ins

DIY & Reuse Opportunities

- Repurpose old notebooks or file folders for your log
- Use masking tape and markers to color-code food types
- Turn a thrifted whiteboard into a rotation dashboard
- Clip pages to shelves using binder clips or clothespins
- Use binder clips to attach labels directly to shelves or bins
- Reuse junk mail envelopes as log pockets for each shelf
- Cut cereal boxes into DIY dividers for categories or dates

Step 1: Choose Your Tracking Format

Use a printed log, whiteboard, or spreadsheet—whichever fits your style. Include columns for item name, quantity, storage date, and expiration or "use by" date.

Step 2: Categorize and Label Storage Areas

Group foods by type (grains, canned goods, freeze-dried, etc.) and organize them by expiration date. Use visible labels or color-coded tape to simplify rotation.

Step 3: Set Inspection & Rotation Intervals

Schedule regular checks (monthly or quarterly) to inspect for damage, spoilage, or nearing expiration. Use the FIFO method: First In, First Out.

Step 4: Track Usage Patterns

Note what you use most often and how quickly. This helps you restock smarter and avoid overbuying low-use items or running out of essentials.

Step 5: Update Your Inventory Monthly

Make it a habit—update your log when you restock or use something. Staying consistent ensures you don't run out of essentials when they matter most.

 CHECKLIST
Building a Resilient Food Storage System

A reliable food storage system balances short-term, mid-term, and long-term reserves to ensure sustainability and adaptability in any situation.

Short-Term Food Storage (2 Weeks - 3 Months)
Essential for Daily Use and Minor Disruptions

- [ ] Stock fresh and frozen foods – Produce, dairy, meats.
- [ ] Store pantry staples – Flour, sugar, salt, rice, pasta.
- [ ] Keep canned goods – Vegetables, beans, meats, soups.
- [ ] Have quick-prep foods – Instant rice, pasta, canned proteins.
- [ ] Add MREs and freeze-dried meals for no-cook emergencies.

Mid-Term Food Storage (3 Months - 1 Year)
- [ ] Extends Beyond Daily Use and Supports Stability
- [ ] Dehydrate and store fruits, vegetables, and meats for nutrient retention.
- [ ] Pressure-can meats and vegetables for preservative-free, long-term meals.
- [ ] Stock bulk grains and legumes – Wheat berries, oats, rice, lentils.
- [ ] Store essential fats – Olive oil, coconut oil, and lard for cooking and health.
- [ ] Rotate inventory using FIFO (First In, First Out) to prevent spoilage.

Long-Term Food Storage (1 Year+)
Ensures Sustained Food Security

- [ ] Seal grains and beans in Mylar bags with oxygen absorbers for 25+ years.
- [ ] Stock freeze-dried meals for emergencies requiring minimal prep.
- [ ] Use a root cellar for fresh storage of potatoes, onions, and squash.
- [ ] Store fermented foods for preservation and gut health.
- [ ] Keep honey, salt, and sugar for indefinite storage.

Food Storage and Rotation Strategies

Maximize Freshness and Prevent Waste

- [ ] Follow FIFO (First In, First Out) to ensure older items get used first.
- [ ] Store food in cool, dry, and dark conditions (50-70°F ideal).
- [ ] Use airtight containers and oxygen absorbers to prevent pests and spoilage.
- [ ] Regularly inventory supplies and track expiration dates for freshness.
- [ ] Diversify storage methods – canning, drying, freezing, and fermenting.

SCAN ME

Take it a step further. Put your knowledge into action.
Exclusive access to the Off-Grid Survival Companion—with printable checklists, guides, visual aids, and troubleshooting charts from the book, plus practical tools to help you adapt and build with confidence.

Survival Gardening & Small-Scale Food:
Quick-Start Survival Gardening

Growing your food is a critical survival skill, ensuring nutrition beyond stockpiled food. The key to survival gardening is selecting fast-growing, high-yield crops that thrive in small spaces and unpredictable conditions.

Best Survival Crops for Emergency Food Production

Why These Crops? They require minimal resources, grow quickly, and provide maximum caloric return—essential for off-grid survival gardening. Survival Crop Yields & Calories Choose crops for space efficiency and high-calorie yield.

Crop	Yield per Sq. Ft.	Calories per Pound	Best Growing Conditions
Potatoes	0.5–1 lb	~350 kcal	Cool to temperate, well-drained
Sweet Potatoes	1–1.5 lbs	~400 kcal	Hot/dry, sandy soil
Corn	0.25–0.5 lbs	~365 kcal	Warm, full sun, rich soil
Beans (Dry)	0.2–0.4 lbs	~340 kcal	Temperate, trellising increases
Amaranth	0.3–0.6 lbs	~365 kcal	Hot/dry, drought-resistant
Squash (Winter)	1–2 lbs	~200 kcal	Warm, sprawling growth
Carrots	0.5–1 lb	~195 kcal	Cool, loose soil for deep roots
Radishes	1–2 lbs	~20 kcal	Fast-growing, great for small

Off-Grid Gardening That Anyone Can Do

In an off-grid emergency, knowing how to grow your food isn't just smart—it's survival. But most guides stop at a list of "best crops," leaving you wondering: **How do I actually make this work with what I have?**

This section gives you what matters most: real strategies, simple guidance, and visual tools to help you grow food—even if you've never planted anything before.

Fast-Growing Crops
Radishes, lettuce, spinach, turnips, green onions

High-Calorie Crops
Potatoes, corn, beans, squash, sweet potatoes

Best Container Crops
Herbs, bush beans, lettuce, radishes

Drought-Resistant Crops
Amaranth, okra, peppers, cowpeas, sweet potatoes

Where to Begin: Think in Tiers

Not everyone needs the same amount of food from their garden. Your setup should reflect your goals and resources, not someone else's.

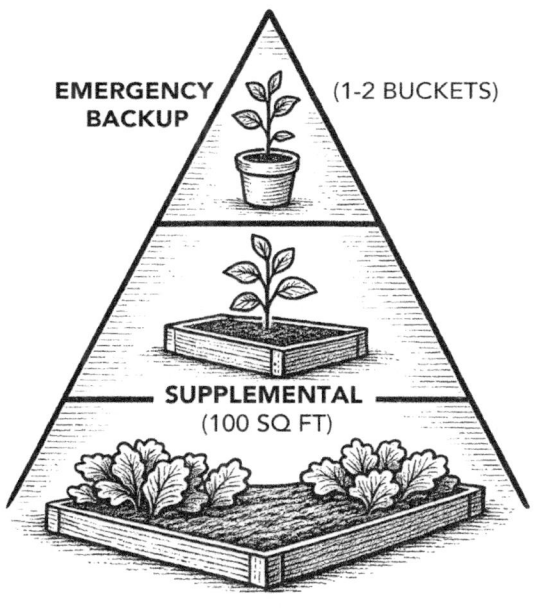

- A backup food source might only require a few containers.

- A supplement to stored food could be built from a handful of raised beds.

- Full self-reliance is possible with ~200 sq ft per adult, with the right planning and crop rotation.

Designing a Resilient Growing Space

Whether you're working with a patio, backyard, or sunny windowsill, start with crops that deliver real return: calories, nutrients, and harvest frequency.

Include crops like:

- 1 root crop for calories (like potatoes or carrots)

- 1 leafy green for nutrition (like kale or spinach)

- 1 legume for protein and soil support (like bush beans)

- 1 bonus crop for flavor or variety (like tomatoes, peppers, or radishes)

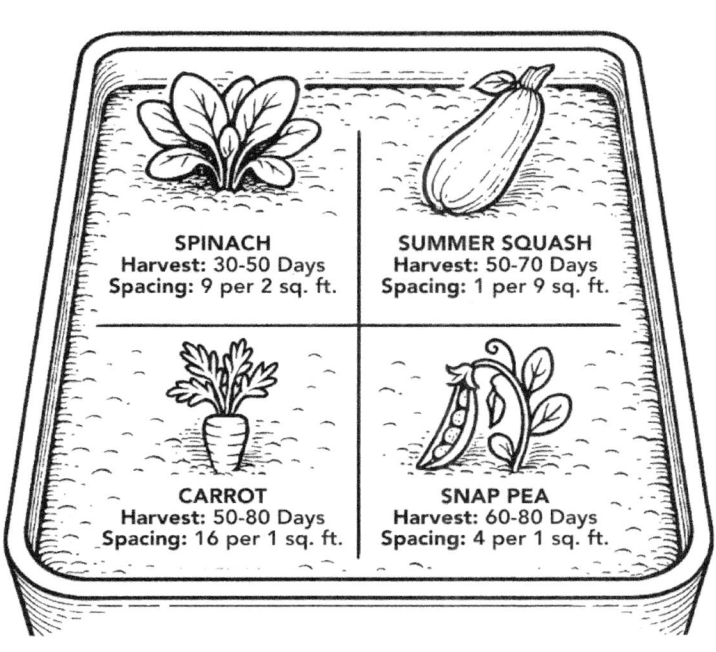

Keep It Growing: The Power of Succession Planting

Many crops mature quickly and can be replanted in the same space. With a little timing, you can double or even triple your yield in small areas. **See Plan Below:**

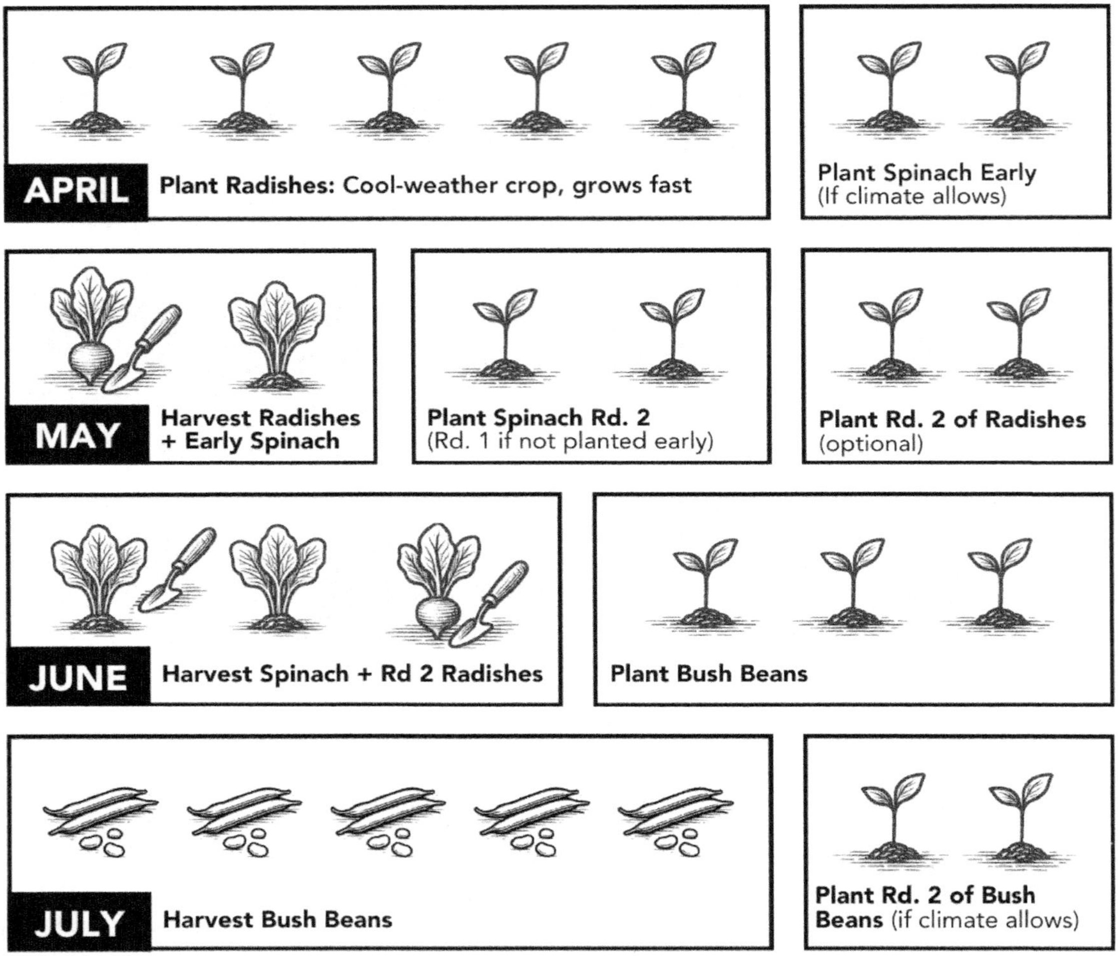

APRIL Plant Radishes: Cool-weather crop, grows fast

Plant Spinach Early (If climate allows)

MAY Harvest Radishes + Early Spinach

Plant Spinach Rd. 2 (Rd. 1 if not planted early)

Plant Rd. 2 of Radishes (optional)

JUNE Harvest Spinach + Rd 2 Radishes

Plant Bush Beans

JULY Harvest Bush Beans

Plant Rd. 2 of Bush Beans (if climate allows)

Harvest Round 2 of Bush Beans by late August-September, depending on the climate.

SCAN ME

Not sure where to start with your growing plan?

Access the free Garden Plan Builder—part of the Off-Grid Companion—to customize your layout, crop choices, and planting timeline based on real conditions, not guesswork.

Container Gardening That Doesn't Fail

Growing your food in buckets, bags, or bins works well—but only if the plant has the room it needs. Roots need depth, drainage, and good, rich soil to grow strong and produce. Don't overcrowd. Fewer plants yield more when they have space to thrive, and you'll waste less water, soil, and effort in the long run.

6-8" SHALLOW TRAY	10-12" BUCKET	14-18" MEDIUM POT	18-24"+ POT OR TOTE
GOOD FOR: LEAFY GREENS	GOOD FOR: BUSH CROPS	GOOD FOR: ROOT CROPS	GOOD FOR: DEEP CROPS
EX: LETTUCE, SPINACH, KALE	EX: BEANS, PEPPERS	EX: RADISHES, CARROTS	EX: POTATOES, TOMATOES

If you're short on budget but not on creativity, the solution isn't store-bought—it's smart DIY. With the right materials, you can build tough, low-cost containers that work just as well as the fancy ones.

STEP-BY-STEP PROJECT
Don't Buy It—Build It. DIY Survival Growing Containers

When land isn't an option—or when you just need to start small—container gardening gives you a way to grow food anywhere. It's a flexible, low-cost way to build food security with whatever space and supplies you have.

Before you begin:

Focus on what you already have access to. You don't need raised beds or high-end soil blends to make this work. With the correct container, a decent soil mix, and a bit of sunlight, you can turn almost anything into a reliable survival grow space.

Skill Level: Beginner

Perfect for those just starting food storage. No prior experience needed—just a practical mindset and a bit of pantry space.

Tools Required

- Drill or screwdriver (hole bit optional)
- Scissors or utility knife
- Small shovel or trowel
- Gloves (optional)

Estimated Cost

$ – Fully repurposed setup using salvaged containers and homemade soil mix

$$ - Grow bags or store-bought add-ins

Estimated Time to Complete

30–60 minutes per container
(including container prep and soil mixing)

Materials List

- Food-safe container: 5-gallon bucket, storage tote, grow bag, washtub, large pot, or lined drawer
- Drainage: gravel, clay, or rocks
- Soil mix ingredients:
  - 40% compost or aged manure
  - 40% coconut coir or peat moss
  - 20% perlite, coarse sand, or gravel
- Optional: mesh, window screen, or breathable fabric to protect plants

DIY & Reuse Opportunities

- Use cracked bins, laundry baskets, or dresser drawers lined with plastic
- Reuse broken pots or sidewalk gravel for drainage
- Line wooden boxes with feed bags or food-safe plastic
- Cover with mesh to block pests.

Step 1: Choose a Food-Safe Container

Look for one of the following:

- Repurpose common items like 5-gallon buckets, storage totes, fabric grow bags, large pots, washtubs, or lined dresser drawers.

- Avoid any containers that previously held chemicals, paint, or motor oil.

Step 2: Drill Drainage Holes

- Flip the container upside down.

- Drill **4–6 holes** evenly spaced in the bottom.

- Optional: Add 1–2 holes an inch up the side for overflow drainage.

This prevents root rot and allows excess water to escape.

Step 3: Add a Drainage Layer

- Pour 1–2 inches of small rocks, pebbles, or broken clay into the bottom of your container to create space for water to drain correctly.

- This helps excess water drain through the soil, preventing it from collecting at the bottom and rotting the roots.

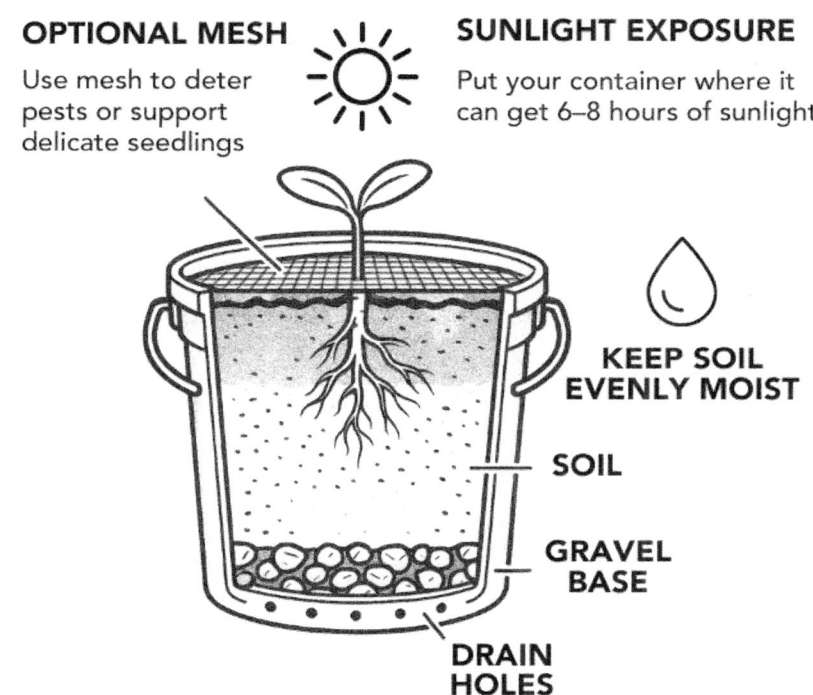

OPTIONAL MESH
Use mesh to deter pests or support delicate seedlings

SUNLIGHT EXPOSURE
Put your container where it can get 6–8 hours of sunlight.

KEEP SOIL EVENLY MOIST

SOIL

GRAVEL BASE

DRAIN HOLES

Step 4: Fill with Soil Mix

Use this survival soil blend:

- 40% compost or aged manure

- 40% coconut coir or peat moss (for moisture retention)

- 20% perlite, coarse sand, or gravel (for drainage)

Mix thoroughly before filling your container. Pre-moisten if needed.

Step 5: Plant and Position

- Select crops that match your container depth

- Place the container in a spot with 6–8 hours of sunlight

- Water deeply after planting and check daily in hot weather

Step 6: Protect Your Plants

- Use mesh, window screen, or lightweight fabric to cover young plants

- This keeps out pests while allowing airflow and rain to pass through

 FROM THE FIRE. STORIES THAT STILL BURN.
No Raised Beds. No Budget. No Problem.

Robbie and Gary didn't wait for perfect conditions. They had no homestead, no raised beds, and no big budget—just old storage bins, cracked buckets, and a backyard. And they used it all.

Instead of hauling in compost or building fancy systems, they composted right inside their containers. Food scraps, dry leaves, and a little soil were enough to create fertile growing space—right where the plants would grow.

You don't need money to start a garden. Just throw food scraps and soil
in a bucket and see what happens. That's how we learn.
—Robbie, Robbie and Gary Gardening Easy

It wasn't pretty, but it worked. Season after season, their "scrap soil" got richer, and their harvests grew. The containers were mismatched, the setup uneven—but the results were solid.

SCAN ME

Want to see low-cost container gardening in action?
Watch how Robbie and Gary build simple raised beds, compost in place, and grow food with almost no digging—perfect for beginners on a budget.

For anyone feeling stuck because they don't have land, gear, or gardening skills—this is the reminder: growing food isn't about perfection. It's about starting with what you have and letting nature handle the rest.

Soil That Delivers

Bad soil is one of the biggest reasons beginners give up. Store-bought "garden soil" isn't enough for containers. Mix your own using easy-to-find materials.

Simple Survival Soil Blend:

- 40% compost or aged manure

- 40% coconut coir or peat moss (holds moisture)

- 20% perlite, sand, or small gravel (adds drainage)

Scan the QR above code to get the Survival Soil Blend Guide, mix tips, and container garden tools.

Grow Anywhere: Turning 10 Square Feet into Food

Where to Place a Small Survival Garden

You don't need a homestead to start growing your food. Even a single 10-square-foot patch—spread across a few containers—is enough to begin. The key is sunlight, a flat surface, and a little resourcefulness.

Here are just a few places to set one up:

- Sunny balcony or patio for herbs and shallow crops

- Driveway/gravel with 6+ hrs sun

- Yard edge for vertical crops

- Trailer or cart for mobile setup

- Trough, crate, or bin garden

- Wall with buckets or verticals

Containers can be grouped or spread out. You can even move them seasonally to chase the sun. Many off-gridders start here—right where they are—with buckets, bins, or whatever they already have.

What You Can Grow in Just 10 Square Feet

With just 10 square feet, you can grow a surprising amount of food—even if you're short on time, space, experience, or money. It's a simple way to start building food security, one container at a time.

Using standard containers:

- 2 potato buckets
- 2 shallow trays of leafy greens
- 1 bean pot
- 1 root crop container (carrots or radishes)
- 1 tomato or pepper plant
- 1 herb pot

Even a setup this small can:

- Supplement your food storage
- Teach essential growing skills
- Build confidence and independence
- Provide fresh harvests throughout the season

It's not about growing everything—it's about **growing something**. When you build small, you build smart—and that's what survival gardening is all about.

Continuous Treatment: Three Fundamental Keys

You don't need a green thumb. You just need to pay attention to three things:

1. Water regularly | 2. Provide plenty of sunlight | 3. Protect them from pests

WATER	SUNLIGHT	PESTS
		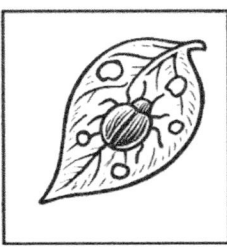
Stick you finger in the soil. If it's dry 2" down, water deeply. Containers dry out fast—daily checks are best.	6–8 hours is ideal. Rotate the pots if sun shifts through the season.	Spray leaves with diluted dish soap for aphids. Use mesh covers for greens.

Last Thing: Start Small, Stay Steady

Your first harvest won't be perfect. That's okay.

What matters most is that you start growing something now. One container, one crop, one meal—that's survival gardening. It's your backup plan, your learning curve, and your homegrown security system.

Even one leafy green can be proof: **you've got this.**

Growing is one layer of security—finding food in the wild adds another. Foraging fills gaps, stretches supplies, and deepens your self-reliance.

Foraging for Wild Edibles: Boost Your Food Supply

Foraging is a direct line to the land, providing highly nutritious food when supplies are scarce. Knowing how to identify, harvest, and prepare wild edibles can be the difference between thriving and struggling in an off-grid situation.

Identifying Common Wild Edibles by Region

Region	Common Wild Edibles
Temperate Forests	Wild onions, dandelions, acorns, blackberries, cattails
Arid/Desert Regions	Prickly pear cactus, mesquite pods, amaranth, wild mustard
Wetlands and Riverbanks	Watercress, wild rice, fiddlehead ferns, burdock root
Mountain/Boreal forests	Wild blueberries, pine nuts, expert-ID'd mushrooms

Always be 100% certain before consuming any wild plant. Many toxic plants resemble edible varieties.

STEP-BY-STEP PROJECT
Universal Edibility Test (For Emergency Use Only)

Use this method only when no known food is available—mistakes can be fatal.

Before You Begin:

This test is a true last resort—never use it as a primary foraging method. Many toxic plants mimic edible ones, and no reaction test is foolproof. If possible, carry a regional foraging guide or learn from a local expert. Your best defense isn't guesswork—it's knowledge.

Skill Level: Advanced Survival

Only for use in true survival scenarios with no access to known safe food.

Tools Required

- Knife or scissors (for sample prep)
- Clean water (for hydration or rinsing)
- Notebook (to track reactions)

Estimated Cost

Free - no special tools or equipment

Estimated Time to Complete

6–24 hours total - Including wait periods between test stages

Materials List

- Unknown wild plant or part being considered for emergency consumption
- Time and safe space to observe your body's response over 6–24 hours

DIY & Reuse Opportunities

- Carry a pocket mirror to monitor delayed skin reactions safely.
- Use a bandana or cloth to separate plant parts carefully
- Repurpose a notebook to track edible vs. questionable species over time
- Use a film canister or mint tin to store test samples separately.

Step 1: Visually Inspect the Plant

Avoid plants with the following traits, which often indicate toxicity:

- **Milky or Discolored Sap** – Snap a stem; milky, yellow, or red sap can signal toxins that irritate skin or cause nausea. Clear sap is safer, but not a guarantee.

- **Spines, Thorns, or Fine Hairs** – These defenses can carry irritants or toxins. If a plant stings, itches, or burns—don't trust it.

- **Strong Almond or Chemical Smell** – A bitter almond scent suggests cyanide compounds. Chemical odors often mean natural toxins. If it smells off, skip it.

- Three-Leaf Clusters – Many poisonous plants, like poison ivy or nightshade, follow this pattern. As the saying goes: "Leaves of three, let it be."

Step 2: Smell the Plant

Crush a small piece of the leaf or stem and inhale gently.

- If the plant smells bitter, soapy, metallic, chemical-like, or like almonds, do not proceed—these scents can signal toxic compounds, including cyanide.

- A strong or unnatural odor is often nature's warning sign.

Step 3: Skin Contact Test

Wait at least 8 hours without washing or touching the area.

- If you experience itching, burning, swelling, rash, or redness, the plant may be topically toxic or allergenic. Do not eat it.

- If symptoms appear, wash the area with soap and water. Use a cool compress or antihistamine cream if available, and monitor for serious reactions.

Step 4: Lip and Mouth Test

Touch a tiny piece of the plant to the edge of your lips.

- Wait 15 minutes for any reaction (tingling, burning, numbness).

- If there's tingling, burning, stinging, or numbness, stop and do not proceed.

- If no reaction occurs, place the piece inside your mouth without chewing, hold it for 15 minutes, then spit it out.

- If irritation starts at any point, rinse your mouth thoroughly with clean water and avoid further testing.

Step 5: Chew Without Swallowing

Chew a very small amount—just enough to break it down.

- Hold it in your mouth for 15 minutes, then spit it out.

- Watch for numbness, burning, excess saliva, or discomfort.

- If symptoms develop, rinse with water, stop the test, and do not eat the plant.

Step 6: Swallow a Small Amount

- Swallow a pea-sized portion or less.

- Wait 6 hours without eating anything else.

- Watch closely for nausea, cramping, dizziness, vomiting, or other symptoms.

- If any occur, drink clean water and rest. Do not induce vomiting unless instructed by a medical professional.

Step 7: Confirm and Proceed Cautiously

- If no symptoms appear, the plant may be safe in small amounts.

- Gradually increase the amount over time, watching closely for any delayed effects.

- Some plants contain toxins that accumulate slowly, so moderation and repeated caution are essential.

- Knowledge from a regional foraging guide or local expert is still the safest path forward.

Wild Foraging:
5 Energy-Rich Plants

While many wild plants are edible, some provide far more calories and nutrition than others. In a survival situation, focusing on high-energy, long-lasting foods is key to sustaining yourself off-grid. (However, while foraging can provide emergency nutrition, it's best used when it's supplemented with stored food for a balanced diet.) These five wild edibles offer the best return for effort and storage potential. Use a local guide or mentor to avoid toxic plants.

ACORNS

Survival Use: Shell and crush. To leach tannins (which make them bitter and potentially harmful), soak the pieces in cool water, changing it several times daily until the water stays clear and the bitterness fades. Dry and grind into flour for bread or soup thickener. Stores 2+ years when sealed.

Hot water leaching is faster but may reduce nutrition.

CATTAILS

Survival Use: Dig up starchy roots any time of year. Scrub clean, peel, and boil or roast to eat. Young spring shoots (cooked or raw) and yellow pollen (used like flour) are also edible.

Roots can be tough—cooked until soft, then scraped out to remove the inner starch.

PINE NUTS

Survival Use: Crack open the pinecones and shell the nuts inside. Eat raw, roast over a fire, or grind into a paste. High-fat fuel that stores for several months when kept dry and cool.

Fresh nuts go rancid quickly—refrigerate or sun-dry to extend shelf life.

WILD BERRIES

Survival Use: Eat fresh when in season. To preserve, sun-dry on a flat surface, string into garlands, or mash and ferment into jam or wild vinegar.

Avoid any berries that are bitter, milky, or unfamiliar—many are toxic.

DANDELION ROOTS

Survival Use: Dig roots in early spring or late fall. Scrub well, slice, and dry fully. Roast in a pan or oven until dark and fragrant. Grind into powder to steep as caffeine-free coffee or brew into broth.

Also usable in tinctures for digestion support.

Wild foods can give you a critical edge, but real security comes from what you can grow and sustain. Once your survival garden is in motion, keeping it productive means protecting the soil, managing pests, and making sure every harvest counts.

Maintaining a Productive Survival Garden:
Essential Soil and Pest Control

A survival garden has to generate food effectively under off-grid conditions. Long-term food security depends on maintaining crops healthy without commercial fertilizers or pesticides. Preserving soil fertility and managing pests naturally guarantees a consistent food supply—even in a crisis.

Maintaining the health of the soil and applying basic, low-tech pest control techniques guarantees that your survival garden stays viable without outside resources.

Basic Soil Health for Survival Gardens

Any survival garden is built on healthy soil; without it, not even the best seeds will flourish. These free, natural methods help you increase fertility and lessen dependence on commercially produced answers:

- **Mulch for moisture retention** – Cover the soil with straw, wood chips, leaves, or dried grass to hold water, suppress weeds, and regulate temperature. This cuts watering needs and prevents nutrient loss in dry spells.

- **Boost soil nutrients with natural amendments** – Save scraps with purpose:

  - Crushed eggshells add calcium to prevent blossom-end rot in tomatoes and peppers.

  - Wood ash supplies potassium and raises soil pH.

  - Bury fish scraps deep to enrich soil with slow-release nitrogen—great for heavy feeders like corn or squash.

- **Compost small-scale** – Layering food wastes, leaves, grass clippings, and aged manure produces rich, live soil over time, even in small areas. Use a bucket, bin, or corner of your garden; no major planning is needed.

  - Weekly rotation with a stick or pitchfork will hasten the process.

Fast, Natural Pest Control Methods

Let bugs ruin your carefully acquired food supply. Though low-tech, these survival-proven techniques are safe to use without damaging your family or your plants:

- **Use barriers** – Row covers, lightweight netting, and even old window screens can protect seedlings from beetles, birds, and bugs. Handpick pests in early morning when they're slow-moving.

- **Use ash or diatomaceous earth** – Wood ash and food-grade diatomaceous earth form a physical barrier that cuts soft-bodied pests like slugs and larvae. Reapply after heavy rain.

- **Use homemade sprays** – Blend garlic, cayenne, or neem oil with water and spray on leaves to deter insects naturally. Always test on one plant first to avoid leaf burn.

Survival gardening is about guaranteeing the bare essentials for long-lasting food security. Even in the toughest environments, by emphasizing high-yield, climate-appropriate crops and augmenting with foraging, you lessen reliance on outside resources and establish actual food independence.

Low-Tech Survival Strategies when Cooking Off-Grid

Maybe you lit some candles, opened a can of beans, and waited it out the first time the power went out for more than a few hours. But should the outage last several days, what then? For weeks? Alternatively, what would happen if the grid never returned on? For many who live off-grid—that is, ready—this is not only a what-if. Daily reality is what we live with. Your ability to cook food, boil water, or just make coffee becomes both a comfort and a survival need when contemporary conveniences vanish.

Fortunately, you can make it work without a homestead kitchen or upscale equipment. From homemade solar ovens to backyard rocket stoves, off-grid cooking appliances are shockingly basic, efficient, and reasonably priced. Whether you're deep in the woods or riding out a storm on the porch, this section will cover low-tech tools and survival-ready techniques that keep meals hot and your options open.

Cooking Without Electricity: Survival Kitchen Work

Cooking without electricity is an immediate survival challenge. In grid failures, long-term outages, or off-grid living, low-tech methods ensure you can prepare food with minimal resources.

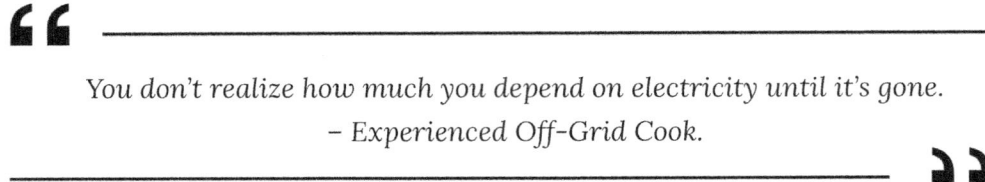

You don't realize how much you depend on electricity until it's gone.
– Experienced Off-Grid Cook.

The best survival cooking method balances fuel, efficiency, and portability, ensuring meals with minimal resources.

Best Off-Grid Cooking Methods for Survival

Off-grid cooking lets you prepare meals without modern tools or abundant fuel. Using rocket stoves, solar ovens, and wood-fired methods builds a resilient, low-tech system for survival.

Cooking Method	Fuel Type	Efficiency	Portability	Best For	Cost
Rocket Stove	Small sticks, twigs, biomass	High – Uses 75% less fuel than open fires	Lightweight and portable	Emergency cooking, camping, homesteads	$10–$80 (DIY to high-end)
Solar Oven	Sunlight	Moderate - No fuel needed but slow cook time	Portable but dependent on the sun	Baking, slow cooking, dehydrating in sunny climates	$0–$300 (DIY to commercial)
Wood-Fired Cooking	Firewood	Moderate - Versatile but requires constant fuel	Not easily portable	Homesteads, survival camps, long-term off-grid cooking	$50–$1,000+ (fire pit to full stove)

Each method has pros and cons, so many survivalists combine them—using rocket stoves for quick heat, solar ovens for fuel-free cooking, and wood-fired setups when fuel is available.

Rocket Stoves: High-Efficiency, Low-Fuel Cooking

Rocket stoves burn small amounts of wood efficiently, generating high heat with minimal smoke. Their vertical combustion chamber reduces wood consumption by up to 75% compared to open fires.

Best Uses: Boiling water, quick frying, high-heat cooking

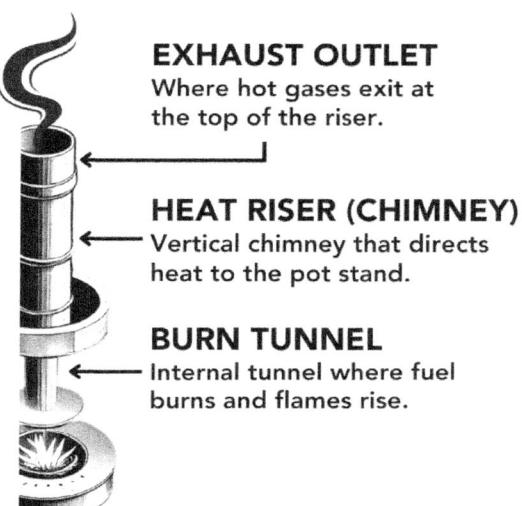

EXHAUST OUTLET
Where hot gases exit at the top of the riser.

HEAT RISER (CHIMNEY)
Vertical chimney that directs heat to the pot stand.

BURN TUNNEL
Internal tunnel where fuel burns and flames rise.

Limitations: Requires dry wood, not ideal for slow cooking

Cooking Tips:

- Use dry wood only to reduce smoke and improve burn efficiency.

- Keep airflow strong by clearing the intake and adjusting fuel as needed.

- Always cook outdoors or in a well-ventilated space to avoid smoke buildup.

" *After switching to a rocket mass heater, we reduced our firewood consumption from 4-5 cords to just half a cord per winter.* "

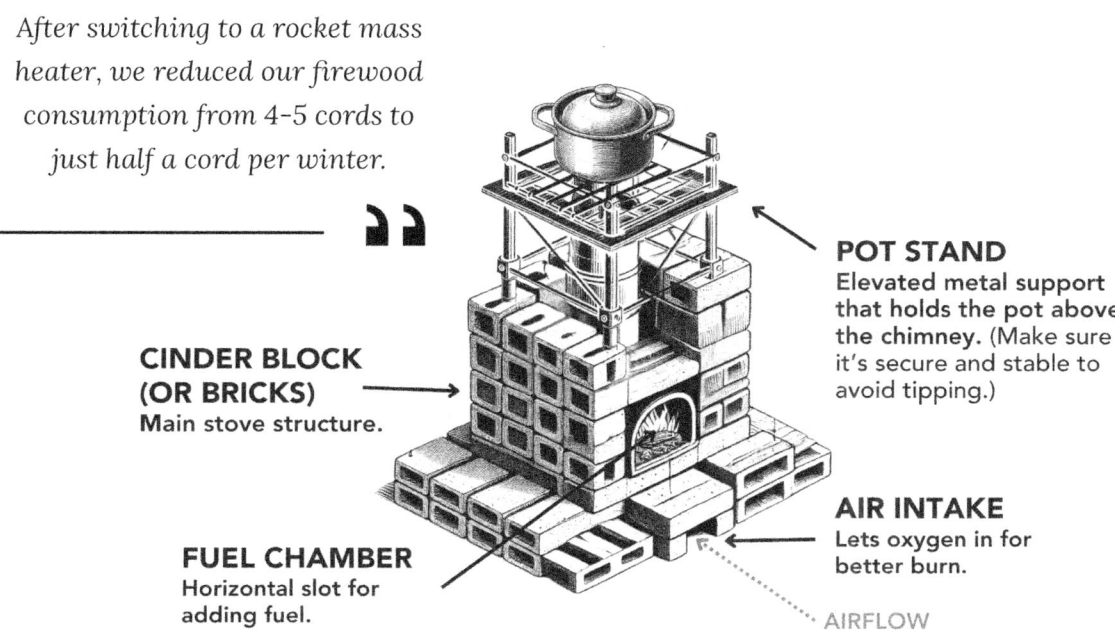

POT STAND
Elevated metal support that holds the pot above the chimney. (Make sure it's secure and stable to avoid tipping.)

CINDER BLOCK (OR BRICKS)
Main stove structure.

AIR INTAKE
Lets oxygen in for better burn.

AIRFLOW

FUEL CHAMBER
Horizontal slot for adding fuel.

Solar Cooking: Harnessing the Sun's Energy

Solar ovens provide a completely fuel-free cooking method, making them essential for off-grid survival. Unlike wood-burning stoves, which require constant fuel, solar ovens operate indefinitely—ideal for long-term emergencies or sunny climates.

Best Uses: Baking, slow-cooked stews, dried fruits, baked potatoes—great for passive, fuel-free prep

Limitations: Requires direct sunlight; longer cook times and weather dependence

Solar Cooking Tips:

- **Use dark-colored cookware** – Absorbs heat more efficiently than shiny or reflective surfaces, speeding up cook time.

- **Plan around peak sunlight hours** – Midday sun provides the highest temperatures and most consistent results.

- **Minimize heat loss** – Avoid opening the oven frequently to preserve internal temperature and cooking consistency.

- **Adjust the reflector panel** – Position it every 30–60 minutes to track the sun and boost thermal efficiency.

> *We live off grid and cook with the sun.*
> *— Off Grid with Doug and Stacy*

Reflective Panel

Transparent Lid
(Plastic Wrap)

Cooking Pot
(Dark-Colored)

Foil-lined Interior
Reflects sunlight to increase
heat inside the oven.

Pot Stand

Cardboard Box

⌐ SCAN ME ──────────────────────

Struggling to plan your off-grid food supply?
Use the checklists and guides to customize a plan that fits your space, season, and household needs. With your exclusive access to the Off-Grid Survival Companion—get printable checklists, growing charts, and storage tools from this chapter, plus bonus content to help you take action and build a food system you can rely on.

Hunger Doesn't Wait

By now, you've built a strong survival food system—from quick-yield crops and wild edibles to fuel-efficient, off-grid cooking. These are the systems that turn panic into preparedness and empty shelves into just another challenge you're ready to face.

Food isn't just about calories. It's control in chaos, peace of mind when things unravel, and the backbone of any off-grid life that's built to last.

You don't need a perfect plan—just one that feeds you when it matters most.

CHAPTER 6: SANITATION ISN'T A CONVENIENCE – IT'S SURVIVAL

In off-grid living, waste isn't hauled away or flushed into hidden systems—it's yours to manage. A reliable sanitation setup is more than a comfort; it's your first line of defense against illness, water contamination, and environmental damage.

Unlike urban areas with sewage treatment and waste pickup, off-grid systems must handle human waste, greywater, trash, and food scraps safely. Poor sanitation can lead to:

- **Waterborne Diseases:** Cholera, dysentery, and E. coli infections can spread through contaminated water.

- **Parasitic Infestations:** Flies, mosquitoes, and rodents thrive in poorly managed waste, transmitting diseases.

- **Respiratory Issues:** Burning trash releases toxic fumes, increasing the risk of lung infections and chronic respiratory conditions.

- **Soil Contamination:** Unprocessed human and organic waste introduce pathogens that can taint food sources.

A reliable waste management system should be low-maintenance, cost-effective, and environmentally sustainable while preventing these health hazards.

Smart Waste Solutions for Real Life

Off-grid waste management solutions must be practical and scalable. Here's a preview of the strategies covered in this chapter:

- **Composting Toilets:** Convert human waste into safe, nutrient-rich compost without water. Reduces disease risk, saves water, and works year-round with minimal maintenance.

- **Greywater Systems:** Filter and reuse water from sinks and showers for irrigation. Preserves clean water, supports gardens, and complies with many off-grid zoning codes.

- **DIY Trash Reduction:** Upcycling, repurposing, and strategic waste disposal to minimize impact. Lowers hauling costs, reduces pests, and turns scrap into usable survival materials.

- **Emergency Waste Solutions:** Safe, temporary waste disposal methods for disasters or short-term crises. Fast to build, budget-friendly, and critical when systems fail or land is undeveloped.

By implementing these strategies, off-grid dwellers can maintain hygiene, protect natural resources, and ensure long-term sustainability.

Environmental Impact of Waste Mismanagement

Waste management directly affects ecosystems, water sources, and long-term sustainability. Without proper disposal strategies, waste accumulates, leading to contamination and resource depletion.

How Poor Waste Management Damages the Environment

- **Groundwater Contamination:** Uncontrolled waste can leak toxins and pathogens into wells and springs, polluting drinking water.

- **Ecosystem Disruption:** Non-biodegradable waste, such as plastics, overwhelms local ecosystems, harming wildlife and plant life.

- **Soil Degradation:** Waste buildup alters soil chemistry, reducing fertility and making land unsuitable for food production.

- **Resource Depletion:** Organic waste, when discarded instead of composted, diminishes soil health and reduces sustainable farming efforts.

To limit environmental harm, prioritize biodegradable materials, compost organic waste, and reduce reliance on plastics.

Climate-Specific Waste Solutions

Different environments require unique waste management strategies. Climate affects composting efficiency, drainage, and sanitation needs.

How Climate Impacts Waste Systems

- **Dry:** Evaporative toilets and low-water composting work best. Hot air speeds up decomposition but may require added moisture. (First image)

- **Wet:** Sealed composting bins and raised latrines to prevent waterlogging and contamination. Proper drainage is critical. (Second image)

- **Cold:** Composting slows or freezes in low temperatures. Insulated or heated bins keep decomposition active. (Third image)

- **Hot & Humid:** Excess moisture accelerates bacterial growth and odors. Extra aeration and drainage are essential for composting. (Fourth image)

Select a composting method suited to your climate. In cold climates, insulated compost bins or worm-based systems work better than open-air piles.

Strategic Waste Planning for Off-Grid Living

Everything we've covered so far—from sanitation risks to climate-specific solutions—has one goal: helping you stay clean, healthy, and prepared. But even with the right tools, success depends on planning. A smart waste system isn't just about surviving today—it's about setting up something that works next week, next season, and next year.

A well-designed off-grid waste system should be:

- **Self-Contained and Low-Maintenance**—Your system should function with minimal daily effort or outside support. For example, a composting toilet with a vented urine diverter needs little more than monthly sawdust and a regular emptying schedule.

- **Climate-Adaptable** – Make sure it works year-round in your specific region. For Example, In freezing climates, dig composting chambers below the frost line or use insulated bins to keep decomposition active.

- **Sustainable** – Aim for closed-loop systems that reuse, reduce, and repurpose. For Example, use composted human waste (after full curing) to fertilize non-edible plants or reforest land, not your food crops.

- **Legally Compliant** – Understand and follow your local regulations before installing anything permanent. For example, some counties ban humanure systems; others require specific setbacks from water sources. Always check septic and sanitation codes.

- **Water-Source Safe** – Avoid contaminating nearby water or wells. For example, never place a composting toilet downhill from a water source. Use lined chambers or leach fields as needed to prevent runoff.

Some off-gridders skip waste planning until it's a problem. Others build smart from day one. The difference? Clean water, safe land, and peace of mind—earned by doing the dirty work right.

FROM THE FIRE. STORIES THAT STILL BURN.
They Didn't Skip the Dirty Work—And It Paid Off

When Jake and Nicole set out to build their off-grid homestead in the Pacific Northwest, they knew managing human waste was one of the most important—and often overlooked—parts of going entirely off-grid. With no septic system and harsh winters ahead, they needed a solution that was low-maintenance, climate-adaptable, and completely self-contained.

They built a dry composting toilet using basic materials, strategically placed downhill and away from water sources to avoid contamination. By insulating the composting area and using sawdust after each use, they created a system that worked year-round with minimal upkeep. It wasn't complicated—and it worked.

But what really set their approach apart was their attention to legal compliance. Before building anything permanent, they researched local regulations and made sure their system met code.

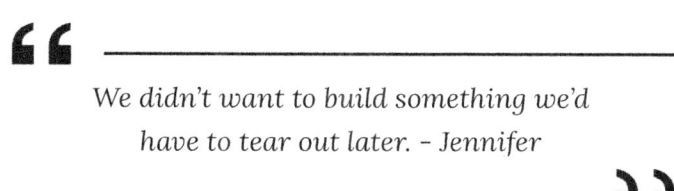

We didn't want to build something we'd have to tear out later. - Jennifer

That mindset—plan ahead, do it right the first time—helped them avoid costly mistakes and unnecessary stress. By treating waste as a manageable system, not a burden, they built something that not only protects their environment but actually gives back by producing compost for non-edible landscaping.

What They'd Do Differently

Jake and Nicole later shared that they wished they had built a second composting chamber from the start. Having a backup would have allowed one pile to fully cure while the other was in use, making the system even more efficient and reducing the risk of overfilling during peak use.

⌐SCAN ME

Want to see off-grid waste done right?

Watch how Jake & Nicole built a simple, low-cost composting toilet system that works year-round—even in a cold climate—with minimal tools and smart planning. "Off Grid Waste Management | Simple Solution for Sewage Treatment"

Once the core principles are in place, use the checklist below to build or assess your setup and avoid the most common pitfalls.

 ## CHECKLIST
Off-Grid Waste Management Setup

Human Waste System

☐ Install an off-grid toilet system (composting toilet, incinerating, or septic).

☐ Verify your system is functional in all seasonal/climate conditions.

☐ Set up a backup toilet solution (bucket toilet, portable unit, or latrine).

Composting & Organic Waste

- [ ] Set up a compost system for food scraps and biodegradable material.
- [ ] Maintain a balanced ratio of green (nitrogen) and brown (carbon) materials.
- [ ] Use sealed, pest-proof containers to prevent odor and critters.

Solid Waste

- [ ] Establish sorting bins for recyclables, reusables, and non-compostables.
- [ ] Identify the nearest disposal/recycling option or repurposing strategy.
- [ ] Reduce incoming waste by buying in bulk and avoiding single-use items.

Greywater System

- [ ] Divert greywater from sinks, showers, and laundry into filtration or irrigation.
- [ ] Avoid pooling or runoff to reduce bacterial growth.
- [ ] Ensure your setup meets local liquid waste guidelines.

Emergency & Long-Term Waste Planning

- [ ] Stock portable sanitation supplies in case of system failure.
- [ ] Design with flexibility for seasonal shifts or future needs.
- [ ] Review regularly to reduce waste and boost efficiency.

Once your waste systems are in place, take it a step further: view waste not as a problem to manage, but as a resource to repurpose.

Repurposing and Upcycling: Waste as a Resource

Waste isn't just something to dispose of. It's an opportunity to create new resources. Off-grid living thrives on maximizing available materials, reducing dependency on outside supplies, and turning waste into functional tools, structures, and essentials. Why it matters:

- **Reduces Reliance on Purchased Materials** – Less need for costly new supplies.

- **Minimizes Waste Output** – Keeps landfills and burn pits from accumulating unnecessary trash.

- **Encourages Self-Sufficiency** – a mindset of making do with what's available.

- **Eco-Friendly and Sustainable** – Repurposing reduces the need for manufacturing and transportation, lowering the environmental footprint.

Practical Upcycling and Crafting Projects

Repurposing everyday materials can provide essential off-grid solutions. Here are some simple but effective projects:

Turning Pallets into Furniture and Garden Beds

What It Solves: Provides free building materials for furniture, shelving, and raised garden beds.

How to Do It: Break down pallets into planks, sand them down, and use them for DIY projects like compost bins, chicken coops, or fencing.

Heat-treated pallets (stamped with "HT") are chemical-free and safe for indoor use.

> *Sustainability isn't just about growing food or generating power—it's about using every resource to its fullest potential.*
> *— Marjorie Wildcraft, Self-Sufficiency Expert.*

Reusing Glass Jars for Food Storage and Functional Utility

What It Solves: Glass jars reduce reliance on plastic storage, keeping food safe and organized.

Uses: Store dried goods, herbs, and homemade preserves. Ferment foods like sauerkraut and kimchi. Create DIY oil lanterns for emergency lighting.

Always sterilize jars before reusing them, especially for food storage.

Using Old Textiles as Insulation and Quilts

What It Solves: Provides warmth and insulation in cold climates without buying expensive materials.

How to Do It: For Insulation: Stuff old clothing, blankets, or fabric scraps into wall cavities or between window gaps to retain heat.

For Quilts: Sew patchwork blankets from old clothes for layered winter warmth.

Wool-based textiles work best for insulation due to their moisture resistance and durability.

 # FROM THE FIRE. STORIES THAT STILL BURN.
They Built It With What They Had–And It Worked

Minnesota outdoor enthusiast C.H. Woods and family created a robust, predator-proof chicken coop out of just recycled materials. They turned what most people would toss— scrap wood, leftover roofing, bits of fencing from past projects—into a useful refuge for his flock. There is no running in stores. Not any pointless expenditure. Just grit, creativity, and a stack of overlooked materials.

The goal was to spend nothing—and I mean nothing. — C.H. Woods

Based on the design, one can meet pragmatic needs with what is now on hand, given enough time and effort. Beyond simple financial savings, they reduced waste and refined critical off-grid skills, including simple carpentry, creative problem-solving, and predator-proof design. Their project reminds us that off-grid living need not start with perfect tools or materials. It starts with using what you now have.

What He'd Do Differently: If they could do it again, C.H. says they would reinforce the base framing earlier to save time and frustration during construction. They also learned that pre-planning ventilation can reduce heat buildup without compromising security.

Adding a hinged access panel for easier clean-out would have made daily maintenance smoother, especially in winter. But none of that stopped the build from working—and that's the win. It wasn't fancy. It was functional, safe, and built with what they had.

SCAN ME

Want to see a budget-friendly chicken coop build?

Watch how C.H. Woods constructs a backyard chicken coop using scrap wood, demonstrating that with creativity and resourcefulness, you can build a functional and attractive coop without breaking the bank. "Backyard Chicken Coop Build from Scrap Wood"

Off-Grid Sanitation Solutions

Whether repurposing materials for a chicken coop or building a waste system from scratch, the principle is the same: self-reliance begins with practical, low-cost solutions that work. Nowhere is this more vital than managing human waste. Off-grid, a reliable toilet system isn't a luxury—it's essential for sanitation, safety, and sustainability. That's where composting toilets come in.

Composting Toilets:

The Foundation of Off-Grid Sanitation

A waterless, ecologically conscious way to handle human waste are composting toilets offer. By aerobic breakdown, they turn it into safe, usable compost.

- **Self-sufficient** – No plumbing, no septic, no grid dependency.

- **Saves water** – Prevents 6,600 gallons of water waste per person annually.

- **Reduces pollution** – Eliminates groundwater contamination risks.

- **Creates compost – Properly processed humanure enriches soil.**

*A composting toilet saves thousands of gallons of water per year
while turning waste into a valuable resource. The key to success?
Proper ventilation and the right balance of materials.*
— Paul Wheaton, Eco-Engineer and Permaculture Expert

Choosing the Right Composting Toilet

Your ideal system depends on budget, climate, size, and maintenance.

Type	Pros	Cons
DIY Bucket System	Cheap, easy to build	Requires frequent emptying
Self-Contained Unit	Low maintenance, compact	Limited capacity, regular emptying
Central Composting	Handles large volumes, remote waste processing	Requires ventilation and extra space
Electric-Assisted	Faster composting, odor control	Requires power, costly
Urine-Diverting	Reduces odor, speeds composting	Requires separate liquid disposal

 CHECKLIST
Choosing the Right Composting Toilet

Use this checklist to set up or check your off-grid waste system.

Assessing Your Needs

☐ Decide if you need a temporary or permanent solution.

☐ Determine how many people will use the toilet regularly. Larger households require bigger capacity systems.

☐ Confirm if you need a climate-adapted model. Cold climates require insulation or heating to prevent freezing.

☐ Decide between a waterless or greywater-connected system. Waterless models require less maintenance.

Evaluating Features and Installation

- [ ] Check if the system requires ventilation. Proper airflow prevents odor buildup.

- [ ] Ensure it can handle liquid waste properly. Urine-diverting models help manage excess moisture.

- [ ] Measure your space to confirm the toilet will fit. Some models require extra clearance for venting pipes.

- [ ] Determine if installation is DIY-friendly. Bucket systems and self-contained units are easy; central composting systems require more setup.

Long-Term Usability and Maintenance

- [ ] Choose a system with the right emptying frequency for your lifestyle.

- [ ] Select a bulking material that is easy to source. Options include sawdust, peat moss, or coconut coir.

- [ ] Check local sanitation laws before installing a composting toilet.

- [ ] Plan for long-term maintenance. Keep spare parts (fans, seals, and extra bulking material) on hand.

Maintaining and Using a Composting Toilet

A well-run system stays odor-free, safe, and efficient. Follow these key tips:

- **Odor Control:** Add dry material (sawdust/peat moss) after each use. Ensure proper ventilation to prevent buildup and discourage pests.

- **Emptying and Composting:** Transfer waste to an outdoor compost bin for further decomposition in a safe, contained environment.

- **Legal Considerations:** Check local laws on human composting before applying it to soil—regulations vary and can carry serious fines or setbacks.

COMMON OFF-GRID WASTE MISTAKES TO AVOID

Never place uphill to a water source | Don't appy composte waste to edible crops | Open waste draws pests & pollutes water

— SCAN ME —

Take it a step further. Put your knowledge into action.

Exclusive access to the Off-Grid Survival Companion—with printable checklists, guides, visual aids, and troubleshooting charts from the book, plus practical tools to help you adapt and build with confidence.

STEP-BY-STEP PROJECT
How to Use & Maintain a DIY Composting Toilet

Whether you're building a long-term off-grid home or upgrading your emergency setup, a composting toilet is one of the most practical, sustainable ways to manage human waste without water or plumbing.

Before You Begin:

This project assumes you already have a composting toilet built or purchased. If not, refer to the DIY Build Guide in this chapter to construct your own. Regular upkeep is key to keeping the system odor-free, sanitary, and legally compliant.

Don't Overthink It

You don't need the perfect setup to start composting. A simple pile, bin, or bucket can make a real impact. Focus on learning the rhythm, then upgrade as you go. Even a few scraps kept out of the trash make a difference off-grid.

Skill Level: Beginner

Simple routine tasks and no technical knowledge needed

Tools Required

- Scoop or cup for bulking material
- (Optional) Stir stick or compost agitator
- (Optional) Thermometer for compost pile

Estimated Cost

$ (if already installed) – Minimal cost for bulking material and occasional parts.

Estimated Time to Complete

Daily: 2–3 minutes per use
Weekly: 10–15 minutes
Monthly: 20–30 minutes
Seasonal: Up to 1 hour (bin maintenance)

Materials List

- Bulking material (sawdust, peat moss, or coconut coir)
- Vinegar-water cleaner
- Gloves and compost-safe waste bins
- Optional: Urine-diverting insert (for odor/moisture control)

DIY & Reuse Opportunities

- Reuse food-grade buckets, barrels, or scrap wood for compost bins
- Use salvaged lumber to build an insulated outdoor compost station
- Collect sawdust or leaf mulch from local sources for free bulking material
- Repurpose old trash bins with holes for compact composting.

Step 1: Prep the Setup

- Build or install your composting toilet with a secure seat, enclosed base, vent pipe, and collection bucket.

- Place dry bulking material (like sawdust, peat moss, or coconut coir) nearby in a sealed container.

Step 2: Use the Toilet

- After each use, cover the waste with a layer of bulking material.

- Ensure the vent system is allowing proper airflow to prevent moisture buildup and odor.

Step 3: Manage Urine (If Applicable)

- For urine-diverting models, regularly empty the liquid container.

- Avoid mixing too much liquid into the compost bucket to maintain the right balance.

Step 4: Weekly Care

• Check for odors. If present, increase dry material use or improve ventilation.

• Wipe down surfaces with a vinegar-and-water solution to keep things sanitary.

Step 5: Monthly Maintenance

• Stir or rotate compost contents (if applicable) to speed decomposition.

• Inspect the vent pipe to ensure there are no clogs or pest issues.

Step 6: Seasonal Adjustments

• **Winter:** Insulate the enclosure to prevent freezing.

• **Summer:** Boost airflow and monitor moisture levels to keep materials dry.

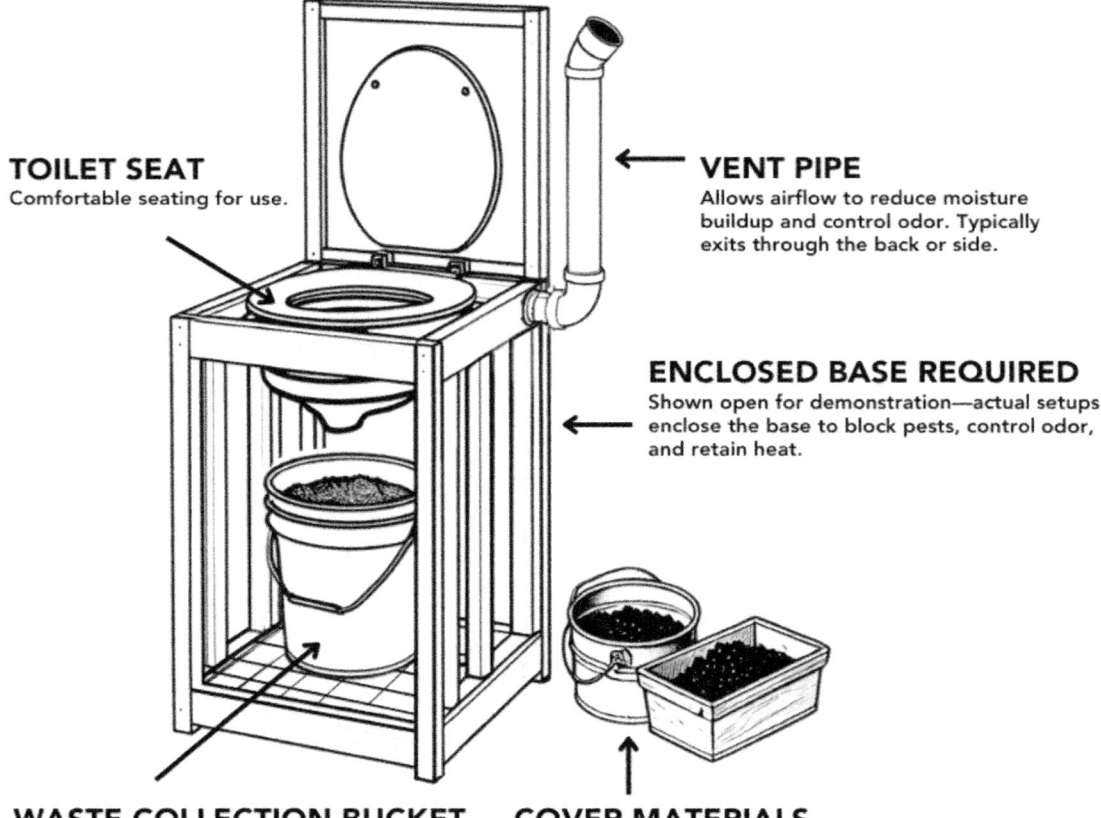

TOILET SEAT
Comfortable seating for use.

VENT PIPE
Allows airflow to reduce moisture buildup and control odor. Typically exits through the back or side.

ENCLOSED BASE REQUIRED
Shown open for demonstration—actual setups enclose the base to block pests, control odor, and retain heat.

WASTE COLLECTION BUCKET
Placed inside the enclosure to collect waste. Sawdust or peat moss is added after each use to aid decomposition and control odor.

COVER MATERIALS
Cover materials should be stored in a sealed container to keep them dry and prevent pests. A bucket with a lid or a closed bin works best.

Representative illustration of a DIY composting toilet setup.
Design details may vary depending on the materials used and climate-specific needs.

Step 7: Composting and Disposal

- Transfer full buckets to an outdoor composting bin for final decomposition.

- Follow local laws regarding compost use—humanure often must be composted for 1–2 years before being used on non-edible plants.

 FROM THE FIRE. STORIES THAT STILL BURN.
She Kept It Simple—And It Works Off the Grid

Savannah, an off-grid DIYer and founder of *"The Off Grid Homesteader"* needed a reliable, low-cost sanitation solution for her family's remote bathhouse setup. With no access to plumbing or septic, she built a composting toilet that's as practical as it is replicable.

Using a 5-gallon bucket inside a wood frame and topped with a standard toilet seat, she added a urine-diverting insert to keep solids dry and minimize odor. The materials were affordable—plywood, basic lumber, and hand tools—making it easy for others to follow her lead without special skills or expensive parts.

You don't need anything fancy to make it work—just a good setup and regular maintenance. — Savannah

Her build proves that with a little planning, anyone can create a functional, off-grid toilet system—no plumbing, septic, or power required. It's a reminder that self-reliance isn't about perfection but purpose.

Effective off-grid systems start with simple materials, thoughtful design, and a willingness to do the work.

┌─ SCAN ME ─────────────────────

Want to see a DIY compost toilet that works?
Watch Savannah & Casey from <u>The Off Grid Homesteader</u> show how they built theirs using simple tools and materials.

Survival Sanitation: Why It Matters in Crisis

When sewer systems fail or plumbing is unavailable, waste management becomes a critical survival factor. Improper disposal can contaminate water sources, spread disease, and lead to outbreaks of cholera, dysentery, and other infections. Disaster recovery studies show that poor sanitation significantly increases illness and mortality rates after natural disasters and infrastructure failures.

To protect health and prevent contamination, waste disposal methods that can be set up quickly with minimal resources are needed.

Short-Term Waste Solutions

When plumbing fails during an outage, storm, or short-term crisis, you need a quick, reliable way to manage waste. These simple setups work for hours to weeks but must be used safely and hygienically.

 STEP-BY-STEP PROJECT
How To Set Up an Emergency Bucket Toilet

When plumbing fails or sanitation systems go offline, a bucket toilet provides a fast, affordable backup that's easy to build, maintain, and store. It's a practical

Skill Level: Beginner

No tools or technical skills needed

Tools Required

• None required
• Scoop or cup for cover material -optional

Estimated Cost

$-$$ - usually under $25 with reused parts

Estimated Time to Complete

5–10 minutes (initial setup) - Ongoing: 2–3 minutes per use, with weekly care

Materials List

• 5-gallon bucket with tight-fitting lid
• Heavy-duty trash bags or compostable toilet liners
• Dry cover material (sawdust, peat moss, shredded paper)
• (Optional) Snap-on toilet seat
• (Optional) Urine diversion container

DIY & Reuse Opportunities

• Repurpose buckets or containers
• Use scrap wood or fabric for privacy
• Shred junk mail or paper for bulking
• Store sawdust in old pet food bins

solution for natural disasters, power outages, evacuations, or early off-grid setups —especially in areas where waste management quickly becomes a health risk.

Before You Begin:

This setup is ideal for short-term emergencies, bug-out kits, or off-grid shelters. Keep one assembled and ready to deploy, even if you already have a composting or flush-based system. Redundancy matters—especially during storms, water shutoffs, or supply chain disruptions when your main option might fail or fill up faster than expected.

Step 1: Line the bucket

Use a heavy-duty trash bag or compostable liner to line a 5-gallon bucket. This makes emptying and cleanup easier and safer.

Step 2: Add dry cover material

Add 1–2 inches of sawdust, peat moss, or shredded paper to absorb moisture and control odor.

Step 3: Use and cover each time

After each use, add another layer of dry material. This keeps the contents dry, supports decomposition, and controls odor; for even better results, consider using a separate container to divert urine.

Step 4: Seal the bucket

Keep the lid tightly closed when not in use to block odors and keep out flies.

Step 5: Empty responsibly

When the bucket is two-thirds full, tie off the bag and dispose of it using safe emergency waste disposal methods. Bury, burn (if legal and safe), or store in a designated containment zone until it can be handled properly. Diverting urine to a separate container helps keep solids dry, which speeds up decomposition and cuts down on smell.

This method is highly effective in emergencies—quick to set up, waterless, and easy to manage with the right dry materials.

STEP-BY-STEP PROJECT
Quickstart: How To Set Up an Emergency Latrine Pit

For group use in short-term emergencies, a latrine pit is a fast, low-tech way to manage waste and prevent contamination with minimal tools.

Before You Begin:

Best for rural or wilderness use. Avoid frozen, flood-prone, or high-density areas. Always dig downhill and at least 200 feet from water.

Quick Set-up

- **Skill Level:** Suitable for beginners with basic digging and site setup skills.
- **Materials Needed:** A shovel, plus soil, sawdust, or ash for covering waste.
- **Optional Materials:** Use a tarp, poles, or scrap wood to add privacy.
- **Tools Required:** A shovel or mattock; a hammer or mallet if building a shelter.
- **Time Required:** 30–60 minutes to set up, and 2–5 minutes of upkeep per use.
- **Estimated Cost:** Typically free if using on-hand or scavenged materials.
- **DIY Tips:** Repurpose wood or fencing for privacy, use wood ash as cover, and pre-mark future pit sites for rotation.

Step 1: Choose a safe site

Pick a location at least 200 feet from water sources and downhill from living areas to prevent contamination.

Step 2: Dig the trench

Use a shovel or digging tool to create a pit roughly 12–18 inches wide and about 3 feet deep.

Step 3: Cover after each use

After each deposit, add a layer of soil, sawdust, or ash to reduce odor and keep insects away.

Step 4: Add basic privacy if needed

If time and resources allow, build a simple shelter around the pit for privacy.

Step 5: Backfill and relocate

When two-thirds full, cover with soil and dig a new pit nearby. This method is easy to set up with basic tools and works well for group use in rural or wilderness areas. It's not suited for frozen ground or densely populated spaces and does require ongoing maintenance.

 # STEP-BY-STEP PROJECT
How To Burn Waste (Caution Required)

Burning waste can be a last-resort solution when sanitation systems fail, but it must be done carefully to avoid environmental and health risks.

Before You Begin:

Burning waste is a last resort, best for rural areas without fire restrictions. Check local laws, keep suppression tools nearby, and never burn hazardous materials.

Quick Set-up

- **Skill Level:** Beginner to intermediate—requires site awareness and fire safety.
- **Materials Needed:** A metal barrel, fire ring, or dug-out burn pit; long-handled tools for tending the fire.
- **Tools Required:** Shovel or digging tool, fire poker or metal rod.
- **Time Required:** 30–45 minutes per burn session, depending on waste volume.
- **Estimated Cost:** $ – Often free using salvaged barrels or natural pits.
- **DIY Tips:** Use a metal grate or mesh to contain debris; keep a water bucket or sand nearby for emergencies.

Step 1: Choose a safe burn site

Select a remote, open-air location far from shelters, water sources, and flammable materials. Never burn waste indoors or in enclosed spaces, and always check local burn restrictions—even during emergencies.

Step 2: Dig a shallow burn trench

Dig a small trench or pit to contain the waste and control the fire.
Keep water and tools nearby for safety, and use a metal barrel if available for better containment and airflow.

Step 3: Burn in small amounts

Add waste in small, manageable amounts, letting each portion burn completely before adding more. Never burn large quantities at once, and monitor the fire closely at all times.

Step 4: Extinguish and cover the ash

Once the fire is fully extinguished and cooled, cover the ash with soil to prevent contact or wind dispersal, and dispose of any remaining materials responsibly.

This method can reduce waste volume but produces toxic fumes and carries legal and environmental risks. Use only when all other options are exhausted.

Why Preppers Keep a Burn Barrel–Even Unused

In long-term grid-down scenarios, waste buildup can become a serious health hazard. Having a designated burn setup—barrel, pit, or fire ring—provides a fallback solution if other systems fail. The key is storing it safely, out of sight, and using it only when absolutely necessary.

Burn Smart: What to Avoid

Avoid burning plastics, treated wood, or anything synthetic—these release harmful toxins into the air and soil. Stick to paper, cardboard, and organic waste. If unsure, don't burn it.

Preventing Disease in Waste Management

In the aftermath of a disaster or when living off-grid, sanitation can mean the difference between survival and widespread illness. Waterborne diseases like cholera and dysentery can spread rapidly when waste contaminates drinking water and living areas. While many people focus on securing food and shelter, failing to plan for sanitation can quickly lead to life-threatening conditions.

Establishing proper waste management and hygiene routines in survival situations is critical. Here's how to prevent disease when traditional systems are unavailable.

Hand Washing and Hygiene Alternatives

When running water is unavailable, alternative hand-washing methods ensure hygiene remains a priority.

DIY Hand-Washing Station:

- A gravity-fed container with a spigot and catch basin mimics a sink. To reduce contamination, use biodegradable soap and place it near waste areas.

Alcohol-Based Sanitizers:

- When water is scarce, use sanitizers containing at least 60% alcohol to kill bacteria and viruses. However, sanitizers do not remove dirt or toxins, so handwashing is necessary when possible.

Ash and Sand Scrubbing:

- Wood ash has mild antibacterial properties, and sand provides an abrasive effect to remove grime. Rubbing hands with either, followed by rinsing, offers an effective alternative in off-grid conditions.

Rainwater Collection for Hygiene:

- A simple catchment system (gutters, tarps, barrels) can provide sustainable hand-washing water. Filtering removes debris for external use, while boiling or UV treatment ensures drinking safety.

Natural Disinfectants for Waste Areas

Store-bought cleaning chemicals aren't necessary for maintaining sanitation. These natural alternatives are effective for keeping waste areas clean:

White Vinegar:
- It kills bacteria and mold and can be made through simple fermentation when commercial supplies are unavailable.

Hydrogen Peroxide (3% Solution):
- A non-toxic disinfectant for toilets, latrines, and waste containers. It breaks down into water and oxygen, making it environmentally safe.

Charcoal Ash:
- Absorbs moisture and neutralizes odors in bucket toilets and latrines.

Lime (Calcium Hydroxide):
- It speeds decomposition, reduces odor, and prevents pathogen growth.

Safe Disposal of Contaminated Materials

Burn contaminated materials like diapers, medical waste, and soiled bandages only when fire risk is low and conditions are safe. If burning isn't an option, seal the items in secure containers for later disposal. Never dispose of any waste in natural water sources or storm drains, as this can cause serious environmental and health hazards.

 CHECKLIST
Preparing for Safe Waste Management

Use this checklist to confirm that your waste management system is safe, sanitary, and sustainable in off-grid or emergency situations.

1. Waste Containment and Disposal

- [ ] Have I set up a secure waste containment system (composting toilet, vented latrine, or septic alternative)?

- [ ] Is my waste disposal site located at least 200 feet from water sources (streams, wells, lakes)?

☐ Am I properly covering waste after each use with sawdust, ash, or dry soil to aid decomposition and reduce odor?

2. Odor and Pest Control

☐ Do I have ventilation in place for composting toilets or latrines to prevent moisture buildup and odors?

☐ Am I checking for flies, rodents, or pest activity around waste areas?

☐ If pests appear, have I improved covers or waste control?

3. Handwashing and Hygiene Setup

☐ Have I set up a handwashing station near waste disposal areas?

☐ Do I have soap, sanitizers, or alternative cleaning agents available?

☐ Am I ensuring handwashing after toilet use or waste handling?

4. Disinfection and Waste Treatment

☐ Have I set up a handwashing station near waste disposal areas?

☐ Am I regularly treating waste areas with natural disinfectants like vinegar, lime, or charcoal ash?

☐ If using a composting toilet, am I maintaining the right balance of moisture and dry material?

☐ Have I ensured that no untreated waste is being dumped near water sources?

5. Long-Term Sustainability and Maintenance

☐ Am I regularly emptying composting toilets or maintaining latrine pits before they become overfilled?

☐ Do I have a backup waste containment plan if my primary system fails or the emergency extends longer than expected?

☐ Have I stocked enough bulking material (sawdust, peat moss, or ash) for continued waste treatment?

SCAN ME

Need a full emergency sanitation plan?
The CDC's emergency hygiene guide covers safe waste handling,
temporary toilet setups, and disease prevention when systems fail.

Off-Grid Waste Reduction and Composting

Why Composting is Essential in Off-Grid Living

Composting reduces waste and creates a closed-loop system that turns organic material into a valuable resource. Without traditional waste disposal, off-grid households must minimize accumulation while enriching their environment.

A well-managed composting system can:

Composting reduces household waste by up to 60%, improves soil health and moisture retention, controls odors and pests, and eliminates the need for fertilizers or municipal waste systems.

Everything that grows must return to the soil. The more we embrace that cycle, the more self-sufficient we become.
— Marjorie Wildcraft, Self-Sufficiency Expert.

Choosing the Right Composting Method

Different composting methods suit different climates, spaces, and effort levels.

Method	Best For	Challenges
Hot Composting	Fast decomposition (weeks)	Requires high temperature monitoring
Cold Composting	Low maintenance	Slow breakdown (6-12 months)
Vermicomposting	Small spaces, efficient breakdown	Requires temperature control for worms
Humanure Composting	Off-grid sanitation and waste repurposing	Needs careful pathogen management

✅ CHECKLIST
Choosing the Right Composting Method

Use this checklist to find the best composting system based on your space, effort level, and needs.

1. What do you need composting for?

- [ ] Human waste and organic waste → Composting Toilet
- [ ] Large amounts of food/yard waste → Outdoor Compost Bin or Tumbler
- [ ] Small-scale kitchen composting → Worm Bin (Vermicomposting)
- [ ] Indoor, odorless composting → Bokashi Bin or Fermentation System

2. How much space do you have?

- [ ] Large yard → Outdoor Hot or Cold Composting
- [ ] Small yard, patio, or garden → Tumbler or Worm Bin
- [ ] No outdoor space → Bokashi or Indoor Vermicomposting

3. How much effort are you willing to put in?

- [ ] Frequent maintenance and turning → Hot Composting
- [ ] Minimal effort, slow process → Cold Composting
- [ ] Hands-off system → Bokashi or Indoor Composting

STEP-BY-STEP PROJECT
How to Compost Organic and Human Waste Off-Grid

Turning organic and human waste into safe, usable compost supports food security, reduces waste, improves soil resilience, and provides a sustainable alternative to trash or septic systems, especially in long-term off-grid scenarios.

Before You Begin:

This system is for composting food scraps, garden waste, and bucket toilet contents (humanure). For human waste, compost must cure for at least 6 months before soil use. Always follow local health and safety regulations.

Quick Set-up

- **Skill Level:** Beginner – Requires basic upkeep and observation
- **Materials Needed:** Dry browns (leaves, cardboard, sawdust), wet greens (scraps, grass, manure), compost bin or pile
- **Tools Required:** Shovel or pitchfork for turning; optional thermometer
- **Time Required:** 10–15 min/week; 6–12 months for full decomposition
- **Estimated Cost:** $ – Low or no-cost using salvaged bins or materials
- **DIY Tips:** Stack pallets into a 3-bin system, use junk mail as browns, bury full toilet buckets in center of pile for safe composting

Step 1: Choose a Location

Pick a well-drained, shaded area that is at least 50 feet from living spaces and food storage. Avoid low-lying ground where water can collect and slow decomposition.

Step 2: Create Your Bin or Pile

Use an open-air bin, a three-sided structure, or just a compost heap directly on the ground. Heighten slightly or place a base layer of sticks and twigs to improve airflow.

Step 3: Add Brown Materials First

Start with a base layer of carbon-rich "browns" like dry leaves, shredded cardboard, or sawdust. This helps absorb moisture and prevents early odors.

Step 4: Layer Green Materials

Add a layer of nitrogen-rich "greens" such as food scraps, grass clippings, or manure. Alternate layers of browns and greens as new material is added.

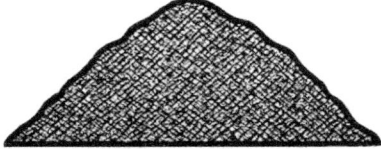

FINISHED COMPOST
Moisture = Sponge-like

CURE 6+ MONTHS
If human waste was used, before soil use

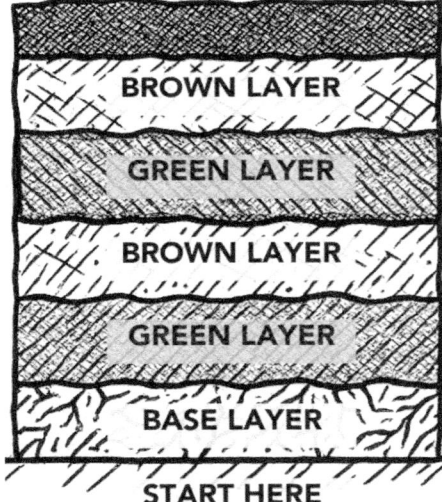

BROWN LAYER

GREEN LAYER

BROWN LAYER

GREEN LAYER

BASE LAYER

START HERE

Step 5: Maintain the Right Ratio

Aim for roughly two parts brown to 1 part green. This balance reduces odor, speeds decomposition, and prevents the pile from getting too wet or too dry.

Step 6: Turn the Pile Weekly

Use a pitchfork or shovel to turn the compost once a week. This introduces oxygen and helps materials break down faster.

Step 7: Monitor Moisture and Temperature

Your pile should feel like a wrung-out sponge—add browns if too wet, or greens/ water if too dry. A warm center means it's actively composting.

Step 8: Use When Ready

Finished compost is dark, crumbly, and earthy-smelling, with no visible food scraps. If composting human waste, ensure it cures for at least 6 months before use on soil.

Quick Composting Troubleshooting Guide

Issue	Solution
Compost isn't breaking down	Balance greens and browns, maintain a 3-foot pile, and turn regularly to speed decomposition.
Compost smells bad	Add more dry brown materials like leaves, sawdust, or cardboard. Turn the pile for better airflow and avoid adding meat or dairy.
Compost is too wet	Mix in dry brown materials to absorb moisture. Cover with a tarp if excess rain is a problem.
Compost is too dry	Add more food scraps and grass clippings for moisture. Lightly water the pile in hot climates.
Pests are present	Bury food scraps under brown material to deter animals. Avoid composting meat, dairy, or oily foods. Use sealed bins in pest-prone areas.

Before using finished compost:

Finished compost should be dark, crumbly, and smell earthy, with no visible food scraps or undecomposed material. For human waste, allow at least six months of decomposition before use.

Using Finished Compost for Survival and Preparedness

In grid-down scenarios, composting is more than a gardening practice—it's a survival tool. It reduces waste, improves food security, and even generates heat. When modern infrastructure fails, composting keeps your systems resilient.

Survival Uses for Compost

1. Sanitation in Long-Term Emergencies

If the sanitation services collapse, composting provides a sustainable way to manage waste and reduce disease risk.

- Use composting toilets when plumbing fails.
- Compost food scraps to prevent trash buildup.
- Control pests by properly managing organic decomposition.

2. Food Security and Soil Fertility

Without access to store-bought fertilizers, compost maintains soil health and keeps crops growing.

- Enrich garden soil with nutrient-rich finished compost.
- Use in raised beds or remote bug-out locations.
- Preserve long-term fertility in survival gardens.

> **Prepper's Note:**
> **Waste Is a Survival Asset**
>
> In grid-down scenarios, fuel shortages are a major threat. Biogas turns waste into fuel, cutting reliance on propane or firewood.
>
> **Maintenance and Troubleshooting**
> - **Low gas output:** Add manure or baking soda to rebalance pH.
> - **No gas production:** Check for air leaks—system must be airtight.
> - **Cold weather:** Insulate with straw or bury part of the digester.
>
> **Estimated Output:** Enough gas to cook daily for a small household.
> **Scalability:** Multiple drums can be connected for larger energy needs.

3. Passive Heat Generation

Decomposing compost produces heat, an often overlooked survival resource that can help keep small spaces or water supplies from freezing in cold climates.

- Build a compost heating system for a greenhouse.

- Place compost piles near shelters for added insulation.

- Run water pipes through compost to warm emergency water supplies.

Quick Check: Is Your Compost Ready?

☐ Dark, crumbly texture with an earthy smell (not foul)—a sign it's mature and ready.

☐ No visible food scraps or undecomposed material—just clean, stable compost for planting.

☐ If human waste is composted, it's been cured for at least six months.

Immediate Survival Applications

- **Sanitation:** Use for human and food waste management in emergencies or off-grid setups.

- **Food Security:** Boost soil fertility for self-reliant growing and long-term productivity.

- **Heating:** Generate off-grid heat to support shelters or greenhouses during cold seasons.

SCAN ME

Waste and sanitation feel easier said than done?
Use the diagrams to pick a system that's practical and low-maintenance. Access to the Off-Grid Survival Companion—with printables, planning worksheets, and setup charts from this chapter, plus bonuses to help you create a system that's clean, safe, and sustainable.

Don't Let Waste Undermine Your Survival

In off-grid life, managing waste isn't optional—it's essential. A solid system protects your health, safeguards your land, and keeps your water sources clean. From composting toilets to greywater setups, these aren't just hygiene solutions—they're tools of resilience.

Handle waste well, and your homestead becomes stronger, safer, and more self-sufficient—no matter what comes your way.

Off-Grid Survival Companion Access

You've made it this far—now it's time to build.

To unlock the printable checklists, project diagrams, troubleshooting tools, and extra content that goes with this book, Scan the QR code to enter.
When prompted, use the password below.

Password: scout

This site is for book buyers only, thanks for supporting independent publishing and building something real.

You Took the First Step.
Want to Help Someone Take Theirs?

A quick review can point someone else in the right direction.

You started reading this book for a reason—maybe to feel more prepared, more independent, or just more in control. Whatever brought you here, you've taken the first step.

By now, you've likely applied a core strategy—starting a basic system, prepping more intentionally, or transitioning off-grid in a way that fits your life.

If this book helped you build something useful or feel more capable—even just one small win—would you consider sharing that in a quick review?

Your words could help...

...someone gets through their first power outage without panic.
...someone grows their first food, they don't have to buy it.
...someone finally believes they can do this, too.

> *"Every part of this life teaches you something—one project at a time."*
> — *Jay and Jen, "Off Grid with Jay and Jen"*

⌐SCAN ME⌐

Share what you've learned—it matters more than you think.
Your voice could be someone else's turning point.
Scan the QR code or visit: https://mybook.to/Off_Grid_JD_Wright

---

Thank you for being here—and for taking the kind of steps most people only dream about. You've already done one of the hardest things: you started. But remember, you're not doing this alone. Every win, every lesson, and every story adds to a growing community of people choosing a more self-reliant life.

Keep going. You're part of something bigger now.

J.D. Wright

CHAPTER 7: YOU CAN'T PREDICT THE THREAT – BUT YOU CAN BE READY

You are your first line of protection in an off-grid environment. Your security precautions have to be self-reliant and quite strong without the safety net of law enforcement or watched alarm systems. Not only is one responding to threats, but also aiming forward. It is meant to deter them before they start.

A well-designed off-grid security system combines visibility with unpredictability. Motion lights, warning signs, and fences all around tell invaders they have been observed. Tripwires, covert cameras, guard dogs—a hidden system guarantees they won't know what else to expect.

Note: Your objective is to alert and discourage, not to cause injury. Avoid setups that might do just that. Always follow municipal rules and liability issues.

 —————————————————————————————

Security is layered—perimeter, lights, hidden storage. Deterrents make intruders move on. — Selco Begovic, Survivalist and Author.

—————————————————————————————

LAYERED SECURITY FOR OFF-GRID PROTECTION

No single tactic will keep you safe. A strong off-grid security system relies on layers—each one creating more friction for intruders and more time to respond. Think of every layer as a silent warning. The more unpredictable and well-placed your defenses, the more likely a threat moves on without confrontation.

Layer 1: Outer Perimeter Barriers & Boundaries

The first step is to define your space. A mix of natural and man-made fencing—thorn bushes, rock piles, privacy fencing, or barbed wire—can slow entry and direct movement. Add clear signage like "No Trespassing" or "Private Property" to send a firm psychological message.

Natural Barriers (Living & Non-Living)

| Thorny Bush Fences | Cactus & Desert Barriers | Thorn & Rock Barriers |

Physical Fencing (Man-Made)

Basic Wooden Fence

Reinforced Chain-Link & Barbed Wire Fences

Privacy Wooden Fences with Barbed Wire & Spikes

Layer 2: Detection, Deterrance & Surveillance

Detection alerts you to intruders; surveillance shows you their numbers, movements, and intent, providing reaction time when seconds matter. Together, they give you a critical edge—letting you respond proactively, not reactively.

EARLY DETECTION STRATEGIES

Detection gives you early warning, alerting you to movement before it becomes a threat. Even seconds of notice can mean the difference between panic and a plan.

1. Motion Lights & Infrared Detectors

Solar-powered motion lights expose anyone moving at night, making them one of the most effective low-maintenance deterrents.

- Place near driveways, sheds, livestock pens, and entry doors to eliminate critical blind spots.

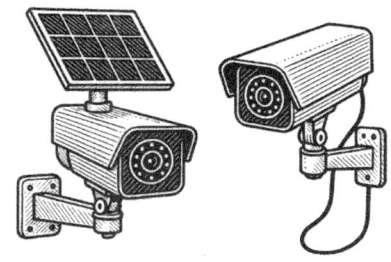

- Pair with sirens or infrared motion detectors for added defense when threats are heightened.

- Test units regularly and keep backups for cloudy seasons or emergency power failures.

Rearrange lights and alarms regularly—predictable setups are easy to map, but randomness makes you harder to target. Motion-activated solar lights aren't set-

and-forget; test them often, especially before winter, and keep backups ready for cloudy or snowy conditions.

2. Guard Animals

Train them to alert and protect—dogs, geese, or donkeys provide early warning and act as active deterrents without relying on electricity.

Start with basic obedience, then train for perimeter alerts using scent, sound, and unfamiliar movement, similar to focused watchdog training.

Guard Dogs: Reliable and Always On

Unlike alarms or lights, dogs don't lose their signal or run out of batteries. Most dogs serve as excellent early warning systems, but only trained guard dogs should be trusted for physical confrontation. Some of the best breeds for protection include German Shepherds, Rottweilers, Belgian Malinois, and others. Keep in mind the costa of care for the animals.

Smart Use Cases: Unless professionally trained, dogs should be used primarily for alert barking and perimeter awareness. Kennels should be placed near gates or high-traffic areas for visibility, and a motion-triggered latch or tripwire system for emergency release should be considered.

3. Audible Alarms

They startle intruders and warn others nearby—battery-powered or manual systems that can function even during power outages to buy you time and get help.

Tripwire Alarms

A basic tripwire system can alert you before someone even reaches your home. Stretch the fishing line or paracord across paths or trails, driveways, or hidden entry points at ankle or knee height. When tripped, it should trigger a noise or a visual cue for you to check.

Bell Tripwire Alarm

" " ——— 🔥 From the Fire ————————

*A tripwire may be simple, but it buys you time—
time to react, reach safety, or stop a threat.*

" "

Spring-Loaded Mechanical Alarm
Triggers noise or signal when disturbed with no power.

Tripwire Placement

- Use natural choke points like trails, gates, or driveways as movement funnels.

Electric Tripwire Alarm
Loud siren activates when the pin is pulled. Battery-powered.

- Set wires at multiple heights, such as ankle and knee level, to increase the chance of contact.

- Camouflage with leaves or dirt.

Tin Can Rattle Alarm
When tripped, cans knock together, creating noise.

- Vary placement occasionally to prevent patterns from becoming predictable.

4. Advanced Option:

A battery-powered pull-pin alarm can be attached to the tripwire using clips or tape, providing a loud, immediate alert that startles intruders and signals danger.

5. Low-Tech Options:

Crushed gravel walkways create noise underfoot, while hinged metal plates on gates sound off when disturbed—simple, passive alerts that signal movement.

These kinds of builds cost less than $20 and use materials you probably already have. For budget-conscious readers, simple doesn't mean weak—it means smart and repeatable.

Psychological Deterrents: Look Defended—Even If You're Not

Most intruders won't take a chance if the property looks alert and occupied. These simple cues create doubt without costing much:

- **Dummy Cameras & Warning Signs** – Post "24/7 Surveillance" signs and use dummy cams at entry points to create doubt and delay intruders.

- **Motion-Sensor Barking** – No dog? Use a speaker that plays barking on motion detection to deter intruders.

- **Signs of Life** – Muddy boots, recent tire tracks, or a well-used axe by the porch send a clear signal: *Someone's here—and paying attention.*

Remember: Don't try to look aggressive. Try to look unpredictable. That's what makes people walk away.

Psychological barriers slow intruders, but effective defense demands physical surveillance—cameras, mirrors, or patrols.

Eyes on Your Perimeter

Whether you're home or away, visibility equals control. Surveillance doesn't always mean high-tech—it means having a system that fits your land, lifestyle, and power limitations. The goal? Spot intruders before they get too close. Below are practical surveillance methods that balance cost, coverage, and off-grid reliability, so you can act before it's too late.

Surveillance Type	Cost	Power Source	Best Use Case	Effectiveness
Solar-Powered Cameras	$$$ High	Solar panels with battery backup	24/7 monitoring of key entry points, remote properties	★★★★☆ Reliable if placed properly
Battery-Operated Cameras	$$ Mid	Replaceable or rechargeable batteries	Backup security in areas without solar access	★★★☆☆ Limited by battery life
Wildlife Trail Cameras	$ Low	Long-lasting batteries	Motion-triggered monitoring for driveways, trails, and sheds.	★★★☆☆ Good for passive surveillance
Dummy Cameras	$ Very Low	None	Visual deterrent when placed strategically	★★☆☆☆ Deterrent only
Mirror-Based POVs	$ Very Low	None	Monitor blind spots and entries without exposure.	★★★☆☆ For early detection
Camouflaged Observation Posts	$$ Moderate	None	Observe property from concealed long-range positions	★★★★☆ Effective but manual monitoring

Surveillance methods compared by cost, power needs, and off-grid effectiveness. All options are scalable—layer multiple types for best results.

Layer 3: Physical Barriers Fortify Your Entry Points

Defensive Landscaping and Concealment

Landscaping can be used for more than aesthetics—it can physically prevent access and slow intruders down. The best security makes access difficult before an intruder reaches your home.

- **Strategic Thorny Bushes:** Blackberries, holly, and cacti under windows and fences create painful barriers.

- **Obstacle-Based Landscaping:** Stacked wood, rock piles, and raised garden beds make foot travel difficult.

- **Hidden Storage:** Essential tools, food, and supplies should be concealed in secondary locations.

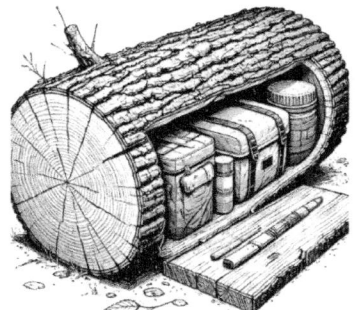

BURIED SUPPLY CACHE   **HOLLOWED-OUT LOG**   **SUBFLOOR STASH**

These physical obstacles slow intruders and help you hear or spot movement earlier, giving you critical time to respond, secure your shelter, or alert others.

Blending In vs. Standing Out

Security is about controlling perception. An off-grid home should either look extremely secure or completely uninteresting to avoid being a target. A visible deterrent suggests resistance, while camouflage removes temptation entirely.

- **Signs and Psychological Barriers:** "24-Hour Surveillance" and "Beware of Dog" signs create uncertainty.

- **Mock Security Setups:** Dummy cameras and fake alarm boxes make intruders second-guess surveillance risks.

- **Camouflage and Concealment:** Keep valuable equipment, fuel, and tools out of sight to avoid attracting interest.

Layer 4: Emergency Response

Once a threat is detected, response time matters most. This final layer prepares you to act decisively when it counts.

Personal Defense Tools

Whether you choose non-lethal or lethal options, the goal is simple: defend yourself effectively, without hesitation, confusion, or unsafe mistakes.

Common Off-Grid Options:

- **Bear Spray or Pepper Spray:** A powerful deterrent that buys you time to escape. Keep by main entries and in high-risk zones like outdoor work areas.

- **Tactical Flashlight with Strobe Mode:** This flashlight temporarily blinds intruders in the dark and doubles as a blunt-force tool. Look for models with a rugged grip and rechargeable batteries.

- **Stun Guns or Tasers:** Legal in many areas, these non-lethal tools require close contact but can quickly disable an intruder. Some models require a background check—know your local laws.

- **Firearms (If Legal and Desired):** Shotguns and handguns are common for rural defense but require secure storage and consistent training. Never rely on ownership alone—practice matters more than power.

DIY Alternatives:

- **Slingshot with Steel Pellets:** Silent, reusable, and effective with practice.

- **Homemade Spear or Staff:** Simple wood tools that extend reach and increase defense range increase range without using ammo.

Safe Handling Starts with Training:

- Take a certified self-defense or firearm safety course—many are low-cost or offered online, locally, or through clubs.

- Dry run drills monthly: Practice drawing and aiming in safe conditions using empty or disabled equipment.

Four Rules of Safe Weapon Use: - Teach every capable adult in your household

1. Treat every tool as if it's live, even during practice or routine checks.

2. Never point at anything you're not prepared to disable.

3. Keep it secure but within reach. Access speed beats overly hidden storage.

4. Know the difference between warning and action, and practice both.

Survival skills aren't about having the most gear. It's about knowing exactly how and when to use what you've got.

Community Defense in a Collapse Scenario

In a long-term crisis, security shifts from occasional trespassers to organized looters and resource raids. A well-prepared community deters threats, protects supplies, and maintains order when external law enforcement is no longer reliable.

- **Backup Communication is Critical** – Use encrypted radios and silent signal codes.

- **Resource Protection is Key** – Store supplies in multiple hidden locations and use decoy caches to mislead intruders.

- **Deterrence is the First Line of Defense** – Keep signs of activity visible, rotate patrols, and avoid predictable patterns.

Security isn't just gear—it's rotation, relationships, and readiness. The most defended homesteads during long-term collapse are the ones with trusted watch networks and hidden fallback supplies.

Why a Community Security Network Works

In off-grid or collapse scenarios, where law enforcement may be delayed or absent, a structured community security network strengthens protection, speeds up response, and builds resilience. Isolated properties are often the first to be targeted—visibility and coordination are your best defense. Assign clear roles to ensure accountability and a fast response.

Communication Coordinator

Manages radios and emergency alerts. Ensures fast, reliable contact across your property and team.

Surveillance Manager

Oversees cameras, motion sensors, and visibility. Keeps key zones covered, logged, and operational daily.

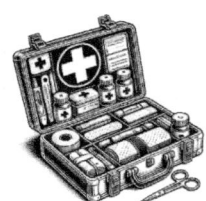

Emergency Response Leader

Maintains supplies and response skills. Provides first-aid confidence when seconds truly matter most.

Training Coordinator

Leads drills and basic defense training. Builds readiness and neighbor trust through regular practice.

Strong community security starts with shared awareness, simple routines, and mutual trust. It doesn't take advanced tech—just neighbors who know what to watch for and how to respond. With the right framework, even a few households can become a powerful deterrent. Strong community security starts with shared awareness, simple routines, and mutual trust.

 # STEP-BY-STEP PROJECT
Building a Community Security Network

Even a small, organized group can create a reliable off-grid security network. By assigning clear roles, assessing vulnerabilities, and establishing communication protocols, your community can be prepared to detect, deter, and respond to threats—even without external support.

Before You Begin:

This project works best with two or more households, a shared perimeter or communication plan, and basic tools or radios. Even small neighborhoods or family compounds can benefit from a simple security network.

Skill Level: Beginner - Intermediate

Easy to set up with roles, teamwork, and basic communication—no skills required.

Tools Required

- Basic tools: screwdriver, pliers, zip ties, nails/screws, hammer
- Optional: whiteboard, flashlights, whistles, or markers for drills & planning

Estimated Cost

$–$$ - Depending on number of radios, signage, and alarm systems; low-cost or reused gear can keep costs minimal

Estimated Time to Complete

4–6 hours: Initial setup to assess, assign, and install key systems
1–2 hours/month: Ongoing maintenance for drills and updates

Materials List

- Printed or hand-drawn map
- Weatherproof signage (e.g., "Patrolled Area," "No Trespassing")
- Radios (CB [citizen-band], HAM, or walkie-talkies)
- Battery or solar security lights
- Low-cost Kits: tripwire or motion
- Emergency supplies for drills
- Shared logbook or digital tracker

DIY & Reuse Opportunities

- Repurpose trail cameras or old mirrors for surveillance
- Use secondhand radios or hand-me-down tools
- Print signage at home or repurpose political sign stakes
- Convert old maps or satellite images for perimeter layout
- Mark paths with rocks or scrap wood

Step 1: Assign Security Roles and Responsibilities

Structure is critical in an emergency. Designate clear responsibilities before a crisis, not during, to avoid confusion, panic, or duplicated effort. Every second counts when your safety is on the line.

In a Family or Group Setting: Assign roles based on age, ability, and skill.

- **Lead Communicator** – Handles radios, alarms, or calling for help (ideal for calm, tech-savvy adults or teens)

- **Perimeter Check** – Scans entry points and secures doors/windows (adults or older teens)

- **Child or Elder** – Safely moves vulnerable household members to a secure spot (older sibling, parent)

- **Tool Grabber** – Retrieves self-defense tools, flashlight, or emergency pack (whoever is nearest or fastest)

With Kids:

Involve them with simple but empowering tasks:

- Blow a whistle
- Grab the family walkie-talkie
- Stay quiet and hidden in the designated safe zone

If You're Solo:

Mentally rehearse your sequence:

- Where you go
- What tool will you grab
- How do you signal for help or record what happened

Keeping People Accountable: Review roles regularly. Post a copy in your shelter. Run drills and debriefs to stay sharp. Clear roles build confidence under pressure.

Step 2: Security Risk Assessment

Walk your perimeter and note vulnerabilities like unlit paths, blind corners, and unsecured gates. Log past incidents—trespassing, theft, wildlife—and factor in off-grid threats like looters or unrest. Prioritize risks by location and history.

Patrol Key Checkpoints: Driveways, Blind Spots

Update your map or notes after major weather events, seasonal changes, or land use shifts. Involve your household—fresh eyes can catch blind spots or new patterns you might overlook.

Step 3: Set Up Reliable Communication Systems

Without cell service, use backup systems for outages and distance.

Best Off-Grid Communication Tools:

- **HAM and CB Radios** – Reliable for long-range contact across valleys, ridgelines, or rural distances. Licensing may be required for HAM (citizen-band), but many off-gridders use them for regional check-ins or mutual aid networks.

- **Walkie-Talkies** – Ideal for short-range communication between household members, neighbors, or outbuildings. Choose waterproof, rechargeable models with privacy codes and backup batteries.

- **Encrypted Messaging Apps (Signal, Zello)** – If you have intermittent Wi-Fi or satellite internet, use these for discreet, secure messaging. Great for coordination during outages or public disturbances when cell towers are overloaded.

- **Emergency Light Signals** – Flashlight, lantern, or headlamp codes (such as three quick blinks for help) offer silent, no-tech signaling. Position lights at windows or use reflective surfaces to signal from a distance.

Make It Actionable:

Assign communication tools based on location, age, and ability. Rehearse response codes for common emergencies like intrusions, fires, or medical events until they're second nature. Example: 2 radio clicks = stay quiet and hold; 3 clicks = regroup at safe zone.

Remember: Keep a waterproof notepad near each radio or station to log messages or signals—especially useful when stress is high or silence is necessary.

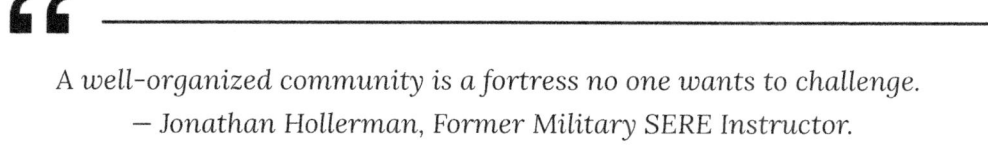

A well-organized community is a fortress no one wants to challenge.
— Jonathan Hollerman, Former Military SERE Instructor.

Security Training and Drills

A trained household or community reacts faster and more effectively under pressure. In high-stress situations, preparation prevents hesitation—and hesitation costs time you may not have. Regular drills build muscle memory, reduce panic, and help even younger or less adept members make a difference.

Core Training Areas:

- **Self-Defense** – Practice practical, situational techniques like stance, escape moves, and non-lethal tools. Train with age-appropriate options—pepper spray for teens, breakaway holds for adults, noise signals for kids.

- **Firearm Safety and Coordination** – Ensure weapons are handled legally, responsibly, and with clear household protocols. Designate who is trained and where the tools are stored. Practice dry runs without ammo.

- **Home Fortification** – Learn to reinforce entry points with improvised barriers, locks, and visual deterrents. Assign zones to defend and practice securing them quickly under timed conditions.

Emergency Response Drills:

- **Medical Training** – Practice CPR, wound packing, choking response, and using a tourniquet. Even one trained responder can stabilize a crisis until help arrives —or isn't coming.

- **Fire Evacuation Plans** – Map escape routes, use fire blankets and extinguishers, and train family members to exit blindfolded or in smoke conditions.

- **Break-In Simulations** – Run scenarios where a "mock intruder" tests your response. Switch roles, practice moving to your safe room, and reinforce communication plans under pressure.

Mental Preparedness: Staying Calm Under Pressure

Training your gear is easy—training your brain is harder. Mental readiness is often overlooked, but in off-grid survival, it's just as important as physical tools.

- **Practice scenarios** regularly to reduce hesitation and freeze responses.

- **Use timed drills** to simulate decision-making under stress.

- **Incorporate stress inoculation techniques** like shouting commands, navigating in low light, or completing tasks under pressure.

- Encourage all members to focus on breathing and verbal clarity—panic spreads, but so does calm.

In a real threat, your mind is your first weapon. Train it well.

Training builds trust—but shared action turns prep into protection. Use the checklist below to launch a simple, practical watch that fits your land and lifestyle.

 **CHECKLIST**
Quick Start: Setting Up Your Community Watch

Whether it's three neighbors or a full rural network, this checklist turns ideas into action. With structure, readiness, and real-world drills, your group can detect, deter, and respond effectively.

Are You Organized?

- [ ] Assigned roles for lookout, communications, response, and medical support
- [ ] Property risk assessment completed, including threat mapping and collapse scenarios
- [ ] Shared, printed plans for crime, raids, or looting scenarios
- [ ] Regular review of roles and plans during seasonal or threat-level changes

Is Communication Secure?

- [ ] Every member is equipped with radios, backup batteries, or low-tech signaling methods.
- [ ] Pre-assigned emergency distress signals (radio codes, light flashes, physical markers)
- [ ] Communications are tested during real drills or under simulated stress

Are There Tactical Defenses in Place?

- [ ] Hidden surveillance at choke points, trails, and blind spots
- [ ] Trained patrol routes with varied timing and overlapping visibility
- [ ] Secured backup supply caches, hidden and known only to trusted members
- [ ] Agreed-upon rally point and response strategy in case of intrusion or lawlessness

Securing your perimeter is just the first layer. What happens inside your home—how you prepare, respond, and stay in control—can mean the difference between chaos and clarity when a threat breaches the line.

Inside-the-Home Readiness

Perimeter defenses are vital—but inside your home is just as important for protecting lives, deterring threats, and maintaining control during a crisis.

1. Lock down your home at night with a consistent routine.

2. Keep flashlights, radios, or personal alarms in easy-to-reach spots.

3. Use three simple code words: danger, regroup, and all clear—practice often.

4. Designate safe fallback points (e.g., reinforced room, escape route).

Practicing calm responses inside your home can buy you critical time and prevent panic during a real threat. A breached perimeter means your internal defenses—plans, communication, and safe zones—must activate quickly.

SCAN ME

Protect what you've built—before you hand is forced.
Use checklists and visuals to spot gaps and shore up defenses. Scan the QR code for exclusive access to the Off-Grid Survival Companion—with printable references, threat assessment guides, and defense-planning tools from this chapter, plus bonus content to help you stay ready, not reactive.

Turning Protection into Real Community Power

Security matters—but without reliable communication and trusted connections, even the best defense falls short. In a crisis, knowing who you can reach—and how —can mean the difference between isolation and action.

When disaster strikes, preparation turns fear into confidence.

CHAPTER 8:
WITHOUT COMMUNICATION, EVEN STRONG SYSTEMS FAIL

The grid goes silent. No cell signal. No internet. No news broadcasts. With the power out, communication networks collapse, and it could take days or even weeks before anything is restored. For off-grid living, this isn't a hypothetical scenario. **It's reality.**

A reliable communication system is your lifeline—essential for calling for help, tracking weather, and staying connected to others. Actual preparedness means having more than one way to reach out.

The 4 Layers of Reliable Communication

A resilient communication system uses multiple methods—short-range, long-range, and backup—to keep you connected when it counts.

Layer 1: Short-Range Communication (1-5 miles)

This is your local network, allowing contact with family, homestead workers, or nearby security teams—ideal for coordinating daily tasks, sharing updates, alerts, or urgent responses.

Best Options:

- **FRS Walkie-Talkies** – No license required, easy to use, limited range.

- **GMRS (General Mobile Radio Service) Radios** – Stronger than FRS, up to 5+ miles, and require an FCC license.

- **CB (Citizen-band) Radios** – Common among truckers, useful for vehicles and homesteads.

Signal Tips for Mountains, Forests & Fog

Dense trees, steep hills, and heavy fog can weaken radio signals. Use VHF radios for open terrain, and UHF for forests or buildings. Raise antennas for better reach, and know that solar storms or bad weather may still disrupt even advanced systems.

Scenario: You're working in the fields while your spouse is at the main house. Instead of walking back, you check in via GMRS radio. A storm alert comes in on your NOAA emergency radio, giving you time to secure the property.

Layer 2: Mid-Range Communication (10-100 miles)

To stay connected with neighbors, nearby towns, or emergency services, Ham radio is the go-to tool.

Why Ham Radio?

- Operates on VHF (open terrain) + UHF (dense areas like forests and buildings).

- Repeaters amplify signals, extending reach far beyond standard radios.

Quick Start Guide: Getting on the Air with HAM Radio

1. Buy a Baofeng UV-5R (an affordable Ham radio).

2. Study for and obtain a Technician License (free online resources available).

3. Join a local Ham radio network for practice.

Scenario: Your nearest neighbor lives 15 miles away, too far for GMRS. With a VHF HAM radio and a local repeater, you check in daily, even if cell towers go down.

Survival in Action: Ham Radio Saves a Life

On September 21, 2024, Greg Owen (WX7Z), a Ham radio operator, intercepted an emergency call from Ed Clark (K7ELC), reporting a four-wheeler accident in a remote, mountainous area in Idaho. With no cell service, Owen relayed the distress call to local emergency services, leading to a successful rescue.

Lessons Learned: Ham radio works where cell service fails—and in remote emergencies, it can mean the difference between life and death. This rescue proved that a simple setup and a listening ear can save lives when nothing else reaches out.

If you own a radio but haven't tested it—or don't yet know how to use it—make today the day that changes.

Layer 3: Long-Range and Emergency Communication (100+ miles and Global)

In major emergencies, long-range communication becomes vital—connecting you to help when everything else goes dark.

Best Options:

- **HF Ham Radio** – Transmits globally by bouncing signals off the atmosphere.

- **Satellite Phones** – Work anywhere, independent of cell towers.

- **PLB (Personal Locator Beacon)** – Sends SOS to rescuers via satellite.

Scenario: You're deep in the backcountry and break an ankle. With no cell service, you activate your PLB, transmitting your exact location. Within hours, emergency responders arrive.

Survival in Action: Wildfire Survival with Emergency Radios

In September 2020, Liz Lawrence and her daughters were camping near Mammoth Pool Reservoir when the Creek Fire trapped them and hundreds of others. Roads were blocked, and cell service failed.

How They Escaped:

A few campers had emergency radios to relay distress calls, and rescuers coordinated a mass helicopter evacuation for 200+ people.

Lessons Learned:
- Cell service is unreliable in wildfires and disasters.

- Emergency radios save lives by providing real-time rescue coordination.

In every vehicle, pack, or camp setup, an emergency radio deserves a permanent spot—it could be your only lifeline.

Layer 4: Backup Methods (Low-Tech and Emergency)

When high-tech fails, simple tools like whistles, mirrors, and hand radios become your last line of communication. Have low-tech options ready:

- Hand-crank or solar emergency radios – Receive NOAA weather alerts.

- Signal Mirrors – Flash sunlight to alert aircraft or distant rescuers.

- Whistles – Produce loud distress signals when lost or injured.

Scenario: Your ATV breaks down deep in the woods. You use your signal mirror to flash sunlight, where a fellow off-gridder sees it and comes to assist.

Family Comms Plans That Actually Work

Create a simple family communication plan before you need it. Choose one place to meet, one method to check in, and three emergency code words (e.g., "safe," "danger," "regroup") that everyone can remember under stress. Practice monthly—even as a game—so every household member responds without hesitation when it counts.

 STEP-BY-STEP PROJECT
Setting Up Your Off-Grid Communication System

Even the most prepared household can miss critical details if they don't test their communication setup. This step-by-step guide walks you through building a reliable, layered system to stay connected—no matter what fails.

Before You Begin:

Map your terrain and identify who you'll need to reach—family, neighbors, emergency responders—and how often. Consider local signal barriers like trees or hills. This will help you choose the right gear and avoid wasted time or money.

Skill Level: Beginner to Intermediate

Most devices are plug-and-play with basic practice.

Step 1: Assess Your Needs

- Who do you need to reach? (Family, neighbors, responders?)

- What is your terrain like? (Flatland, mountains, forests—this affects range.)

- How far do you need to reach? (1 mile? 100 miles? Worldwide?)

Step 2: Acquire the Right Equipment

- **Short-Range:** Walkie-talkies (FRS/GMRS)

- **Mid-Range:** Ham radio (VHF/UHF)

- **Long-Range:** HF Ham radio or Satellite phone

- **Backup:** Hand-crank emergency radio, PLB

Step 3: Install and Maintain Infrastructure

- Place antennas 30–50 feet high for better range.

- Use solar or battery backups.

- Store extra antennas, cables, and batteries for emergency redundancy.

Preventive Maintenance for Communication Devices

- **Weekly:** Test all radios and satellite phones.

- **Monthly:** Rotate and charge backup batteries.

- **Seasonal:** Update emergency contacts and clean solar panels.

Step 4: Run a No-Grid Communication Drill

Test your preparedness by disconnecting from all modern communication for 24 hours. After the drill, identify weaknesses and improve your setup.

Time Block	Task
Hour 1-3	Turn off cell phones, WiFi, and landlines.
Hour 4-6	Use GMRS radios for household check-ins.
Hour 7-12	Contact a neighbor using Ham radio.
Hour 13-18	Attempt to reach an emergency relay via HAM or Satellite phone.
Hour 19-24	Log issues, adjust system, document improvements.

How to Find an Off-Grid Community

Living off-grid does not mean living alone. Many survivalists and homesteaders thrive in communities, sharing resources, knowledge, and skills. Building a strong off-grid network means faster problem-solving, safer security measures, and more resource-sharing. Here's how to find and connect with others:

1. **Use Online Networks and Forums** – Websites like Permies.com, Homesteading Today, and off-grid Facebook groups connect off-gridders worldwide.

2. **Attend Local Homesteading and Survival Events** – Look for barter fairs, preparedness expos, or farmers' markets where like-minded people gather.

3. **Start a Skill-Sharing or Trade Network** – Connect with nearby homesteaders by trading skills (e.g., "I'll fix your fence if you teach me food canning").

Communication is often overlooked in off-grid living, yet it can be the difference between safety and disaster. A layered strategy with the right tools keeps you connected when the grid goes down.

Building a Local Off-Grid Resource Network

Self-reliance is stronger with support. Local networks help you trade, share, and stay ready together. Here's how to build one that lasts.

The Benefits of Community Networking

A strong local network is critical to off-grid survival, enhancing:

- **Resource Efficiency** – Reducing waste by sharing essential supplies.

- **Sustainability** – Growing food and keeping power reliable by working together.

- **Security and Emergency Preparedness** – Ensuring mutual aid in crises.

Radios aren't enough if they're untested. A real system means knowing your gear, checking your coverage, and running drills.

Organizing Community Meetings

To foster cooperation, regular meetings help maintain structure:

- **Set a Fixed Schedule** – Weekly or monthly check-ins maintain consistency.

- **Use Consensus-Based Decision-Making** – Ensures fair conflict resolution and aligned priorities.

- **Create a Community Directory** - List skills and resources for easy access.

Developing a Resource Exchange System

A barter and resource-sharing system allows communities to thrive independently. Effective exchange models include:

- **Barter Networks** – Trade skills and goods (e.g., carpentry for fresh produce).

- **Local Currency Systems** – Trade-based tools to track shared resources.

- **Shared Tool and Equipment Libraries** – Access to necessary gear without individual ownership.

Quick Start: Launching a Local Barter Network

1. **List Your Trade Skills & Goods** – Start with what you can reliably offer (produce, tools, childcare, repairs, etc.).

2. **Invite Others to Share** – Encourage neighbors to make their own trade lists.

3. **Host a Simple Barter Meetup** – Keep it informal with clear, fair ground rules.

4. **Collect Feedback & Improve** – Adjust based on what works best for your group.

Once it's up and running, use a simple checklist to keep trades consistent, fair, and community-driven.

 CHECKLIST
Quickstart: Running Your Barter Network

Shelter and Insulation

☐ Keep an updated list of barterable items and skills

☐ Rotate meeting times and locations to include more participants and gather broader input over time.

☐ Promote events through local bulletin boards, radio, or word-of-mouth

☐ Set clear trade expectations (item condition, trade equivalency, etc.)

☐ Include a "community needs" board for high-demand items

☐ Encourage members to bring extras—labels, scales, sample kits, etc.

☐ Collect feedback after each meetup to improve the next one

☐ Document successful trades to build trust and accountability

Building Trust in Your Community Network

Key strategies to strengthen relationships:

- **Consistent Engagement** – Attend meetings regularly to foster trust.

- **Reliability** – Fulfill barter commitments on time.

- **Clear Communication** – Define expectations to avoid misunderstandings.

- **Conflict Resolution** – Address issues quickly and constructively.

Conflict Resolution Framework

1. **Identify the Problem** – Clearly state concerns.

2. **Collaborate On Solutions** – Work toward a fair resolution.

3. **Formalize the Agreement** – Document agreed solutions and responsibilities.

4. **Follow-Up** – Ensure continued compliance and effectiveness.

While every barter network will look a little different, the most successful ones follow the same core principles: clarity, trust, and adaptability. The following case study offers a real-world example of how one off-grid community put these principles into action—and the lessons they learned along the way.

 FROM THE FIRE. STORIES THAT STILL BURN.
Sharing Tools, Building Trust

Vashon Island, Washington

In 2015, a group of neighbors on Vashon Island launched a tool library with one simple goal: to stop wasting money buying tools they'd only use once or twice. Today, their shared inventory includes over 1,500 tools—from power washers to post-hole diggers—and it's entirely volunteer-run.

But what makes it powerful isn't just the savings. It's the ripple effect.

Instead of everyone owning their own circular saw or struggling through a job without the right gear, locals borrow what they need and get help using it. Volunteer Neil Wiesblott described the library as "the best neighbor you ever had," where the tools come with advice and support.

It's proof that you don't need to go it alone—even in a place known for independence. Shared systems work. And when they're well organized, they don't just reduce costs—they build trust.

What to Remember: A well-run tool library can reduce waste, cut expenses, and strengthen local networks. It's not just about gear—it's about giving your community a reason to show up for each other. - *The Guardian*, June 3, 2024.

Community Skills and Resource Directory

Regularly update this directory and make it accessible to all community members.

Community Member	Skills/Expertise	Resources Offered
Christopher Pickett	Carpentry, Plumbing	Lumber, tools, repair services
Johanna Wright	Gardening, Herbal Remedies	Vegetables, herbs, canned goods
Mark Lopez	Mechanical Repairs	Vehicle repairs, spare auto parts
Emily Chen	Food Preservation, Cooking	Canned goods, prepared meals

Addressing Common Barter Challenges

- **Missed Commitments?** Set clear rules and encourage early communication.

- **Disputes?** Use agreed trade values and a simple appeals process.

- **Key Members Leave?** Maintain a directory and train backups to fill skill gaps.

Expert Advice: Building a Reliable Barter Network

Community-building expert Diana Leafe Christian emphasizes that clearly defined expectations prevent barter system failures. Many communities struggle due to unclear exchange values, leading to disputes.

Start small with simple trades to build trust before expanding into larger, complex resource-sharing systems.

Resource Sharing Communication Protocols

With a strong barter system or supply-sharing network in place, your community is better equipped to solve problems, reduce waste, and stay resilient. But without reliable communication, even well-built systems can break down when it matters most. Whether you're coordinating a food exchange or organizing a neighborhood response to a storm, communication is the glue that holds the network together.

That's why off-grid communities need structured, self-powered communication tools—not just for routine updates, but for crisis response. The next section will show you how to build long-range, grid-independent systems using HAM radios and other tools that work when cell towers and the internet fail.

In the meantime, reinforce your local network with clear communication channels such as:

- **Community Bulletin Boards** – Use physical boards at shared locations (like gardens or tool libraries), or simple digital versions updated via radio or shared devices. Post trade opportunities, weather alerts, or rotating needs lists.

- **Group Messaging Systems** – Set up a reliable channel through GMRS/FRS radios or encrypted messaging apps (if power and Wi-Fi allow). Use simple call signs or pre-set times to check in.

- **Emergency Response Channels** – Assign trusted leaders or rotating volunteers to coordinate crisis communication. Predefine roles for first aid, supply distribution, and security during local events or grid-down situations.

Standardizing updates and responses reduces confusion and builds trust—essential for a resilient off-grid network.

With strong local systems in place, it's time to scale your reach. Long-range communication gives your community eyes and ears beyond the horizon.

Utilizing Ham Radios for Emergency Communication

When other systems fail, ham radios keep working. They connect communities, coordinate rescues, and deliver real-time updates—no cell towers or internet required. This section shows how to use them when it matters most.

Why Ham Radios Are Essential for Off-Grid Survival

Ham radios provide long-range, independent communication—most pivotal when conventional networks fail. During disasters, ham operators have coordinated rescues, relayed emergency messages, and provided real-time updates when all other communication methods failed.

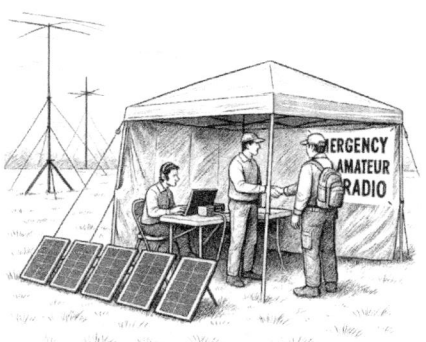

Ham radios:

- Connect with global emergency networks.
- Run on solar, wind, or battery backups.
- Operate without reliance on external infrastructure.

Getting Licensed: Legal Requirements and Regulations

To legally operate a ham radio, you need an Amateur Radio License, which requires passing a test on radio operation, safety, and frequency use. Free online resources, study guides, and practice exams make this process accessible.

Key licensing takeaways:

- **Technician License** – Entry-level, ideal for local and regional communication.

- **General License** – Allows long-distance HF (High Frequency) operation.

- **Extra Class License** – Provides full access to all ham radio frequencies.

Radios aren't enough if they're untested. A real system means knowing your gear, checking your coverage, and running drills.

Start Small. Learn Fast.

You don't need fancy gear to get started. With the right habits and practice, even basic tools can outperform expensive setups. A $35 Baofeng radio and a few YouTube tutorials can outperform a $500 setup if you know how to use it. Build confidence with short-range check-ins and local practice before scaling up.

STEP-BY-STEP PROJECT
How to Set Up a Ham Radio Station

A well-prepared station ensures reliable communication in emergencies. Follow these steps to build a system you can count on when it matters most.

Before You Begin:

You'll need a HAM license to legally transmit—but anyone can start by listening. Define your goals: Do you need regional check-ins, emergency alerts, or long-distance reach? Start simple and expand as your skills grow.

Skill Level: Beginner to Intermediate

No prior technical experience needed—just a willingness to learn. Most users can get licensed with basic study tools and online support.

Step 1: Gather Essential Equipment

- Transceiver (radio unit) for sending and receiving signals
- Antenna system (consider both fixed and portable options)
- Backup power sources: solar panel, hand-crank charger, or battery bank

Step 2: Install the Antenna for Maximum Range

- Mount antennas as high as possible (on a roof, pole, or tree)
- Use directional antennas to target long-distance communication
- Set up a portable antenna option for mobile or emergency use

Step 3: Organize Your Station for Quick Access

- Pre-program emergency and local frequencies
- Keep backup batteries and power sources easily accessible
- Store a printed frequency guide in case digital devices fail

SCAN ME

Take it a step further. Put your knowledge into action.
Exclusive access to the Off-Grid Survival Companion—with printable checklists, guides, visual aids, and troubleshooting charts from the book, plus practical tools to help you adapt and build with confidence.

Troubleshooting Common Ham Radio Issues

Issue	Possible Cause	Solution
Weak signal	Antenna too low or misaligned	Adjust height and positioning
No response	Wrong frequency or licensing issue	Confirm settings and check for repeaters
Dead battery	Solar charge failure or aging battery	Use backup power source or replace battery

Joining Ham Radio Networks

Joining local and regional emergency radio networks strengthens your preparedness, expands communication reach, and builds mutual support.

- **Emergency Response Groups** – Connect with ARES (Amateur Radio Emergency Service) or RACES (Radio Amateur Civil Emergency Service).

- **Online Ham Communities** – Join forums and practice drills to improve skills.

- **Emergency Scenario Drills** – Participate in test situations to ensure readiness.

 FROM THE FIRE. STORIES THAT STILL BURN.
When the power goes out, it's too late to start learning.

Living off-grid in Hawaii comes with unique challenges, especially when storms roll in and knock out power and cell service. One island-based off-gridder, Julian learned this the hard way. Early in his setup, he installed a ham radio system to stay connected during outages—but quickly discovered that just owning the gear wasn't enough.

His first major storm exposed critical weaknesses: poor antenna placement limited his signal range, and static-heavy communication made it nearly impossible to reach other operators. Julian later documented how relocating the antenna, testing different frequencies, and joining local radio nets helped turn things around. Over time, his ham radio became a lifeline—not just for weather alerts, but for community connection and reassurance when other systems failed.

Julian's biggest takeaway? "Set it up, test it often, and don't assume it'll work when you need it most." That experience now shapes how he prioritizes communication in every off-grid system he builds.

You don't have to wait for a storm to learn the same lesson. This chapter walks you through what works, what doesn't, and how to build a system you can count on—no matter where you are. - Modern Off Grid DIY – "How to Ham Radio Off Grid For Off Grid Communication"

Trusted Emergency Communication Networks (U.S.)

These radio networks and volunteer teams keep communication alive during disasters, forming the backbone of U.S. ham radio response and ensuring real-time coordination when other systems fail.

┌─ SCAN ME ─────────────────────────────────┐

Too many to list here—but we've got you covered.

Explore the full list of national emergency radio networks, training organizations, and how to connect with one near you. Includes: ARES, RACES, MARS, SKYWARN, SATERN, and more.

└──┘

Advanced Ham Radio Strategies for Off-Grid Survival

Once you've mastered the basics, consider advanced techniques to improve your reach and reliability.

Using Repeater Networks

Repeaters are shared radio towers that receive your signal and re-broadcast it, dramatically increasing your range. Instead of reaching just a few miles, you might reach 50+—even with a handheld unit. These systems are often maintained by local emergency groups like ARES (Amateur Radio Emergency Service) or RACES (Radio Amateur Civil Emergency Service).

When disasters strike and cell towers fail, these volunteer-run repeaters become lifelines—connecting off-grid users to emergency services, rescue coordination, and community updates. Tapping into them means you're never truly alone, even when you're miles from help.

Digital Communication: Packet Radio and APRS

Beyond voice communication, ham radios can also transmit data—allowing you to send messages, coordinates, and status updates even when internet and cell networks are down.

- **Packet Radios** let you send text-based messages without needing internet—perfect for check-ins or relaying supply requests.

- **APRS (Automatic Packet Reporting System)** allows you to broadcast real-time location, weather, and alerts—a powerful tool during storms, wildfires, or search-and-rescue efforts.

These systems are ideal when you need to communicate quietly or over long periods, especially if you're coordinating with multiple people across a region.

Building an Emergency Antenna Array

The right antenna makes the difference between static and clarity.

- **Directional antennas** focus your signal where it matters—letting you connect with specific outposts or repeaters.

- **NVIS (Near Vertical Incidence Skywave) antennas** send your signal upward, allowing it to reflect back down over mountains or obstacles—perfect for regional comms in rugged terrain.

This setup gives you reliable reach when you can't afford dead zones in an emergency. Whether you're calling for help or relaying vital updates, every extra mile counts.

You don't need to master all of this at once. In fact, most off-gridders start small and grow their skills over time. If you're wondering how to begin—or what's truly required—the next section breaks down the most common questions new operators ask.

Common Questions About Ham Radios

1. Is ham radio difficult to learn?

No. Beginners can start with local VHF/UHF communication and expand as they gain experience. Many ham radio clubs provide free training and mentorship.

2. How expensive is it to get started?

Most handheld radios cost under $100, and you can build a DIY antenna with basic materials. It's one of the most affordable off-grid tools to add.

3. What if I fail the licensing test?

You can retake it—often the same day. Most people pass with basic study tools, and your license is valid for 10 years once you do.

Ham radios remain one of the most trusted tools in off-grid survival. Once licensed, you'll unlock a network of resources and community support.

SCAN ME

Worried about staying connected when it matters most?

Staying connected takes more than luck—it takes a plan. Use what you've learned in this chapter to build a system you can trust. Then scan the QR code for checklists, comms plans, product picks, and bonus tools inside the **Off-Grid Survival Companion.**

You're Only Ready If You Can Respond

Reliable communication is more than a backup—it's a lifeline. The layered systems in this chapter—from walkie-talkies to ham radio to community bulletins— are what keep you informed, connected, and capable when the grid goes down.

This week, test a tool: run a no-grid drill, check in with a radio, or create a simple family comms plan. Practicing now means you'll act with clarity when it counts.

Strong communication builds trust. And in a crisis, trust is everything.

CHAPTER 9: PREPARE TO SAVE LIVES – STARTING WITH YOURS

Medical emergencies off-grid aren't rare—they're expected. With no hospital around the corner, you need the tools and training to treat injuries, infections, and chronic conditions yourself. This chapter gives you practical guidance on building a first aid kit, handling emergencies, and using herbal medicine to stay prepared when help is far away.

Disclaimer: This chapter is here to inform and empower, not to replace medical advice. Always talk with a licensed healthcare professional before making health or emergency care decisions. Use what works for you, and stay safe out there.

Building Your Off-Grid First Aid Kit

A well-equipped first aid kit is the foundation of off-grid medical readiness. Unlike standard kits, yours needs to handle both everyday injuries and more serious emergencies, without relying on a nearby clinic or quick resupply.

Here's what to include in your 72-hour vital first aid kit to cover the most likely off-grid injuries:

- **Wound Care:** Gauze, trauma pads, antiseptic wipes, tweezers, triple antibiotic ointment, medical tape, butterfly closures

- **Infection Control:** Gloves, alcohol pads, iodine, oral rehydration salts

- **Pain & Inflammation:** Ibuprofen, acetaminophen, antihistamines, cold packs

- **Splinting & Immobilization:** Elastic wraps, SAM splint, triangle bandage

- **Basic Tools:** Trauma shears, thermometer, headlamp, CPR mask

- **Instructions:** Printed emergency care guide (in case digital access fails)

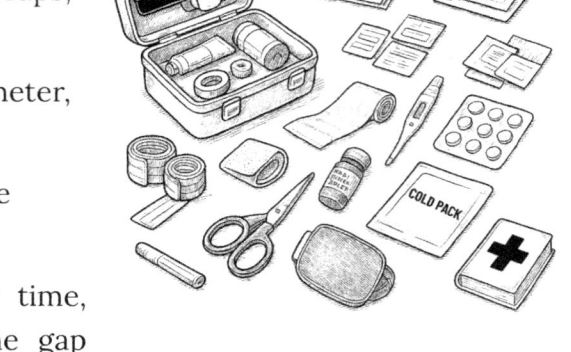

Even a simple kit like this can buy time, prevent complications, and bridge the gap until professional care is available. Start with these basics, then customize based on your location, skills, and household needs.

┌─ **SCAN ME** ─────────────────────────────────

Want a clear starting point to customize for your setup?

For a reliable starting point, check out the **Off-Grid First Aid Kit Guide.** Then, use our printable inventory checklist, modular add-ons for off-grid hazards, and do-it-yourself alternatives for more difficult-to-find items.

Storage and Organization

Medical supplies should be stored in a durable, waterproof case with labeled compartments for quick access. Keeping multiple kits in different locations—home, vehicle, and personal bug-out bag—ensures supplies are always within reach. Regular maintenance is essential—conduct monthly inventory checks, replace expired medications, and restock items after each use.

 FROM THE FIRE. STORIES THAT STILL BURN.
Out here, you don't get second chances. Be ready.

Dennis and Amy, the couple behind Holdfast Alaska, left suburbia to build a remote Alaskan homestead. One winter, Dennis misjudged a swing while chopping wood and badly cut his shin. With roads impassable, Amy had to respond alone.

> *We've learned that you can't afford to freeze or freak out. You have to be your own help out here—and that starts long before anything goes wrong.*

She stopped the bleeding, cleaned the wound, and dressed it with antiseptic and raw honey. They watched for infection over the next few days, and Dennis fully recovered without leaving their land.

The Lesson: In remote conditions, you're the first responder. Being prepared— mentally and medically—can turn a crisis into something you're ready to handle. *"Holdfast Alaska", as featured in the* New York Post

Natural Remedies and Herbal Medicine

Access to pharmaceuticals may be limited in an off-grid environment. Herbal medicine provides an effective alternative for treating injuries, reducing pain, and preventing infections. Understanding how to forage, grow, and prepare medicinal plants is a valuable skill that boosts self-sufficiency.

Common Medicinal Plants and Their Uses

These time-tested plants offer powerful support when medicine shelves are empty. Learn to identify and use them safely to strengthen your off-grid care.

ALOE VERA

How to Identify in the Wild: Thick, pale green spiked leaves; gel inside when cut; grows in dry, rocky soil.

Primary Use: Soothes burns and skin irritation; speeds healing.

How to Apply: Slice leaf; apply gel directly to clean, dry skin.

YARROW

How to Identify in the Wild: White or pink flower clusters; feathery leaves; found in fields and on roadsides.

Primary Use: Stops bleeding, reduces fever and swelling.

How to Apply: Apply fresh/dried as a poultice; drink as tea.

How to Identify in the Wild: Bright orange/yellow daisy-like flowers; sticky, aromatic leaves.

Primary Use: Eases rashes, cuts, and skin infections.

How to Apply: Infuse petals in oil or salve; apply to skin.

How to Identify in the Wild: Tall shrub with white flower clusters and dark purple berries; find in moist shade.

Primary Use: Fights colds and flu; supports immune health.

How to Apply: Simmer berries in syrup or tea; do not eat raw.

How to Identify in the Wild: Dark green leaves; square reddish stems; strong mint scent when crushed.

Primary Use: Relieves nausea, indigestion, and headaches.

How to Apply: Brew as tea or inhale calming steam.

How to Identify in the Wild: Grows near water; long, narrow leaves; bark peels in strips; twigs snap cleanly.

Primary Use: Natural pain and fever relief.

How to Apply: Dry and steep bark as tea; use tincture internally.

How to Identify in the Wild: Pale purple flower spikes; narrow gray-green leaves; strong floral scent.

Primary Use: Calms nerves, improves sleep, soothes skin.

How to Apply: Drink as tea or apply diluted oil to skin.

How to Identify in the Wild: Underground bulb; flat leaves; flower stalk with round bloom; pungent smell.

Primary Use: Fights infection; boosts immunity.

How to Apply: Eat raw, infuse in oil, or mash into a poultice.

Always research dosage and contraindications before using herbal remedies. Natural remedies can be powerful allies—but knowing when to use them (and when to seek help) is just as important.

Using Herbal Medicine Effectively

Herbal remedies can be prepared in different forms that enhance their potency, shelf life, and ease of use depending on the situation:

- **Tinctures** – Alcohol-based extracts with a long shelf life, ideal for pain relief and immune support.

- **Teas and Infusions** – Quick, practical solutions for digestion, colds, and general wellness.

- **Salves and Poultices** – Applied directly to wounds, burns, and infections for rapid healing.

- **Oils and Syrups** – Used internally or externally for various health benefits.

SCAN ME

Want clear, printable recipes for tinctures, and more?
Find beginner-friendly recipe cards inside the **Off-Grid Companion**—rooted in practicality and built for your herbal toolkit.

Integrating Herbal Medicine with Conventional Treatment

Herbal remedies can be highly effective, but they should be used with proper knowledge and caution:

- Check for interactions between herbs and medications. Track your top remedies and flag possible conflicts ahead of time.

- Test for allergic reactions before using a new herb. Try a small skin patch or diluted tea first to avoid surprise reactions when stakes are high.

- Keep a record of treatments to track effectiveness and avoid overuse. Log what you tried, what worked, and any side effects in a field journal.

> *Gear is useless if you freeze in a crisis. Train now so action comes naturally later. — Dr. David M., Wilderness Medicine Specialist and Survival Trainer*

Emergency Medical Procedures and Training

When professional medical assistance is unavailable, having the knowledge and confidence to perform emergency procedures can be lifesaving.

Top 5 Medical Mistakes Off-Gridders Make

1. **Ignoring Early Infection Signs:** Even minor cuts can turn serious. Watch for red streaks, swelling, or pus.

2. **Relying Too Much on Herbal Medicine:** Herbal remedies are great, but cannot replace antibiotics for serious infections. Know when to escalate care.

3. **Not Practicing First Aid Techniques:** Reading about medical skills is not enough—practice with family regularly so you don't freeze under pressure.

4. **No Emergency Evacuation Plan:** Even the most prepared off-gridder might need professional help. Have a plan for getting to the nearest medical facility.

5. **Not Rotating Medications:** Expired antibiotics, painkillers, and first aid supplies may be ineffective when you need them most.

Avoid these mistakes by training regularly, staying vigilant with wound care, and knowing when to seek outside help.

STEP-BY-STEP GUIDES
Basic Life Support: CPR and AED Use

When you're living off-grid or far from medical help, knowing how to perform CPR and use an AED can be the difference between life and death. These life-saving steps are simple to learn—and critical to act on when seconds matter.

Before You Begin:

Practice matters. Review these steps regularly and walk through them with your household so no one hesitates under pressure. Keep a printed guide near your first aid kit, and make sure your AED (if you have one) is charged, accessible, and tested monthly.

Quick Set-up

- **Skill Level:** Beginner – Requires hands-on practice and confidence under pressure.
- **Tools Required:** CPR dummy or pillow, timer or metronome
- **Time Required:** 10–15 min/month; regular refreshers improve muscle memory
- **Estimated Cost:** $ – Minimal cost with free tutorials and low-cost mannequins
- **Practice Notes:** Use a pillow or foam pad to rehearse compressions. Mark hand placement with tape and train your rhythm using "Stayin' Alive" to build muscle memory and reduce panic under pressure.

CPR for Adults (Hands-only)

Whether you're helping an adult or a child, CPR can restart a stalled heart or buy precious time until help arrives. These techniques are simple, powerful, and easy to practice, so you can step in when every second counts.

Step 1: Check for Response

Shake the person gently and check if they are breathing or showing signs of life.

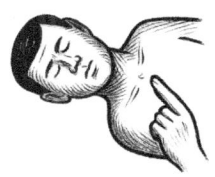

Step 2: Call for Help

Call for help or trigger your alert—then start CPR immediately.

Step 3: Begin Chest Compressions

Place both hands in the center of the chest. Push hard and fast, about 100–120 times per minute (use the rhythm of the song "*Stayin' Alive*" as a guide).

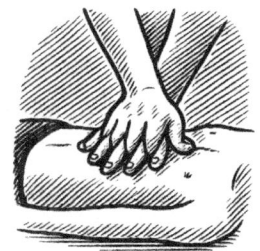

Step 4: Continue Until Help Arrives

Do not stop CPR unless the person begins breathing, trained help arrives, or you are physically unable to continue.

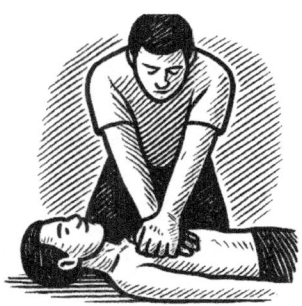

CPR for Children and Infants: When Seconds Count

Step 1: Check for Response

Tap the child or infant gently on the shoulder or foot and look for any signs of breathing or movement.

Step 2: Begin Chest Compressions

Place two fingers (infant) or one hand (child) in the center of the chest. Give 30 compressions at a steady rhythm, allowing full rebound.

Step 3: Give Rescue Breaths

Tilt the head back slightly, lift the chin, and seal your mouth over the child's mouth (and nose for infants). Give two gentle breaths, watching for chest to rise.

Step 4: Repeat the 30:2 Ratio

Continue cycles of 30 compressions followed by two breaths until help arrives or the child begins breathing on their own.

WHEN TO USE HANDS-ONLY VS FULL CPR

Hands-Only CPR
Best for adults who collapse suddenly and aren't breathing. Focus only on chest compressions—ideal if you're untrained or uncomfortable giving breaths.

Full CPR (Compressions + Breaths)
Needed for children, infants, or cases like drowning or overdose—when breathing stops first. Give 30 compressions, then 2 rescue breaths.

When it's a child or infant, stay calm and focused—your confidence will help them too. Gentle breaths and steady compressions matter more than perfection. Keep going until help arrives or the child starts breathing.

Using an AED (Automated External Defibrillator)

When used correctly, an AED can restart a heart in seconds. Learn the steps so you can act quickly and confidently—no medical training required.

Step 1: Turn On the AED

Switch on the device and listen carefully to the voice instructions provided.

Step 2: Attach Pads

Expose the person's chest and apply the electrode pads—one on the upper right side, the other on the lower left chest.

Step 3: Clear the Area

Say "Clear!" and ensure no contact before shock.

Step 4: Deliver Shock

If the AED advises a shock, press the button when prompted. The shock may restart the heart.

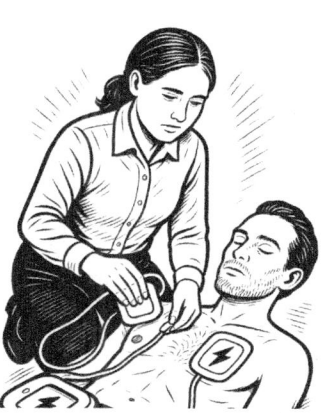

Step 5: Resume CPR

Immediately begin chest compressions again unless the AED instructs otherwise or the person starts breathing.

SCAN ME

Need CPR and AED guidance?

Get up-to-date, medically reviewed training straight from the source. Visit the **Off-Grid Companion** for current protocols and lifesaving instructions.

Wound Management and Infection Control:

Even minor wounds can spiral into major problems when you're far from medical help. Without access to antibiotics or sterile environments, proper cleaning and dressing are your frontline defense. This section helps you turn small injuries into recoverable moments, not survival threats.

STEP-BY-STEP GUIDES
Cleaning and Dressing a Wound

Infection is one of the biggest threats when you're off-grid. These steps will help you clean and protect wounds before they become dangerous.

Before You Begin: Clean hands, clear space, calm mind. Prep materials so once you start, your focus stays on protecting the wound—not grabbing supplies.

Quick Set-up

- **Skill Level:** Beginner – Focus on cleanliness, control, and consistency
- **Tools Required:** Clean water or saline, gauze, antiseptic, gloves, bandages
- **Time Required:** 10–15 min/session; practice monthly to stay familiar
- **Estimated Cost:** $ – Most supplies are low-cost or already in basic kits
- **Practice Notes:** Rehearse washing the wound gently, applying antiseptic, and dressing with clean gauze and tape. Use a dummy arm or fruit (like a banana) to simulate delicate skin and practice pressure without causing damage.

Step 1: Wash Your Hands

Use soap and clean water to thoroughly wash your hands, or wear gloves if available, to prevent bacteria from entering the wound.

Step 2: Flush the Wound

Rinse the wound thoroughly using clean water or sterile saline to remove visible dirt, debris, and bacteria from the area.

Step 3: Apply Antiseptic

Apply antiseptic solution or antibiotic ointment directly to the wound to prevent infection and support healing from the start.

Step 4: Cover the Wound

Place a sterile dressing or clean cloth over the area, then secure it with tape or a wrap to protect the wound from contaminants.

Step 5: Monitor for Infection

Check the wound at least once a day for signs of infection, such as redness, swelling, warmth, pus, or fever in the injured person.

Managing Severe Bleeding Step-by-Step

Severe bleeding can become life-threatening in minutes. Knowing how to respond quickly—with pressure, elevation, and clotting agents—can be the difference between survival and tragedy.

Before You Begin: Set up your tools before you touch the wound. Once pressure starts, your hands need to stay put. Focus, act fast, and stay steady—your response matters most in those first moments.

Quick Set-up

- **Skill Level:** Beginner – Requires observation, consistency, and infection awareness
- **Tools Required:** Gauze, antiseptic, tweezers, gloves, bandages, medical tape
- **Time Required:** 5–10 min/day for care; more for deep or ongoing wounds
- **Estimated Cost:** $ – Affordable supplies; refill from any basic first aid kit
- **Practice Notes:** Learn to monitor for infection (redness, swelling, discharge), change dressings safely, and document progress. Practice handling mock wounds and refreshing bandages cleanly under low-light or field conditions.

Step 1: Apply Direct Pressure

Using a clean cloth or gauze, press firmly and continuously over the wound to help slow or stop the bleeding as quickly as possible.

Step 2: Put Up the Wound

If it's safe, raise the bleeding limb or area above the level of the heart to help reduce blood flow and minimize pressure at the wound.

Step 3: Apply a Hemostatic Agent

If available, use clotting powder or gauze treated with a hemostatic agent (a material that helps blood clot faster) on the wound.

Step 4: Use a Tourniquet as a Last Resort

Apply a tourniquet several inches above the wound only if bleeding is life-threatening and direct pressure fails to stop it.

Once bleeding is under control, your next priority is preventing further damage from broken or unstable bones. Even without formal training, you can protect yourself from injury and buy time with the right stabilization techniques.

STEP-BY-STEP GUIDES
Fractures and Sprains: Treating Fractures

Broken bones and twisted joints are common off-grid injuries—whether from uneven ground, heavy tools, or daily tasks gone wrong. Knowing how to stabilize fractures and manage sprains quickly can prevent further damage, reduce pain, and keep you moving safely until full recovery or medical care is possible.

Quick Set-up

- **Skill Level:** Beginner – Focus on immobilization, stability, and gentle handling
- **Tools Required:** Sticks or splints, cloth strips, duct tape, padding (towel or shirt)
- **Time Required:** 10–15 min/session; repeat monthly to build muscle memory
- **Estimated Cost:** $ – Use household materials or low-cost first aid supplies
- **Practice Notes:** Splint with common materials. Pad well, secure above and below, and drill under pressure to build confidence.

Fractures can happen fast—during falls, heavy lifting, or accidents in rough terrain. Stabilizing the injury early helps prevent further harm, reduce pain, and protect the area until proper care is available.

Before You Begin: Don't rush. Stabilizing a fracture is about steady hands and calm decisions. Scan for other injuries, talk to the person about it, and pad any sharp materials before you touch the limb.

Step 1: Do Not Move the Limb

Leave the injured limb in the exact position you found it. Movement could cause further damage or increase the risk of complications.

Step 2: Create a Splint

Use sticks, foam, rolled cloth, or other rigid materials to brace both sides of the injury and keep the fractured area stable.

Step 3: Secure the Splint

Wrap the splint firmly but not too tightly using tape, cloth, or cord. Check below the injury for warmth, sensation, or discoloration.

Not every injury means a break. When joints are overstretched or twisted, quick action can limit pain, swelling, and long-term damage—no splint required.

Treating Sprains (R.I.C.E. Method)

Sprains are common off-grid injuries—from missteps on uneven ground to heavy lifting accidents. Acting fast helps reduce inflammation, protect soft tissue, and speed up recovery.

Before You Begin: Have your ice, bandage, and elevation set up ready. Small adjustments—like padding under a leg or elevating an arm on a pillow—make a big difference when trying to prevent further strain.

Step 1: Rest the Joint

Avoid using or putting weight on the sprained area. Allowing it to rest helps prevent further injury and supports faster healing.

Step 2: Ice the Injury

Wrap ice in a cloth or towel and apply it to the injury for 15–20 minutes at a time, several times a day, to reduce pain and swelling.

Step 3: Compress the Area

Use a flexible bandage to gently compress the injured area. Make sure circulation isn't restricted, and fingers or toes remain warm.

Step 4: Raise the Limb

Raise the injured area above heart level whenever possible to reduce swelling and help drain fluid from the affected tissue.

Dental Emergencies Off-Grid

Dental emergencies vary, but all require fast action. Here's how to prevent infection, relieve pain, and know when to escalate care and how to act quickly with what you have.

 STEP-BY-STEP GUIDES
Tooth Knocked Out (Avulsed Tooth)

If a tooth gets knocked out, fast action can save it. Here's how to preserve and protect it until professional care is available.

Before You Begin: Stay calm and act fast—time is critical. Avoid touching the root, and prep clean water, gauze, and a container before handling the tooth.

Quick Set-up

- **Skill Level:** Beginner – Requires calm response and gentle handling
- **Tools Required:** Clean cloth, small container, saline or milk, gloves
- **Time Required:** 5–10 min; immediate response is key for success
- **Estimated Cost:** $ – Minimal; most supplies are found in basic kits or the kitchen
- **Practice Notes:** Rehearse picking up the tooth by the crown (not root), rinsing gently, and placing it in a container with milk or saline. Practice with a clean object to simulate urgency and control under stress.

Step 1: Don't scrub the tooth

Be careful with the root—gentle handling helps the tooth reattach.

Step 2: Rinse gently

Use clean water or saline to remove dirt. Do not use soap or chemicals.

Step 3: Reinsert the tooth

If possible, place it back in the socket. Hold it in place with gauze or a clean cloth.

Step 4: Store if reinsertion fails

If reinsertion fails, store in cold milk or saline and seek dental care quickly.

Dental issues are more than just painful—they can become life-threatening if ignored. These guides walk you through how to act fast, reduce risk, and know when it's time to get help.

SEVERE TOOTHACHE OR ABSCESS STEP-BY-STEP

Tooth infections spread fast and often without warning. These steps reduce pain, control infection, and give you time to seek help if needed.

Before You Begin: Pain can mask deeper problems. Rinse gently, gather supplies, and look for swelling, fever, or drainage—signs the infection may be spreading.

Quick Set-up

- **Skill Level:** Beginner – Focus on pain relief and infection control
- **Tools Required:** Salt, water, pain reliever, cold pack, clove oil
- **Time Required:** 5–10 min for relief; monitor daily until symptoms improve
- **Estimated Cost:** $ – Most items are low-cost or already in your home
- **Practice Notes:** Practice saltwater rinses, cold compress use, and clove oil for pain. Know signs of serious infection and when to get help.

Step 1: Rinse with saltwater

This helps reduce bacteria and inflammation.

Step 2: Apply pain relief

Use clove oil or garlic for relief. Apply a warm compress to ease swelling.

Step 3: Take antibiotics if available

If safe to take, use antibiotics for the infection. Seek help if symptoms worsen.

BROKEN OR CRACKED TOOTH STEP-BY-STEP

A chipped or cracked tooth may seem minor but can spiral into nerve exposure or infection fast. These quick actions protect the tooth and give you the best chance of saving the tooth.

Before You Begin: Clean the area gently and avoid extremes in temperature. Gather soft wax, gauze, and pain relief before touching the tooth.

Quick Set-up

- **Skill Level:** Beginner – Start with core skills and build confidence over time
- **Tools Required:** Basic first aid kit, CPR dummy or pillow, training videos or guides
- **Time Required:** 1–2 hours/month for hands-on practice, drills, and regular review
- **Estimated Cost:** $ – Free or low-cost with DIY setups and online resources
- **Practice Notes:** Rotate core skills monthly and include team drills for CPR, bleeding, wounds, and evacuation

Step 1: Cover the exposed area

Use dental wax or temporary filler to protect the tooth.

Step 2: Relieve pain

Use clove oil and over-the-counter pain meds like ibuprofen.

Step 3: Avoid irritation

Don't eat hard, hot, or cold foods until professional treatment is available.

You've now walked through the most critical off-grid medical skills—now it's time to build confidence through training, drills, and community support.

STEP-BY-STEP GUIDE
Training and Skill Development

Preparedness isn't just about gear—it's about knowing what to do. This plan helps you build and maintain the hands-on skills every off-gridder needs.

Before You Begin: Knowing what to do is one thing—being able to do it under stress is another. This section helps you build muscle memory through realistic practice, so your response becomes second nature when emergencies hit.

Step 1: Get Certified

Take a CPR and first aid course through the Red Cross, CERT, or wilderness-focused organizations. Certification builds confidence and skill.

Step 2: Practice Emergency Drills

Conduct practice emergencies with your family or group to build muscle memory, stay calm under pressure, and test your gear and plan.

Step 3: Build a Medical Support Network

Connect with others in your area who have medical training. Share skills, compare gear, and make plans for mutual aid during crises.

First Aid Training Plan

Having supplies isn't enough—you must practice key medical skills regularly, under pressure, and in real-world conditions before an emergency happens. *Drill in different lighting, weather, and energy levels. The more you simulate stress, the better you'll perform when it counts.*

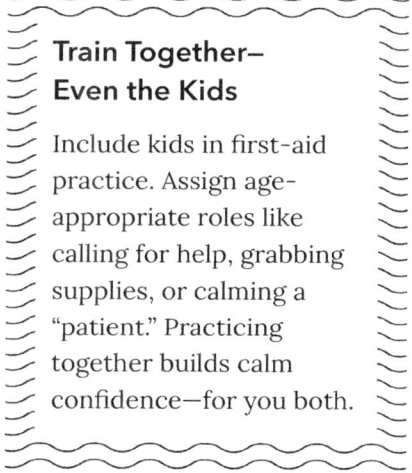

Train Together— Even the Kids

Include kids in first-aid practice. Assign age-appropriate roles like calling for help, grabbing supplies, or calming a "patient." Practicing together builds calm confidence—for you both.

 CHECKLIST
Quick-Action Medical Guide

Practice this drill often—there's no time to look it up in an emergency. This checklist covers core skills from CPR to evacuation. Use it to assess, respond, and act confidently until it becomes second nature.

- ☐ **Assess the Person** – Check breathing, alertness, and responsiveness. Watch for signs of shock or internal injury before taking action.

- ☐ **Call for Help** – Use your radio, signal, or alert system to get help. If communication fails, follow your evacuation plan or send someone to assist.

- ☐ **Start CPR if Needed** - Choose hands-only or full CPR based on the situation. Reassess often and rotate with others to maintain rhythm and reduce fatigue.

- ☐ **Control Bleeding** – Use clotting agents if available, apply firm pressure, and raise the limb. Get ready for evacuation or advanced care if the bleeding doesn't stop.

- [ ] **Stabilize Injuries** – Splint fractures and use R.I.C.E. for sprains. Pad carefully, check circulation, and avoid wrapping too tightly.

- [ ] **Treat for Shock** – Lay the person flat, keep them warm and calm, and monitor breathing. Elevate legs if safe and limit movement or stress.

- [ ] **Clean and Cover Wounds** – Flush, disinfect, and dress wounds to prevent infection. Change dressings regularly and monitor for worsening symptoms.

- [ ] **Watch for Complications** – Look for signs of infection, bleeding, or decline. Swelling, fever, or confusion can mean it's time to escalate care.

Practice this checklist in real-world conditions—wind, cold, darkness. **Emergencies rarely happen when it's easy.**

Medical Supplies to Cache or Trade

Antibiotics, antiseptics, and dental kits are high-value barter items in long-term disruptions. Keep extras stored securely and rotate stock to prevent expiration.

Already walked through the steps?

Use this challenge to reinforce what you've learned and stress-test your setup—no extra prep required. Adapt each day to match your current gear, skills, and terrain.

7-Day Off-Grid First Aid Challenge

Turn knowledge into muscle memory. Each day targets one essential skill to sharpen your response and reveal real-world gaps.

Day 1: Master Bandaging

Practice gauze wrapping, wound packing, butterfly closures, and pressure dressings on different body parts. Simulate real conditions using improvised materials and timed drills to build speed and confidence.

Day 2: CPR + AED Simulation

Run through adult, child, and infant CPR. Use a CPR dummy or pillow. Practice AED steps out loud—even if you don't have one.

Day 3: Build and Test Splints

Use found materials like sticks, foam, or clothing to stabilize a "fracture." For practice, try immobilizing both arms and legs.

Day 4: Spot and Treat Infections

Review signs of infection on fake wounds or photos. Practice wound flushing, antiseptic application, and redressing over time.

Day 5: Make Herbal Remedies

Using common plants like yarrow, calendula, or garlic, create a simple tincture, poultice, and salve. Note their shelf life and uses.

Day 6: Dental Emergency Drill

Simulate a lost filling, toothache, or abscess. Use clove oil, gauze, or wax to create a temporary fix with what's in your kit.

The Golden Hour: Why Action Saves Lives

"In trauma medicine, we refer to the first 60 minutes after a severe injury as 'The Golden Hour.' In that critical time, stopping bleeding, stabilizing fractures, and preventing shock can mean the difference between survival and death." - Trevor, Off-Gridder

What to do the First 60 Minutes:

- Apply direct pressure or a tourniquet to stop bleeding.
- Keep them warm and lift their legs if they show signs of shock.
- If breathing, place them in the recovery position.
- If help is available, evacuate ASAP—every minute counts.

Day 7: Full Scenario Drill

Run a complete off-grid emergency: from injury discovery to treatment, shock care, and communication.

Practice when it's dark. Use headlamps, low lighting, or no lighting. You'll learn fast what needs adjusting.

Red Flags for Evacuation: When Your Care Isn't Enough

Some conditions go beyond the scope of first aid and require professional care. Recognizing red flags early—like severe bleeding, head trauma, or signs of sepsis—can make the difference between life and death. Stay calm, act fast, and trust the training you've built to carry you through.

1. Severe Head Injuries

Loss of consciousness, vomiting, seizures, or confusion may signal brain trauma. Swelling can escalate quickly, leading to permanent damage or death. Evacuate within the hour—don't wait to see if it improves.

2. Uncontrolled Bleeding

If bleeding continues after 10 minutes of firm pressure—even with clotting agents—it's time to act. Apply a wrap, elevate the limb, and evacuate to prevent shock or collapse.

3. Compound Fractures

Bone protruding through skin carries a high risk of infection and internal bleeding. Pad and loosely stabilize the limb, avoid movement, and prepare for immediate evacuation.

4. Signs of Sepsis (Infection in the Blood)

Red streaks, high fever, rapid breathing, or confusion following a wound could mean sepsis. Begin cooling and fluids if possible, but this is a life-threatening condition—evacuate without delay.

5. Severe Burns (3rd or 4th Degree)

Burns that are white, leathery, or deep, especially on the face, hands, or groin, require advanced care. Cover with a clean, non-stick dressing and evacuate as soon as possible.

6. Anaphylaxis (Severe Allergic Reaction)

Facial swelling, throat tightness, or difficulty breathing can escalate fast. Use an EpiPen if available, then evacuate—even if symptoms improve—because second waves can occur.

7. Respiratory Distress

Blue lips, wheezing, or labored breathing that doesn't resolve with an inhaler or rest is an emergency. Open airways, monitor closely, and get the person to help immediately.

8. Heart Attack or Stroke Symptoms

Chest pressure, arm numbness, confusion, or slurred speech are critical warning signs. Keep the person calm and still, and evacuate right away—every minute matters.

9. Severe Dehydration

Signs like confusion, weakness, dry mouth, or vomiting that prevent rehydration are serious. Move them to shade, attempt slow sips, and begin evacuation before collapse sets in.

Always have an evacuation plan—by ATV, boat, snowmobile, or through someone who can assist. Don't wait until it's too late to leave.

SCAN ME

Unsure if you're ready off-grid for a medical emergency?
Use the tools in this chapter to build a kit and a plan you can trust. With checklists, herbal prep guides, and hands-on emergency strategies, you now have the knowledge to respond with clarity and confidence when it matters most.

What Comes Next: Expand Your Resilience and Reach

Medical preparedness builds the skills, confidence, and adaptability to handle emergencies without professional help. By mastering wound care, emergency procedures, and natural remedies, you create true medical resilience.

Take action now: practice key first-aid skills, familiarize yourself with herbal treatments, and organize your medical supplies. The knowledge you gain today could mean survival tomorrow.

Health is your first line of defense. Without it, survival is impossible.

CHAPTER 10: THE COST OF INDEPENDENCE IS PLANNING AHEAD

Living off-grid demands financial sustainability. Whether you are preparing for a full transition or already living off-grid, financial planning ensures long-term stability, resource security, and resilience. This chapter explores the essential strategies for budgeting, reducing expenses, generating income, and securing long-term financial independence in an off-grid lifestyle.

Assessing Your Financial Readiness

Many people underestimate how critical financial planning is when preparing for off-grid living. Without a clear strategy, unexpected costs can quickly derail your progress or compromise your setup. Assessing your financial readiness is a key first step in ensuring a smooth and sustainable transition.

Understanding the True Costs of Off-Grid Living

Going off-grid isn't free—and while it's tempting to believe you can simply "live off the land," the reality is more complex. There are significant upfront investments and ongoing expenses to plan for. Before you begin, list out every potential cost across the categories on the next page:

- **Land Acquisition** – Even raw land can come with hidden costs, such as zoning regulations and property taxes.

- **Shelter Construction and Maintenance** – Whether building from scratch or modifying an existing structure, housing costs add up.

- **Water System Installation** –A well or rainwater collection system can cost thousands, especially with filtration or storage needs.

- **Energy Systems** – Solar panels, wind turbines, or backup generators are necessary but require a large upfront investment.

- **Food Production and Storage** – Seeds, soil amendments, greenhouses, livestock, and preservation supplies all cost money.

- **Waste Management and Sanitation** – Composting toilets, septic systems, and greywater solutions are critical for sustainability.

- **Tools and Equipment** – You can't build, repair, or maintain an off-grid homestead without essential tools.

- **Medical and Emergency Preparedness** – Having access to first aid, backup power for medical devices, and emergency supplies is non-negotiable.

- **Insurance & Permits** – Factor in off-grid-specific insurance, well-drilling permits, septic permits, and road-access fees.

- **Time & Labor Costs** – Your sweat equity has a price; budget for days lost to construction, repairs, and harvest.

- **Learning Curve & Training** – Courses in solar wiring, chainsaw safety, or bookkeeping often save money later.

- **Buffer for Regulatory Changes** – Zoning shifts or new code requirements can create surprise expenses.

Refer back to Chapter 1 for a step-by-step Cost Discovery Worksheet that walks you through gathering real quotes before you commit.

Heads Up: Listing expenses is only half the battle—seeing how those numbers stack up in the real world is what tells you whether the dream is six months away or six years out.

How Much Does It Really Cost to Live Off-Grid?

One of the biggest financial concerns for aspiring off-gridders is understanding exactly how much money they need to transition. The reality? There's no one-size-fits-all answer. Your total cost depends on your location, your level of self-sufficiency, and whether you can build or source materials yourself.

The chart below outlines three common off-grid budget levels—from minimalist to full-featured setups—to help you visualize the range of possibilities. These are not fixed rules but flexible benchmarks to guide your planning based on your goals, skills, and available resources.

Setup Level	Estimated Cost Range	What You Get
Minimalist	$7,500 – $25,000	Tiny shelter or RV, basic solar kit, rainwater system, composting toilet. Highly DIY and best for those prioritizing extreme simplicity and self-builds.
Mid-Budget	$40,000 - $80,000	Small cabin (300–600 sq ft), drilled well or advanced rain system, hybrid solar + backup generator, raised garden beds, basic tools and storage. Suitable for modest year-round living with moderate infrastructure.
Full Setup	$90,000 - $150,000+	Full-size off-grid home (400–800+ sq ft), high-capacity solar/water systems, large-scale food production, full toolset, and long-term resilience. Designed for complete self-reliance.

Every off-grid journey is different. Decide what's essential now and what you can upgrade over time. The best approach is to start small, invest wisely, and scale up when it makes financial sense.

Creating a Realistic Off-Grid Budget

A dream only becomes doable when every line item is priced against real quotes, seasonal costs, and a healthy buffer for mistakes. Use the Build-Your-Budget Blueprint below to convert rough guesses into a concrete, decision-ready plan.

Build-Your-Budget Blueprint

1. **Price Local Essentials First** – Call three regional suppliers for each big-ticket line item (land, well, solar array) and record the highest quote—you can always beat it later.

2. **Add a 20 percent Learning-Curve Buffer** – New skills equal extra materials lost to mistakes. Multiply all DIY materials by 1.2.

3. **Forecast Recurring Costs Quarterly** – Plot taxes, feed, propane, phone/data, and healthcare in three-month blocks so you can spot seasonal spikes.

4. **Zero-Day Fund** – Park at least three months of essential cash (or barter-ready goods) in a fire-proof lockbox or digital high-yield savings.

Example Mid-Budget Plan – Upper Peninsula, MI, cold climate, family of 4

Item	Estimated Cost
Land (5 ac)	$18,000
Drilled well	$8,500
6 kW solar + 2 kWh storage	$15,200
750 sq ft cabin shell	$32,000
Greenhouse & seed	$2,000
Tools & equipment	$4,300
Emergency fund	$6,000
Total	**≈ $86,000**

Budgeting with Kids

Off-grid with kids? Include realistic, evolving expenses—like medical supplies, education materials, clothing, and backup food. Kids grow, outgrow, and get injured—your plan should too. Build in buffers for seasonal gear, emergency meds, and learning tools that support independence. It's not just about survival—it's about setting them up to thrive.

Action Steps: List three skills you already have, circle the one easiest to monetize online, and pilot it for 30 days.

SCAN ME

Editable Budget Toolkit
Use the QR link to open a library of editable budget sheets—each pre-loaded with live formulas that recalculate totals as you adjust land size, climate, or project scale inside the Off-Grid Companion.

Numbers matter, but proof matters more. Jeff and Rose's Northern-Canada homestead—with five daughters, solar-hydro hybrid, and community bartering—shows how a tight budget can power a debt-free, year-round off-grid life.

 ## FROM THE FIRE. STORIES THAT STILL BURN.
No Mortgage. No Regrets. A Family Thriving Off-Grid.

Jeff and Rose Burkinshaw and their five daughters set out to build a self-sufficient homestead in Northern Canada, sharing the journey on their YouTube channel, Gridlessness. They bought a remote 20-acre parcel with no road access, paying cash to keep costs low, then cut their own road to reach the site.

Using salvaged lumber, local timber, and plenty of sweat equity, the family raised a mortgage-free home outfitted with rain-catchment, gravity-fed water storage, and composting toilets, eliminating monthly utility bills. Gardens, small livestock, and a mix of side gigs—teaching homesteading skills, milling timber for neighbors, and selling handmade goods—covered food needs and generated steady income.

Strategic land choice, resourceful building methods, and phased upgrades let them stay debt-free while growing true resilience. Their story shows how clear goals, gradual implementation, and diversified income streams can turn an ambitious off-grid dream into a daily reality for a large family.

What they'd do differently: Launch multiple income streams sooner and set firm milestones to keep cash flow steady during the first two years.

Their success wasn't magic—it was the result of relentless cost-cutting and stripping life down to essentials. The next section breaks those tactics apart so you can apply the same "live simple, spend less" mindset from day one.

SCAN ME

 ### Can You Go Off-Grid Debt-Free with Kids?
Use the QR link to watch "Homesteading Debt Free... Off Grid with a Big Family" on YouTube—Jeff and Rose Burkinshaw and their five daughters reveal the costs, systems, and hard-won lessons behind their Northern-Canada homestead.

Cutting Costs and Living Simply

Off-grid living thrives on minimalism and resourcefulness. The less you spend, the less you need to earn. The best off-grid setup isn't the most expensive. —Iit's the one built with creativity, resourcefulness, and financial wisdom.

Where to Find Affordable Off-Grid Essentials

A tight budget doesn't mean sacrificing quality. Many successful off-gridders cut their costs in half by sourcing used, salvaged, or alternative materials. Here's how you can do the same:

- **Used Solar Panels and Batteries** – Buying second-hand or refurbished panels can save up to 40% compared to retail prices. Check local solar companies, government surplus auctions, and online marketplaces.

- **Reclaimed Wood and Building Materials** – Many cities have architectural salvage yards or Craigslist listings offering free or cheap lumber, bricks, and metal roofing from demolitions.

- **Bulk Buying Groups and Co-Ops** – Some communities pool money to buy grains, fuel, water filters, and emergency repair supplies at wholesale prices, cutting freight fees and locking in stock before supply chain disruptions.

- **Barter for Essentials** – Before spending money, ask: "Can I trade for this?" Many off-gridders swap tools, seeds, or manual labor for needed supplies.

Cutting purchase prices is only half the battle; the next leap comes from shrinking day-to-day expenses through mindset and habit shifts.

Minimalism and Resourcefulness Strategies

Living simply frees up cash and headspace for the projects that matter most. Apply these habit-building tactics.

- **Debt Elimination:** Attack high-interest balances first; every payment erases funds for your next infrastructure upgrade.

- **DIY Mentality:** Tackle one repair or build each week to compound skills and slash service bills.

- **Bartering and Community Exchange:** List three tradable assets you already have, and use them before spending cash.

- **Waste Reduction:** Set up a compost and reuse station; aim for zero trash-bag weeks to reveal hidden savings.

- **Energy and Water Efficiency:** Seal obvious drafts and fit low-flow fixtures; bank the monthly utility savings for larger projects.

Live below your means to sustain off-grid life—maximize self-reliance, not deprivation. — Mark Lewis, Financially Independent Off-Gridder

Remote Money Moves

Multiple income streams keep an off-grid budget resilient. Mix remote work, local services, and product sales to match your land, skills, and bandwidth.

Income Idea	Startup Cost	Skill Level	Why It Fits Off-Grid
Freelance graphic or web design	$0–$200	Intermediate	Only requires a data signal and a laptop
Market-garden microgreens	$150	Beginner	High profit per square foot; quick harvest cycle
Portable sawmill service	$3–5 k (used)	Advanced	Turns storm-fallen timber into cash for neighbors
Online course: chainsaw safety, foraging, etc.	Under $100	Intermediate	Monetizes skills without shipping physical goods
Short-term cabin or tent rental	Varies	Advanced	Leverages your land for passive income
Cold-climate seedling sales	$250	Beginner	Fills a niche for locals with short growing seasons

Choose one idea, set a 30-day micro-goal (first client, first sale, or first listing), and track revenue against hours spent to confirm viability.

Want proof that digital hustles thrive beyond the grid? Sammy's story shows how one signal bar and smart product choices turned remote life into reliable income.

FROM THE FIRE. STORIES THAT STILL BURN.
Sammy's Digital Off-Grid Hustle.

Sammy Cummings, known as Alaska's Off-Grid Mommy, has successfully combined off-grid living with a thriving online business. Residing in remote Alaska, Sammy manages an Amazon business, demonstrating that e-commerce can be a viable income source even in off-grid settings.

Sammy Cummings realized that Alaska's wet, gear-heavy culture offered a perfect niche: waterproof dry bags. She sourced small batches, listed them on Amazon, and reinvested profits into larger orders. By batching product photography during long winter nights and uploading when satellite bandwidth was cheapest, she kept operating costs minimal. The business now funds everything from livestock feed to generator diesel—all from a laptop on a plywood table.

What They'd Do Differently: Test-list two products instead of one, so cash flow starts sooner and you learn which item resonates fastest.

SCAN ME

Could One Digital Hustle Fund Your Remote Life?
Use the QR link to hear how Sammy built a profitable online business from her off-grid cabin. Her episode on the Rainmaker Family Podcast breaks down what worked, what she'd change, and how digital income is possible—even in the middle of nowhere.

Digital sales aren't the only path; thriving off-grid communities also run on good-old trade.

Trade Like Your Survival Depends on It

Cash dries up fast in crises, but barter keeps value flowing—eggs for veggies, labor for lumber—so no one is left short on essentials.

In many off-grid communities, bartering replaces traditional cash transactions. Learning to trade goods and services effectively can reduce financial dependence.

- Exchanging fresh eggs for homegrown vegetables.

- Offering construction skills in return for medical care.

- Trading preserved foods for firewood or fuel.

Ready to make trade a habit instead of a panic move? Start here.

 # STEP-BY-STEP GUIDE
How to Build a Successful Off-Grid Barter Network

Bartering isn't just about trading eggs for firewood—it's about creating a sustainable local economy. If you want to maximize value and reduce cash dependence, follow this step-by-step guide:

Before You Begin: Map out your local assets—what you can trade—and your deficits—what you'll need. Agree on clear quality standards up front, because rotten produce or dull tools quickly erode trust. Finally, keep a running ledger, so everyone sees the values and exchanges stay transparent.

Quick Set-up

- **Skill Level:** Beginner – Start with simple trades and build trust over time
- **Tools Required:** Barter log, inventory checklist, list of local contacts or groups
- **Time Required:** 1–2 hours/month to track trades, assess needs, and connect
- **Estimated Cost:** $ – Free or low-cost using existing supplies and skills
- **Getting Started Tip:** Focus on practical goods and skills, and build your first few trades with people you already know and trust

Step 1: Identify What You Can Offer

Make a list of goods or skills you have available for trade. Examples include:

- Fresh produce, dairy, or preserved foods for trade or emergency use

- Carpentry, welding, or construction skills for repairs and shelter building

- Herbal medicine or alternative healthcare for basic treatment and wellness

- Tools, seeds, or raw materials for building, planting, or trade

Step 2: Build a Trusted Bartering Network

Post a trade wish list on local homestead groups, attend one farmers' market, and host a monthly skill-swap afternoon. For example, you could trade two hours of chainsaw work for plumbing help, or suburban readers could swap balcony-grown herbs for car-share rides.

Quick-Win Scenario: A suburban reader trades sourdough starter and online marketing tips to a rural beekeeper in return for raw honey and mentoring—no cash exchanged, both cut grocery bills.

Step 3: Set Fair Exchange Rates

Determine how much your goods/services are worth in barter terms.

- 1 dozen eggs = 1 lb of organic vegetables

- 1 hour of labor = 10 lbs of firewood

- 1 homemade wool blanket = 5 lbs of fresh meat

Regional Value Examples:

> ### Barter Isn't Backup—It's a System
>
> Barter works best when practiced regularly. Don't wait for a crisis—use your network now for tools, labor, or goods. It's a skill, not just a fallback. The more familiar you are with fair trade values and local needs, the easier it is to navigate shortages without stress.

- **Rocky Mountain Winter** – One hour of snowplow labor equals 15 pounds of seasoned firewood.

- **Urban Southeast** – Three dozen quail eggs equal one gallon of biodiesel.

- **Great Lakes** – Five pounds of lake fish fillets equal a weekend canoe rental.

Step 4: Track Your Trades

Some barter networks use "trade credits" instead of direct exchanges. Trade credits are a simple IOU ledger: each item earns points pegged to local labor rates; credits live in a shared spreadsheet or on index cards—no physical currency needed yet.

When your ledger can't cover every need, it's time to expand the toolbox—from paper IOUs to currencies built for tough conditions.

Alternative Currencies and Financial Tools

Cash isn't always king when you're miles from the nearest bank or grocery run. The options below keep value circulating locally, hedge against inflation, and stay usable even when the grid or the internet goes dark.

- **Cryptocurrency and Digital Banking**: Off-grid individuals are increasingly using Bitcoin, Monero, and decentralized finance.

- **Gold and Silver**: Hard assets that retain value in uncertain economies.

- **Community Credit Systems**: Local trade networks that allow bartering without direct item-for-item exchange.

- **Time-Banking** – One hour of skilled labor equals one credit redeemable for any other skill; works well in suburban pockets.

- **Local Scrip** – Printed notes accepted only inside the county, keeping value circulating locally (for example, BerkShares in Massachusetts).

- **Gold-Back Cards** – Micro-denominated bullion laminated into swipe cards; tangible value, no internet needed.

- **Privacy Coins (Monero)** – Useful where power is stable but privacy matters; carry on an encrypted USB stick.

Whichever tool you choose, pair it with paper records—electronics fail, redundancy saves.

FROM THE FIRE. STORIES THAT STILL BURN.
Off-Grid and Trading: A Desert Barter Life

A small desert enclave discovered that trucking in supplies was bleeding everyone dry. They formalized weekly barter meets where one neighbor's welding repairs could purchase another's surplus melon harvest. Over a year, cash use fell by 60 percent, and the group now maintains a communal seed bank and a shared water-hauling trailer.

What They'd Do Differently: Rotate meeting hosts to prevent travel fatigue and designate a neutral mediator to settle occasional value disputes.

Barter, credits, or bitcoin—whichever mix you choose, the numbers still need an annual tune-up.

Adapting Your Off-Grid Budget

Your financial needs will change as your off-grid lifestyle evolves. Maybe you'll upgrade your solar system, expand your food production, or take on unexpected repairs. The key is to monitor, adjust, and plan ahead.

Here's how to manage off-grid finances long-term:

To manage your off-grid finances long-term, start with an annual budget review to compare what you spent versus what you expected—look for areas to cut waste and opportunities to invest wisely. As your income grows, focus on upgrades that lower future costs, like improved insulation. If you face a major setback, such as job loss or a medical bill, reassess immediately and cut non-essentials. Once your core setup is stable, consider diversifying your income with a side business or rental property. Financial freedom isn't just about going off-grid—it's about staying there without the stress.

SCAN ME

Not sure how to plan your off-grid finances?
Use the tools in this chapter to create a flexible, future-proof plan. With budget templates, income strategy guides, and financial checklists, you'll have what you need to stay prepared, adapt through uncertainty, and protect your long-term independence.

Money Mastery Fuels Freedom

By now, you have a toolkit to price your dream accurately, launch income streams that fit your land, and swap value when cash is scarce. Treat money as one more system—plan it, automate it, and revisit it before it breaks.

Own your numbers today, own your independence tomorrow.

CHAPTER 11:
TECHNOLOGY WON'T SAVE YOU – BUT IT CAN STRENGTHEN YOU

When the grid fails, the prepared don't panic. They flip a switch on their solar system, tap into their rainwater reserves, and harvest food from their greenhouse. Sustainable innovation ensures off-grid living uses technology to create a self-sufficient, resilient lifestyle.

This chapter explores cutting-edge advancements that maximize energy production, water security, food sustainability, and waste reduction. These innovations are transforming survival into long-term thriving.

Advancing Renewable Energy Independence

This section covers solar efficiency, hybrid systems, and battery storage for reliable year-round power. Many readers worry about cloudy days, winter output, or overestimating their setup—this chapter helps you avoid common mistakes. You'll learn how to size your system for real-world conditions and combine sources to stay powered, even when the weather—or life—doesn't cooperate.

Choosing the Right Off-Grid Energy System

Your energy setup should balance cost, efficiency, and sustainability. Use this DIY vs. premium comparison to guide your investment. Federal 30 % solar ITC now extended through 2032—check DSIREusa.org for state rebates.

Energy Source	DIY Budget Option	Premium High-End Option
Solar Power	Used solar panels ($100 each), DIY charge controller	Monocrystalline high-efficiency panels ($300 each), professional setup
Wind Power	DIY wind turbine from salvaged materials ($200)	5kW commercial turbine with smart tracking ($5,000)
Micro-Hydro	Small homemade waterwheel ($500) for low-flow streams	Micro-hydro turbine with battery storage ($10,000)

Heads Up: High-altitude Rockies: expect +10 % solar output but wind downtime in winter inversions.

Maximizing Solar Efficiency

Solar remains the backbone of most off-grid power systems, but recent advancements have dramatically improved efficiency and affordability:

- **High-Efficiency Solar Panels** – Monocrystalline or bifacial panels now hit 22–25 % efficiency, tolerate partial shade better than polycrystalline, and can shave one or two additional panels off small-roof arrays.

- **Solar Tracking Systems** – Two-axis trackers boost output 30–40 % and pay for themselves fastest in high-latitude zones or tree-shadowed clearings.

- **Integrated Micro-Inverters** – Panel-level inverters slash DC losses, simplify expansion one panel at a time, and isolate faults so a single failure won't kill the whole array.

Efficiency gains are only half the battle; reliability comes from stacking technologies that cover each other's weak spots. Enter hybrid systems that blend sun, water, and wind so power keeps flowing when any one source drops.

Hybrid Power Breakthroughs

Relying on a single energy source is risky. Hybrid energy setups combine multiple renewables for consistent, year-round power generation:

You've learned the fundamentals—now picture the next rung on the ladder. Mix-and-match kits let you start with used panels and a DIY controller, then plug in wind or micro-hydro later without ripping everything apart. Use the table as a roadmap, not a shopping list: begin cheap, log real loads for a year, then upgrade the single bottleneck that hurts you most.

Maximizing Water Conservation & Purification

The right innovations can reduce water waste, improve purification, and ensure long-term availability, even in drought-prone regions.

Optimizing Off-Grid Water Systems

Sustainable strategies should save work and still last a long time.

- **Greywater systems** – reduce household water use by over 50% and support off-grid reuse for gardens, trees, and cleaning needs.

- **Energy-Saving Water Collection** – Use gravity-fed rainwater harvesting to reduce the need for pumps and pressurized systems.

- **Low-Tech Filtration** – Passive bio-sand and ceramic filters remove contaminants without electricity, ideal for off-grid or emergency use.

Advanced Water Filtration and Recycling

Today's water filtration technology allows for more sustainable collection, purification, and reuse than ever before. Key innovations include:

- **Atmospheric Water Generators (AWGs)** – Extract 5-10 gallons per day from humidity, even in semi-arid regions.

- **Bio-Sand and Ceramic Filters** – Natural, long-lasting filtration that removes bacteria, viruses, and heavy metals without chemicals.

Energy resilience is useless if water runs out. The next tools slash pump time, capture every drop, and purify it with almost no moving parts—because calories and spare parts are precious.

STEP-BY-STEP PROJECT
Activated Charcoal Water Filter

A simple, low-cost method to ensure clean drinking water, activated charcoal removes bacteria, heavy metals, and chemicals without electricity—making it ideal for off-grid, emergency, or backup use in any climate.

Before You Begin: Rinse gravel, sand, and charcoal until runoff is clear; any silt left behind will clog the flow. Work on a clean tarp to keep debris out, and pre-mark the bucket for fill levels so re-packing the filter later is fool-proof in low light.

Quick Set-up

- **Skill Level:** Beginner – Simple build with basic materials—great for first-timers
- **Tools Required:** Bucket, drill, charcoal, sand, gravel, mesh screen, scoop or trowel
- **Time Required:** ~30–45 minutes with prep and clean-up
- **Estimated Cost:** Very Low ($10–$20) – Materials often salvaged or local.
- **Best Use:** Filtering rainwater, pond water, or low-quality groundwater
- **Getting Started Tip:** Use clean, food-grade containers and rinse all materials thoroughly before assembly. For best results, combine charcoal with sand and gravel layers to improve filtration and flow rate.

Step 1: Prepare the Container

Drill a drainage hole near the bottom of a food-grade bucket.

Step 2: Layer the Filter Materials

- **Bottom layer:** Add 3–4 inches of gravel to provide drainage.

- **Middle layer:** Add 10 inches of fine sand for primary filtration.

- **Top layer:** Add 2 inches of activated charcoal to remove toxins and taste.

Step 3: Secure Mesh Screen

Place a mesh screen over the top to prevent leaves, insects, and debris from entering the filter system.

Step 4: Filter Your Water

Pour water into the top and allow it to pass through each layer. Clean water will exit from the drainage hole at the bottom.

Step 5: Maintain the Filter

Replace the activated charcoal every 2–3 months and clean all layers as needed to ensure proper flow and continued filtration.

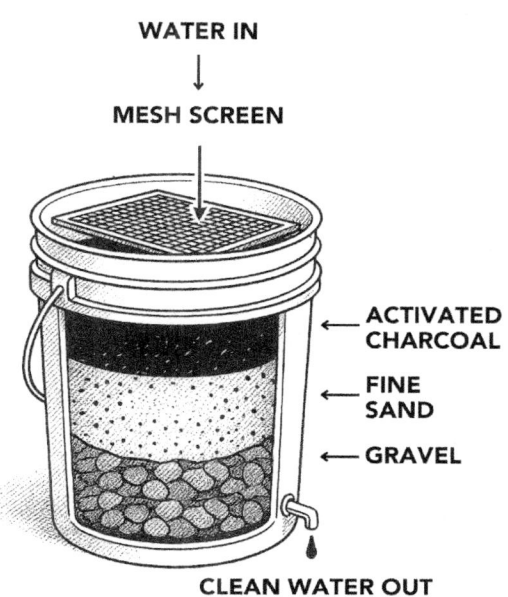

WATER IN

MESH SCREEN

← **ACTIVATED CHARCOAL**

← **FINE SAND**

← **GRAVEL**

CLEAN WATER OUT

Charcoal handles day-to-day microbes, but drought and saltwater need different answers. The next build turns sunshine into a distiller you can forget about until you need a drink.

Water Security Strategies

Off-grid water security requires layered collection and conservation methods:

- **Rainwater Harvesting with Filtration** – Modern systems filter and pressurize collected rainwater, making it potable.

- **Underground Cisterns** – Evaporation-proof storage ideal for hot, dry climates.

- **Solar-Powered Desalination** – Converts salt water into drinking water using solar distillation—critical for coastal and brackish water sources.

Low-Cost Doesn't Mean Low Impact

Many sustainable systems can be built from salvaged or repurposed materials. Focus on airtight seals, smart placement, and solar exposure—not expensive parts. What matters most is function, not perfection.

Even basic builds can outperform store-bought gear if assembled with care. Test your systems early, troubleshoot in real conditions, and document what works—this hands-on insight is worth more than a receipt.

STEP-BY-STEP PROJECT
Solar-Powered Desalination

A passive, zero-electricity way to convert saltwater or brackish water into freshwater—ideal for coastal or island off-gridders.

Before You Begin: Choose a pit site that sees at least six hours of direct sun and sits above high-tide or flood lines. Pre-filter murky water through cloth to extend plastic life and keep salt crust from blocking condensation.

Quick Set-up

- **Skill Level:** Beginner – No electrical wiring required; uses basic solar heat principles
- **Tools Required:** Black tray or shallow basin, clear plastic wrap, small container or cup, weight (stone or similar)
- **Time Required:** 30–60 minutes to set up; ongoing solar operation
- **Estimated Cost:** $ – Low-cost using salvaged or household materials
- **Best Use:** Ideal for coastal areas, brackish water sources, or emergency backup when freshwater is limited
- **Getting Started Tip:** Works best in direct sun. Pre-filter salty or dirty water to extend system life and improve yield.

Step 1: Dig a Collection Pit

Dig a shallow pit about 2–3 feet wide and 1.5 feet deep using a shovel.

Step 2: Place the Collection Container

Place a small container in the pit center to catch water.

Step 3: Cover with Plastic

Lay a clear plastic sheet over the pit, extending it beyond the edges. Secure it with rocks or heavy objects to create a seal.

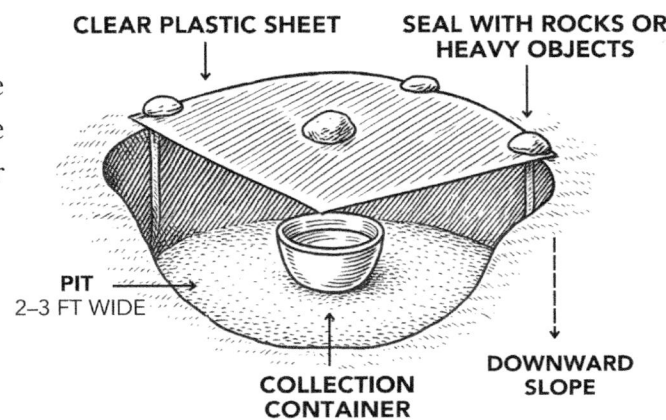

CLEAR PLASTIC SHEET

SEAL WITH ROCKS OR HEAVY OBJECTS

PIT 2–3 FT WIDE

COLLECTION CONTAINER

DOWNWARD SLOPE

Step 4: Create Slope

Place a small rock in the center of the plastic above the container to form a low point for water to drip from.

Step 5: Maintain and Collect

Wipe down the plastic daily. As sunlight heats the pit, water evaporates, condenses on the plastic, and drips into the container, leaving salt and contaminants behind.

With fresh water secured, let's move to food. Smart preservation keeps surplus edible food when seasons or supply chains shut down.

Sustainable Food Production: Grow More with Less

Off-grid food security relies on high-yield, low-labor methods that work in any climate. Whether you're starting a survival garden or refining an existing setup, this section offers practical, scalable strategies to keep your food supply stable, without store runs or refrigeration. It's about growing smarter, not harder—so you can produce more food with fewer inputs and less daily effort.

Solar Dehydration for Long-Term Storage

Shelf-stable food is survival insurance. One of the most effective low-tech preservation methods is solar dehydration, which removes moisture to prevent spoilage while maintaining nutrients, without electricity.

This simple method lets you preserve seasonal harvests and reduce waste while building a dependable food supply.

Let Everyone Own a System

- Assign each person a piece of the sustainability puzzle—building the dehydrator, tracking solar output, or maintaining the water filter. Shared ownership builds skills, confidence, and long-term success.
- When everyone contributes, even small wins feel like a team win. It also takes pressure off one person to manage every system alone—something that can lead to burnout fast.

STEP-BY-STEP PROJECT
Building a Simple Solar Dehydrator

This off-grid food storage solution allows long-term preservation of fruits, vegetables, and herbs without refrigeration.

Before You Begin: Salvage lumber or a block that matches your waist height—comfortable access beats fancy materials. Collect a thermometer now; knowing the inside temperatures during the first frost will tell you whether to add blankets or venting later.

Quick Set-up

- **Skill Level:** Beginner – Basic carpentry and assembly; no wiring needed
- **Tools Required:** Wood for frame, screen or mesh trays, clear cover (glass or plastic), dark backing (metal or painted wood)
- **Time Required:** 1–2 hours to build; ready for daily solar use and food preservation
- **Estimated Cost:** $ – Low-cost using scrap wood and repurposed materials
- **Best Use:** Ideal for coastal areas, brackish water sources, or emergency backup when freshwater is limited
- **Getting Started Tip:** Position the dehydrator to face south with good airflow. Start with thin-sliced fruits or herbs to test drying speed and evenness.

Step 1: Build the Frame

A 12-inch raised bed doubles as insulation and keeps soil from flooding; in windy plains, add two rebar stakes per corner.

Step 2: Attach the Cover

Secure plexiglass or clear plastic on top to trap heat and create a greenhouse effect for efficient drying.

Step 3: Install Heat-Absorbing Tray

Place a black-painted metal tray at the bottom of the structure to absorb sunlight and radiate consistent heat throughout the dehydrator.

Step 4: Add Drying Racks

Install mesh racks above the tray, allowing warm convective air to circulate for faster, even drying.

Step 5: Position in Direct Sunlight

Place in the sun; adjust angle throughout midday for maximum heat absorption. Most foods dry in 8–24 hours. Wipe the clear cover weekly to keep temps high.

Step 6: Store Food Properly

Rotate items periodically for even drying, then transfer to airtight containers once fully dehydrated to preserve freshness.

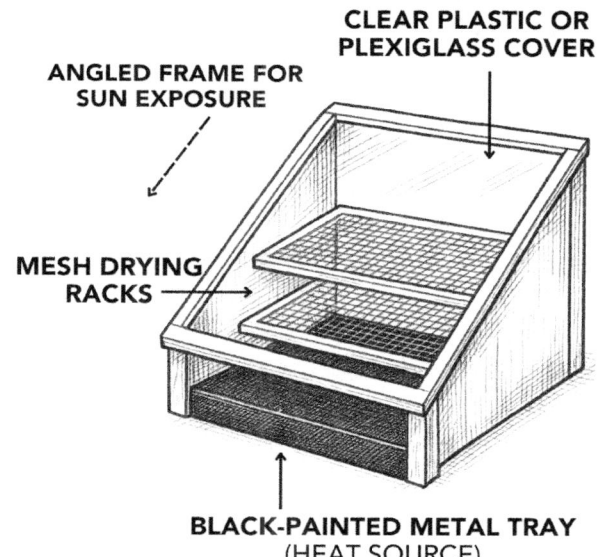

CLEAR PLASTIC OR PLEXIGLASS COVER

ANGLED FRAME FOR SUN EXPOSURE

MESH DRYING RACKS

BLACK-PAINTED METAL TRAY
(HEAT SOURCE)

Best Use: Shelf-stable food storage for survival preppers—extends food usability without electricity.

Off-Grid Gardening for Survival Food Security

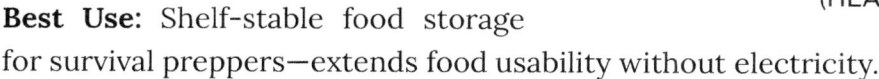

Traditional gardening requires heavy irrigation, fertilizers, and time, not realistic in survival situations. Instead, off-grid gardening prioritizes low-labor, drought-resistant, and resilient food production methods.

Key Survival Gardening Strategies:

- **Deep Mulching for Moisture Retention** – Reduces evaporation, protects soil, and suppresses weeds.

- **No-Till Gardening for Soil Health** – Prevents soil depletion, retains nutrients naturally, and reduces water use.

- **Drought-Resistant Crops** – Hardy plants like squash, amaranth, and Jerusalem artichokes require minimal watering.

Grow Food That Grows Itself

In a real crisis, you may not have time—or water—for daily garden upkeep. Low-labor methods like deep mulch, no-till beds, and drought-tolerant crops let your garden survive even when you're focused on security, repairs, or relocation. Survival gardening isn't about yield per square foot—it's about food that grows while you handle everything else.

Cold Frames for Four-Season Harvests

Unlike high-tech greenhouse systems, cold frames are a low-tech, survival-friendly way to extend your growing season.

STEP-BY-STEP PROJECT
Building a Cold Frame for Off-Grid Gardening

Cold frames are a simple, low-cost way to extend your growing season. This build traps heat and protects crops, keeping food growing longer in colder months.

Before You Begin: Choose a sunny, well-drained south-facing spot. Gather 12-inch lumber or blocks and a clear lid (a salvaged double-pane window works). Keep a soil thermometer ready for first-night checks, and pre-mark cuts plus pilot holes indoors to speed outdoor assembly.

Quick Set-up

- **Skill Level:** Beginner – Basic carpentry and layout; great for first-time builders
- **Tools Required:** Saw (hand or circular), drill or screwdriver, tape measure, soil thermometer for early use. Optional: clamps for holding pieces steady and wood sealer for longer frame life.
- **Time Required:** 1–2 hours to assemble; ongoing daily use for early/late-season
- **Estimated Cost:** $ – Low-cost build using salvaged materials like scrap lumber and old windows or glass shower doors.
- **Best Use:** Extending the growing season in cold or variable climates
- **Getting Started Tip:** Cut and pre-drill lumber indoors to save time outside. Position with the high back facing north, low front facing south for best sun exposure.

Step 1: Build the Base

Use wood or cinder blocks to construct a raised, enclosed growing area.

Step 2: Add the Cover

Reclaimed double-pane windows cut night heat loss by 30% compared with single glazing.

Step 3: Install Hinges

Hinge the cover to allow easy opening during warm days and prevent overheating.

Step 4: Insulate the Base

Surround the base with straw bales, rocks, or other natural insulation materials to help retain warmth overnight and protect plants from cold snaps. Yield: Extends growing season by 2-3 months

Season extension saves groceries, but true thrift means turning every scrap into something else, like fuel or tools. The following section shows how waste becomes an asset pile, not a trash pile.

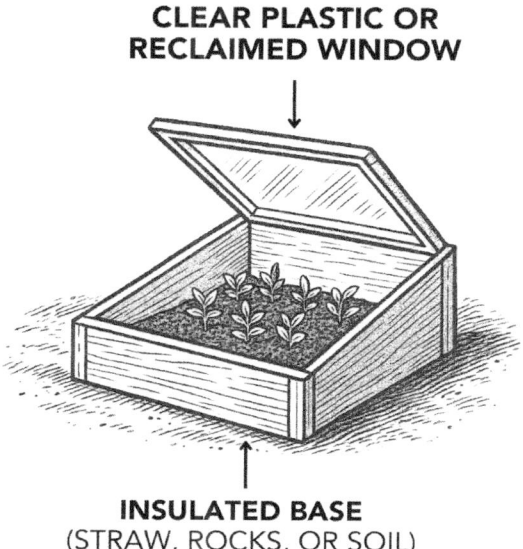

CLEAR PLASTIC OR RECLAIMED WINDOW

INSULATED BASE
(STRAW, ROCKS, OR SOIL)

Waste Reduction and Resource Use

Every pound you divert from the burn barrel or landfill lightens resupply runs and emergency stockpiles. Modern off-gridders bank "waste" as future calories, BTUs, or building stock. With a few low-tech setups, you'll cut expenses, cut hauling, and harden your retreat against shortages, without adding hours of chores.

Turning Waste into Resources for Survival

Off-gridders who thrive long-term don't see waste as a burden—they see it as an opportunity. Organic waste, human waste, and even discarded materials can be converted into fuel, soil nutrients, and functional tools. The key is adopting simple, low-maintenance systems that maximize survival efficiency.

Practical Waste Solutions for Off-Grid Survival

* **Biogas Digesters** – Convert kitchen scraps and manure into cooking fuel and liquid fertilizer using anaerobic breakdown in sealed systems.

* **Humanure Composting Toilets** – Safe, low-maintenance toilets that eliminate septic needs, reduce waste, and improve soil health over time.

* **Practical Upcycling** – Repurpose scrap materials for tools, shelter reinforcements, heating aids, and emergency structural repairs.

Ready to turn kitchen scraps into stove gas? The biogas digester below costs less than a single propane refill and scales from an apartment balcony to a barnyard.

STEP-BY-STEP PROJECT
Biogas Digester for Emergency Fuel

Relying on propane or firewood for cooking is costly and unsustainable. A biogas digester provides free cooking gas from food scraps, manure, and plant waste, making it a valuable waste-to-fuel survival tool.

Before You Begin: Once mature, this digester replaces at least one 20-lb propane cylinder per month, but only if you keep it above 70°F. Plan to bury or insulate the drum in cold climates and position the outlet downhill to prevent back-pressure.

Quick Set-up

- **Skill Level:** Intermediate – Basic plumbing, sealing, and safe waste handling needed.
- **Tools Required:** Airtight barrel or container, PVC pipe and fittings, sealant, one-way valve, gas storage bag or hose, organic waste (manure, kitchen scraps)
- **Time Required:** 2–4 hours to build; gas forms in 7–14 days.
- **Estimated Cost:** $$ – Moderate cost for containers and fittings; lower with salvage and local sourcing
- **Best Use:** Reliable off-grid fuel for cooking, heating, or emergencies.
- **Getting Started Tip:** Keep the system warm (above 70°F) for faster gas production. Stir gently and feed small amounts regularly for consistent output.

Step 1: Set Up the Digester Tank

- Drill two holes near the top edge of the drum—one for the inlet pipe, one for the outlet pipe.
- Secure with rubber gaskets and sealant to make both connections airtight.
- Paint the drum black for passive heat if temperatures drop below 60°F.

Step 2: Connect the Gas Storage System

- Attach the outlet pipe to your storage bladder using hose clamps.
- Make sure all connections are tight and leak-free.

Safety Note:

Never store biogas in a sealed, rigid container like a propane tank. Use soft bladders or expandable storage only, and keep the setup in a ventilated outdoor space.

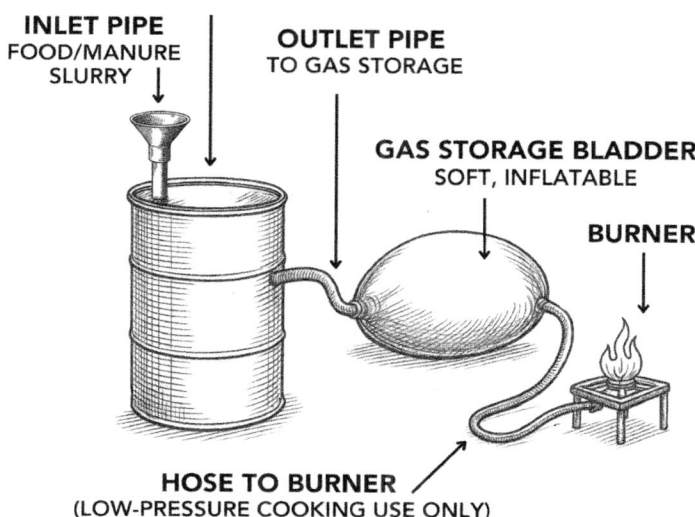

55-GALLON DIGESTER TANK

INLET PIPE FOOD/MANURE SLURRY

OUTLET PIPE TO GAS STORAGE

GAS STORAGE BLADDER SOFT, INFLATABLE

BURNER

HOSE TO BURNER (LOW-PRESSURE COOKING USE ONLY)

Step 3: Fuel It with Food Scraps and Manure

- Feed in a mixture of kitchen scraps, manure, and water weekly.

- Aim for a slurry consistency to help bacteria thrive.

- Keep the feed ratio 50 % manure, 50 % veg scraps; too much citrus or meat slows bacteria.

Step 4: Give It Time to Start Cooking

- Biogas production starts in 2–4 weeks.

- Stir gently once a week to improve fermentation.

- If bubbles smell like rotten eggs, add a cup of garden lime to cut sulfur.

Step 5: Fire It Up

- Once gas accumulates, attach a hose from the bladder to a simple burner.

- Open the valve, light the flame—clean cooking fuel from waste.

- Test flame at a safe distance; a blue flame signals good methane concentration.

Fuel from yesterday's scraps proves waste is just an untapped supply. Next, turn the rest of your cast-offs into gear, shelter, and cooling hacks that cost little more than creativity.

Scrap-to-Survival Hacks

In survival situations, waste is a liability or an asset—depending on how you use it. Beyond composting and biogas, repurposing materials for practical survival use ensures nothing goes to waste.

- **Salvaging Metal and Mechanical Parts** – Old machinery, scrap metal, and broken tools can be reworked into functional equipment.

- **Reclaimed Wood for Emergency Repairs** – Pallets, fencing, and scrap wood become fuel, building material, or tool handles.

- **Simple DIY Wind Generator** – Small motors from old appliances can be converted into low-power wind generators.

- **Desert Southwest** – Evaporative swamp-cooler pads re-stitched into shade sails cut cabin temps 10 °F.

- **Great Lakes Families** – Old boats sail, waterproof woodpiles, and double as storm shutters.

- **Arctic Solo Off-Gridders** – Broken snow-machine skis reshaped into sled runners for hauling firewood.

- **Urban Balcony Preppers** – Food-grade 55-gal drums become stacked barrelponics for greens.

Your off-grid survival becomes a self-refilling hardware store when scrap begins to solve problems. Let's now also take a look at some new technologies that might quadruple today's achievements tomorrow.

What's Next in Sustainable Tech?

Innovations in sustainability and automation are reshaping off-grid living. These systems aren't just futuristic—they're becoming more accessible, reliable, and integrated into real-life homesteads.

Emerging Tech to Watch:

Bleeding-edge gear shows up first at trade shows (RE+), open-source forums (Low-Tech Magazine), and grant-funded prototypes featured on platforms like

TEDx or NASA's Tech Briefs. Follow those feeds plus the Off-Grid Companion's quarterly roundup to spot breakthroughs before they hit retail.

- **AI-Driven Smart Grids** – Home-level controllers already trim battery cycling 15 % in cloudy Appalachian winters; expect plug-and-play kits in big-box stores within five years.

- **Solar Paint** – Field tests in Arizona desert claim 8 % efficiency; coastal users could spray small sheds today for trickle-charge sensors.

- **Bio-engineered Filters** – Kenyan NGOs deploy mycelium membranes to strip arsenic; similar cartridges will soon retrofit into countertop filters.

- **Modular Hydrogen Cells** – Pacific Northwest pilots use surplus micro-hydro at night to store hydrogen that fuels cooking stoves; see rural kits by 2028.

Future-Proof Reminder: The skills you learned in this chapter—sizing loads, sealing joints, maintaining simple systems—never go obsolete. Tech should serve those skills, not replace them, so invest only in tools you can repair or safely bypass if chips fail.

Here's what happens when tech adoption outruns bandwidth, sunlight, and sheer human energy.

FROM THE FIRE. STORIES THAT STILL BURN.
Overbuilt, Overwhelmed—Then Rewired for Resilience

Ivan built his off-grid tiny house with the latest technologies: high-efficiency solar panels, LiFePO4 batteries, and smart-home controls. His goal was to create a self-sufficient, tech-savvy living space. However, the integration of these advanced systems brought unforeseen complications. When glitches occurred, simple problems became complex puzzles, highlighting the risks of over-automation.

Ivan's experience underscores the importance of simplicity and gradual implementation. By prototyping one system at a time and allowing for thorough testing, he learned to build a more resilient and manageable off-grid setup.

SCAN ME

Would your systems still run if the smart tech failed?

Watch on the Off-Grid Companion site how Ivan navigated the challenges of a tech-forward off-grid lifestyle—and what he'd change if he had to do it again.

Troubleshooting Off-Grid Innovations

Off-grid tech can fail in unexpected ways. If you're relying on a solar-hybrid system, biogas digester, or advanced filtration, small errors in setup or conditions can lead to major slowdowns. Use this quick-reference table to diagnose common issues and get back on track quickly.

Issue	Possible Cause	Quick Fix
Hybrid Energy System (Solar + Wind + Batteries) Not Charging Properly	Battery misconfiguration, inverter incompatibility, charge controller limits	Check battery charge settings, upgrade controller, ensure inverter can handle mixed inputs
Solar Tracking System Fails to Follow the Sun	Mechanical motor jam, dirty sensors, incorrect alignment	Clean sun sensor, recalibrate tracker, test motor function
Water Recycling System (AWG + Greywater) Producing Low Output	Clogged filters, low humidity, poor system pressure	Replace pre-filters, move AWG to a more humid area, adjust system pressure valves
Biogas System Producing Low Methane Output	Improper feed ratio, low temperature, blocked gas outlet	Increase organic waste input, insulate digester for warmth, check for leaks

Quick-fix skills matter, but staying calm cuts downtime in half. When the table runs out of rows, firsthand pivots fill the gap and prevent costly repeat mistakes later on. Jay and Jen's first off-grid winter shows how real-world failures point to smarter upgrades.

FROM THE FIRE. STORIES THAT STILL BURN.
Returning to Jay & Jen—What They Didn't See Coming

You met Jay and Jen in the Introduction, where they showed how they built an off-grid solar system step by step, without debt and without doing everything at once. But their first winter revealed hidden gaps. Short days and thick cloud cover drained batteries faster than they could recharge, and frigid temps crept upward.

> *We'd grown confident. But when the sun stopped, it changed.*
> *We weren't ready for how fast things slipped.* — Jen

They didn't panic—but they did pivot.

What They'd Do Differently: Size a battery bank for at least two sun-less weeks from day one, keep a propane backup generator for heavy loads, swap to an inverter with live-usage readouts, and log every appliance to expose hidden energy leaks.

Off-grid success isn't getting everything perfect the first time—it's correcting fast when reality disagrees. They adapted and built something stronger.

SCAN ME

Not sure which off-grid tech is worth it?
Plan smart, scalable upgrades. Use the QR code to open the Off-Grid Survival Companion for printable checklists, system comparisons, and tools tailored to your land, goals, and budget.

Stronger Through Smart Systems

Technology is a force multiplier, not a crutch. When you match the right innovations to solid fundamentals—solar, you can service, water you can trust, food that stores itself—you trade fragility for freedom. Master the basics, add tech that earns its keep, and pull the plug on anything that doesn't.

Own the tools, own the outcome.

CONCLUSION: YOU CAN

You now have the knowledge to control your energy, water, food, and security systems for off-grid living. But knowledge alone isn't enough—consistent action is what transforms preparedness into lasting resilience.

The good news?
Off-grid living isn't an all-or-nothing leap. Your path to self-sufficiency unfolds step by step—with small, meaningful victories along the way.

This final chapter brings everything full circle, summarizing what matters most and giving you a practical plan to move forward with clarity and confidence.

Moving from Knowledge to Action

What Off-Grid Living Truly Means

Off-grid living means controlling your essential resources *before* disaster strikes. Water, power, food, and waste systems are the pillars of long-term independence.

The more control you have over your essential resources, the less reliant you are on unstable systems. – Marjory Wildcraft, F.

Start Here: Key Actions to Build Your Resilience

- Secure a dependable water source—rain catchment, well, or emergency storage.

- Establish a backup power system—solar, wind, generator, or hybrid.

- Begin food security—grow something, preserve something, store something.

- Build or improve home security and connect with your local community.

- Create a maintenance plan to keep your systems reliable.

Schedule a monthly "resilience tune-up": review systems, practice one skill, celebrate wins.

It's a Process, Not a Flip of a Switch

Off-grid living doesn't require a sudden, dramatic shift.
It's a lifestyle you build layer by layer—each decision reinforcing your freedom.

Common mistakes to avoid:

- Underestimating daily resource needs

- Overspending on tech-heavy systems without mastering the basics

- Neglecting maintenance or system testing

- Going it alone—connection matters

Smart Systems Work Together

The most efficient off-grid setups are interconnected. Here's how to make your systems work smarter, not harder:

Pair Water + Energy

- Use solar-powered pumps with rainwater storage.

- Install a water catchment under solar panels.

Turn Waste Into Power

- Composting toilets and greywater can enrich your soil.

- Biogas digesters convert waste into usable fuel.

Grow More in Small Spaces

- Use vertical gardening, companion planting, and passive solar greenhouses.

- Aim for < $500 total in your first 30-day kit—proof you don't need deep pockets to start.

Create Redundant Energy

- Start with solar, then add wind or a backup generator.

- Use DC appliances to reduce energy waste.

Strengthen Community

- Trade tools, knowledge, and bulk goods.

- Build local barter relationships before you *need* them.

From Ideas to Action: What Happens Now?

If the grid went down tomorrow, would you have:

- Clean water?

- A way to cook and store food?

- Backup energy?

If you're not sure—or know the answer is no—you're not alone. That's exactly why this book was written.

What to Tackle (and When):

You've read the pages. You've seen what's possible. Now it's time to turn insight into action—and start building a life that truly works for you.

If the grid fails tomorrow, would you be ready?
Could you get clean water, cook without power, or stay warm if the heat shuts off?

If your answer is "not yet"—you're in the right place. This book isn't just a read. It's a roadmap designed to guide, encourage, and equip you every step of the way.

Whether you're preparing for a crisis or simply reclaiming your independence one system at a time, this journey puts you back in control.

Your Practical Action Plan In the First 30 Days

- Stock emergency water and backup food.
- Set up a portable stove or battery bank.
- Practice a weekend off-grid run to test your basics.

In the Next 6 Months
- Build your first sustainable system: rainwater, solar, or food garden.
- Track your usage and tweak your setup for better efficiency.
- Learn to store and rotate supplies the smart way.

By the End of Year One
- Add redundancy—multiple ways to power, cook, and stay warm.
- Start bartering with local makers or growers.
- Create a rhythm of seasonal prep so you're always one step ahead.

Keep this guide within reach—real change starts the moment you begin building.

SCAN ME

Not sure which off-grid tech is worth it?
Use the QR code to open the Off-Grid Survival Companion—revisit your Chapter 1 planning guides, early checklists, and the new system tools from this finale, all in one place. Cross-check goals, compare upgrades, and download printables tailored to your land, budget, and next steps.

LIVE PREPARED. LIVE FREE.

Take control, create boldly, and thrive—whatever comes next.
Perfection isn't required; action is.

Preparedness never asks permission—start now, and lead the way.

Share Your Spark

You've turned pages into progress—whether that's your first rain-barrel install or a full system upgrade. If this book pushed you forward or saved you a costly misstep, a quick review can do the same for another reader.

Why your review matters:

- Inspires the next person to take that first off-grid step

- Proves small, steady wins beat waiting for "perfect"

- Strengthens a growing network of self-reliant doers

> *"After a decade off-grid, we've learned simplicity and shared know-how keep us thriving."* — **Doug and Stacy.**

⌐ SCAN ME ─────────────────────────────

Could your insights inspire someone else's change?
Turn your hard-won lessons into the momentum others need.
Use the QR code or go to https://mybook.to/Off_Grid_JD_Wright

---

Thank you for adding your voice—every lesson you share strengthens our community, spreads practical know-how, shortens someone else's learning curve, and sparks fresh collaborations that push self-reliance even further.

Coming Soon

Practical Projects for Off-Grid Homesteading.

We're building the next volume with you in mind. Stay tuned.

Until then,

J.D. Wright

J.D. Wright

Born in the Midwest and still riding out the same tornado alley today, J.D. Wright learned early how to turn chaos into clarity, first while leading high-stakes projects for demanding clients. That same skill now powers Wright's career pivot: simplifying complex topics into grounded, accessible, and thoroughly researched information.

Wright saw an opportunity while compiling scattered resources on Off-Grid Survival. The goal? Bring together proven strategies from seasoned professionals, government guides, and real-life off-gridders—and turn them into step-by-step DIY instructions, checklists, printables, and tools that connect reliable survival systems with the mindset required to use them.

Life brings unexpected obstacles. But being actively prepared levels the field.

When not writing, Wright slips away in a kayak or heads out to explore new climates and cultures—always looking for the next challenge worth unraveling and sharing.

References & Further Reading

Introduction

The following sources were directly referenced, quoted, or linked in this chapter.

- Plohetski, T. (2021, March 15). Texas winter storm death toll now at 246, revised state data shows. Austin American-Statesman. https://www.statesman.com/story/news/2021/03/15/texas-winter-storm-2021-death-toll-updated-246-people-died/4696101001/

- Weersink, A., von Massow, M., Bannon, N., Ifft, J., Maples, J., McEwan, K., ... & Wood, B. (2021). COVID-19 and the agri-food system in the United States and Canada. Agricultural Systems, 188, 103039. https://doi.org/10.1016/j.agsy.2020.103039

- U.S. House of Representatives. (2012). Weathering the storm: How can we better communicate weather warnings? Committee on Science, Space, and Technology. https://www.govinfo.gov/content/pkg/CHRG-112hhrg76174/html/CHRG-112hhrg76174.htm

- U.S. Department of Energy. (2021). Grid resilience: DOE efforts to strengthen the power grid. https://www.energy.gov/oe/grid-resilience

- Rustic Spirits Homestead. (2023, July 27). We seriously MISCALCULATED when we set up our off-grid solar system [Video]. YouTube. https://youtu.be/_yXPfABDCAo

- Off Grid with Jay and Jen. (n.d.). Off-grid solar build and upgrades [YouTube channel]. YouTube. https://www.youtube.com/@OffGridwithJayandJen

Supplementary Reading & Source Influence

The following resources were consulted during the development of this introduction to shape its framing, tone, and survival strategy approach. While not directly quoted, they helped reinforce the mindset, preparedness principles, and practical structure.

- Federal Emergency Management Agency. (2021). Are You Ready? An In-Depth Guide to Citizen Preparedness. https://www.ready.gov/are-you-ready-guide

- EcoWatch. (2022). Texas grid failure: What really happened and how to prepare for future outages. https://www.ecowatch.com

- Backwoods Home Magazine. (n.d.). What does it mean to live off the grid? https://www.backwoodshome.com

- Living Off Grid Guide. (2023). The difference between homesteading and off-grid living. https://livingoffgridguide.com

- Medium. (2022). Off-grid mindset series: Lesson 1 – Getting past fear and taking action. https://medium.com/to-the-summit
- Off Grid World. (n.d.). How to get started with off-grid survival – The basics of water, power, and food. https://offgridworld.com

Chapter 1: Mindset First, Tools Second

The following sources were directly referenced, quoted, or linked in this chapter.

- Camp Out West. (2023, June 19). We made a mistake... Building a life off-grid with no experience [Video]. YouTube. https://youtu.be/aRr9W10sMzI
- Off Grid with Chris and Kristie. (2023, October 15). The true cost of living off grid | Our first winter results [Video]. YouTube. https://youtu.be/VFddeYs7F6I
- Off Grid with Curtis Stone. (2021, April 26). What I'd do differently with my off-grid power system [Video]. YouTube. https://www.youtube.com/watch?v=-GnQO6ceAxA
- Doug and Stacy. (2023, April 8). Off-grid living 12 years later – Doug and Stacy [Video]. YouTube. https://youtu.be/CNbilEbx7Ic

Supplementary Reading & Source Influence

The following resources were consulted during the development of this chapter to inform strategy, structure, and survival frameworks. While not quoted directly, they contributed to the content's accuracy and scope.

- U.S. Department of Energy. (2023). Energy Transitions Playbook: Seven phases to scale your clean energy project. https://energy.gov/islands
- EcoFlow. (2023). Off-grid living essentials guide. https://www.ecoflow.com/us/blog/off-grid-living-essentials-guide
- Mindful SWFL. (2023). Transitioning to an off-grid, intentional life: A beginner's guide. https://mindfulswfl.com
- The Survival Mom. (2022). Off-grid living: What skills do you need to survive? https://thesurvivalmom.com/off-grid-living-skills-survival/
- Truoba. (n.d.). The ultimate guide to off-grid house plans. https://www.truoba.com/off-grid-house-plans/
- Elena Foukes. (2023). The mindset shift: Why off-grid living is more about intention than isolation. https://elenafoukes.com

Chapter 2: Water Isn't Optional. It's Everything

The following sources were directly referenced, quoted, or linked in this chapter.

- KSL News. (n.d.). Utah rainwater harvesting and water rights conflict [Reported story referenced in Mark Miller case]. (Original article unavailable; story summarized in-book based on public reporting.)

- U.S. Department of Energy. (n.d.). Rainwater harvesting tool. https://www.energy.gov/femp/rainwater-harvesting-tool

- World Water Reserve. (n.d.). Is it illegal to collect rainwater? https://worldwaterreserve.com/is-it-illegal-to-collect-rainwater/

- Congress.gov. (n.d.). State legislature websites. https://www.congress.gov/state-legislature-websites

- Urban Farmer Store. (2021). Rainwater Harvesting Manual. https://www.urbanfarmerstore.com/wp-content/uploads/2021/05/5_Rainwater-Harvesting_RRH7-Rainwater-Harvesting-Manual.pdf

- Off Grid with Doug and Stacy. (2023, July 11). How safe is your off-grid water? [Video]. YouTube. https://www.youtube.com/watch?v=oxvIJ_qThfU

- Centers for Disease Control and Prevention (CDC). (n.d.). Emergency water supply planning guide. https://www.cdc.gov/water-emergency/about/index.html

Supplementary Reading & Source Influence

The following resources were used to guide structure, best practices, and survival recommendations in this chapter. They were not quoted directly, but they informed the chapter's accuracy, legality, and DIY strategy depth.

- The Berkey. (n.d.). Understanding Berkey water filters. https://www.berkeyfilters.com

- Sawyer Products. (n.d.). Sawyer water filtration systems overview. https://sawyer.com/products/water-filtration/

- FEMA. (2021). Water and sanitation preparedness guide. https://www.ready.gov/water

- Off Grid World. (n.d.). DIY rainwater harvesting system guide. https://offgridworld.com/diy-rainwater-harvesting/

- Environmental Protection Agency (EPA). (2020). Water reuse and conservation in drought-prone areas. https://www.epa.gov/waterreuse

- Oasis Design. (n.d.). Greywater system basics and legal guidelines. https://www.oasisdesign.net/greywater/

- The Humanure Handbook. (Jenkins, J., 2019). A guide to composting human waste for sustainable sanitation. [Publisher: Chelsea Green Publishing]

Chapter 3: Take Control of Your Power – and Keep It

These sources were directly referenced, quoted, or linked in this chapter.

- Off Grid with Jay and Jen. (2022, November 3). Simple solar setup and our DIY solar shed [Video]. YouTube. https://www.youtube.com/watch?v=18P_D8Kiw10
- Mo. (2023, May 20). DIY off-grid cabin wind turbine install [Video]. YouTube. https://youtu.be/0WbXrjpX-1s
- Backwoods Home Magazine. (2021). A small creek provides plenty of power for this off-grid home. [Print article summary as cited in text].
- The Provident Prepper. (n.d.). Building resilient communities through bartering and preparedness. https://theprovidentprepper.org

Supplementary Reading & Source Influence

These trusted resources informed the structure, technology guidance, and safety practices of this chapter. While not directly quoted, they were used to verify feasibility, safety standards, and system design advice.

- National Renewable Energy Laboratory (NREL). (2023). Small solar electric systems. https://www.energy.gov/energysaver/small-solar-electric-systems
- Wind Empowerment. (n.d.). DIY wind turbine designs and troubleshooting. https://windempowerment.org
- Microhydropower Systems – U.S. Department of Energy. (n.d.). Planning and installing micro-hydro systems. https://www.energy.gov/energysaver/microhydropower-systems
- Jackery. (2023). Portable solar generator safety guide. https://www.jackery.com/pages/safety
- Renogy. (2022). Battery comparison and solar system setup guide. https://www.renogy.com/learn/
- Backwoods Solar. (n.d.). Off-grid solar system kits and technical resources. https://www.backwoodssolar.com
- Prepper's Long-Term Survival Guide (Cobb, J., 2014). Food, shelter, security, off-the-grid power, and more life-saving strategies for self-sufficient living. Ulysses Press.

Chapter 4: Shelter Is Your Freedom – Build It to Withstand Anything

These sources were directly referenced, quoted, or linked in this chapter.

- U.S. Department of Energy. (n.d.). Rainwater harvesting tool. https://www.energy.gov/femp/rainwater-harvesting-tool
- World Water Reserve. (n.d.). Is it illegal to collect rainwater? https://worldwaterreserve.com/is-it-illegal-to-collect-rainwater/

- Holdfast Alaska. (2023, November 4). Homesteading in Alaska: Preparing for our first storm of winter [Video]. YouTube. https://youtu.be/aehfXEPc9bo
- New York Post. (2025, January). Off-grid couple survives brutal winter with smart design. [Summary cited in-book; original article not directly linked]
- Winter Like When We Were Kids. (2023, December). How we reinforced our homestead after the storm [Video]. YouTube. https://youtu.be/doMphJKwq38

Supplementary Reading & Source Influence

These sources were used to inform structure durability, building techniques, insulation strategies, legal research advice, and regional shelter adaptations—even if not directly quoted.

- Backwoods Home Magazine. (2021). Designing low-impact off-grid cabins. https://www.backwoodshome.com
- Earthbag Building. (Hunter, K. & Kiffmeyer, D., 2004). The Earthbag Building Guide. New Society Publishers.
- International Code Council. (2023). 2021 International Residential Code (IRC) for One- and Two-Family Dwellings. https://www.iccsafe.org
- FEMA. (2021). Building codes toolkit for shelter resilience. https://www.fema.gov
- The Natural Building Blog. (n.d.). Rubble trench foundations: A natural alternative. https://www.thenaturalbuildingblog.com
- Sun Surveyor. (n.d.). Solar app tools for off-grid builders. https://www.sunsurveyor.com
- The Homestead Survival. (n.d.). A-frame cabin blueprints and off-grid building hacks. https://thehomesteadsurvival.com
- The Provident Prepper. (n.d.). Legal risks and zoning traps for off-grid landowners. https://theprovidentprepper.org

Chapter 5: Your Food Supply Is Your Lifeline

These sources were directly referenced, quoted, or linked in this chapter.

- Finley, R. (2013, May). A guerrilla gardener in South Central LA [TED Talk]. TED. https://www.ted.com/talks/ron_finley_a_guerilla_gardener_in_south_central_la
- Off Grid with Doug and Stacy. (n.d.). We live off grid and cook with the sun [Video quote referenced]. https://www.youtube.com/@OFFGRIDwithDougandStacy
- Robbie and Gary Gardening Easy. (n.d.). Simple raised beds and composting in containers [Video]. https://www.youtube.com/@RobbieandGaryGardeningEasy

Supplementary Reading & Source Influence

The following resources shaped storage guidelines, preservation methods, gardening techniques, and emergency food planning presented in this chapter. They were not quoted, but informed about the instructional and survival strategies used.

- U.S. Department of Agriculture (USDA). (2022). FoodKeeper app: Storage guidance and shelf life info. https://www.foodsafety.gov/keep-food-safe/foodkeeper-app

- Ball Canning. (n.d.). Ball Blue Book Guide to Preserving (37th ed.). Newell Brands.

- National Center for Home Food Preservation. (n.d.). How do I... Can, Freeze, Dry? https://nchfp.uga.edu

- Mother Earth News. (n.d.). Solar dehydrators and off-grid food drying. https://www.motherearthnews.com

- The Provident Prepper. (n.d.). Emergency food storage strategies. https://theprovidentprepper.org

- USDA Plants Database. (n.d.). U.S. wild edible plant profiles. https://plants.usda.gov

- Green Deane. (n.d.). Eat the Weeds – Foraging guide for edible wild plants. https://www.eattheweeds.com

- Practical Self Reliance. (n.d.). Foraging, food preservation, and DIY off-grid living tips. https://www.practicalselfreliance.com

- Backwoods Home Magazine. (n.d.). Gardening and self-reliant food production archives. https://www.backwoodshome.com

Chapter 6: Sanitation Isn't a Convenience

The following sources were directly quoted, cited, or QR-linked in this chapter:

- Centers for Disease Control and Prevention. (n.d.). Emergency sanitation: Safe waste handling when systems fail. https://www.cdc.gov/healthywater/emergency/sanitation/index.html

- The Off-Grid Homesteader. (n.d.). How we built a simple composting toilet [Web article and video]. https://www.theoffgridhomesteader.com/all/kr1jh0avwl8595nl7qwsgy90x6u9rl

- Jake & Nicole. (2022, February 21). Off-grid waste management: Simple solution for sewage treatment [Video]. YouTube. https://youtu.be/gUEOhMBRRdY

- C.H. Woods. (2023, July 18). Backyard chicken coop build from scrap wood [Video]. YouTube. https://www.youtube.com/watch?v=NWvfAgwXUUE

- Wheaton, P. (n.d.). Composting toilet design and maintenance [Permies.com quote reference]. https://permies.com/f/170/composting-toilets

Supplementary Reading & Source Influence

The following sources helped inform composting strategies, sanitation setup designs, and survival waste management best practices. They were not directly quoted, but helped shape the instructional structure and recommendations.

- Jenkins, J. (2019). The Humanure Handbook: A guide to composting human manure (4th ed.). Chelsea Green Publishing.

- Marjorie Wildcraft. (n.d.). Waste management and self-sufficiency insights [Public interviews and quotes]. https://www.growyourowngroceries.org

- U.S. Environmental Protection Agency (EPA). (n.d.). Composting basics and guidelines. https://www.epa.gov/recycle/composting-home

- The Provident Prepper. (n.d.). Off-grid sanitation and waste planning. https://theprovidentprepper.org

- Mother Earth News. (n.d.). DIY compost bins, latrines, and sanitation tips. https://www.motherearthnews.com

- Wheaton Labs. (n.d.). Rocket mass heaters and composting systems. https://www.wheaton-labs.com

- Survival Dispatch. (n.d.). Emergency waste disposal for off-grid and crisis living. https://survivaldispatch.com

Chapter 7: You Can't Predict the Threat – But You Can Be Ready

The following sources were directly quoted, named, or QR-linked in this chapter:

- Begovic, S. (n.d.). Layered defense and survival strategy advice [Quoted in-text]. https://www.shtfschool.com

- Jake & Nicole. (2022, November 5). Off-grid waste management | Simple solution for sewage treatment [Video]. YouTube. https://youtu.be/gUEOhMBRRdY

- Robbie and Gary Gardening Easy. (n.d.). Tin can alarms and perimeter deterrents [Video reference]. https://www.youtube.com/@RobbieandGaryGardeningEasy

- Hollerman, J. (2016). Survival Theory: A Preparedness Guide. Creative Texts Publishers. [Quoted as "Former Military SERE Instructor"]

- The Off-Grid Homesteader. (n.d.). DIY off-grid security and surveillance setup [Blog/ video referenced]. https://www.theoffgridhomesteader.com

Supplementary Reading & Source Influence

These trusted sources were not directly cited but informed many of the defense, detection, surveillance, and training strategies outlined in this chapter. They supported scenario logic, tools, and system design for both solo and community-level off-grid preparedness.

- Survival Dispatch. (n.d.). Off-grid perimeter defense and survival tactics. https://survivaldispatch.com

- Tactical Intelligence. (n.d.). Low-tech alarms, tripwires, and alert systems. https://tacticalintelligence.net

- Selco Begovic. (n.d.). The Dark Secrets of SHTF Survival: What to Expect When Everything Falls Apart. One Year in Hell Publications.

- The Provident Prepper. (n.d.). Neighborhood watch systems and crisis defense. https://theprovidentprepper.org

- FEMA. (2020). Community Emergency Response Team (CERT) Basic Training Manual. https://www.ready.gov/cert

- Signal.org. (n.d.). Private communication tools for emergency use. https://signal.org

- Zello. (n.d.). Push-to-talk app for encrypted voice communication. https://zello.com

- Off-Grid Survival. (n.d.). Practical defense plans and emergency security guides. https://offgridsurvival.com

Chapter 8: Without Communication, Even Strong Systems Fail

The following sources were directly quoted, named, or QR-linked in this chapter:

- The Guardian. (2024, June 3). "The best neighbor you ever had": How a tool library transformed a community. https://www.theguardian.com

- Modern Off-Grid DIY. (n.d.). My ham radio setup for off-grid communication [Blog post and video reference]. https://www.youtube.com/@ModernOffGridDIY

- Permies.com. (n.d.). Off-grid forums and community-building resources. https://www.permies.com

- ARRL (American Radio Relay League). (n.d.). How to get started with ham radio. https://www.arrl.org/getting-licensed

- U.S. Federal Communications Commission (FCC). (n.d.). Amateur Radio Service licensing requirements. https://www.fcc.gov/wireless/bureau-divisions/mobility-division/amateur-radio-service

- Owen, G. (WX7Z) & Clark, E. (K7ELC). (2024, September 21). Emergency ham radio rescue relay in remote Idaho [Event reference].

- Lawrence, L. (2020, September). Creek Fire rescue coordinated by emergency radio users [Event summary].

Supplementary Reading & Source Influence

The following sources were not quoted directly but informed the chapter's structure, examples, and recommended tools for off-grid communication and community-building.

- RACES. (n.d.). Radio Amateur Civil Emergency Service. https://www.ready.gov/races

- ARES. (n.d.). Amateur Radio Emergency Service. https://www.arrl.org/ares

- SKYWARN. (n.d.). NOAA emergency weather alert system and ham radio integration. https://www.weather.gov/skywarn

- SATERN (Salvation Army Team Emergency Radio Network). (n.d.). Emergency comms during disaster response. https://www.satern.org

- Survival Dispatch. (n.d.). Emergency communication protocols. https://survivaldispatch.com

- The Provident Prepper. (n.d.). How to build a resilient communication plan. https://theprovidentprepper.org

- Signal.org. (n.d.). Encrypted messaging tools. https://www.signal.org

- Zello. (n.d.). Push-to-talk encrypted communication app. https://www.zello.com

Chapter 9: Prepare to Save Lives – Starting With Yours

The following sources were directly quoted, named, or QR-linked in this chapter:

- American Heart Association. (n.d.). CPR & AED training and resources. https://www.heart.org/cpr

- The Guardian. (2024, June 3). "The best neighbor you ever had": How a tool library transformed a community. https://www.theguardian.com

- Holdfast Alaska. (n.d.). Homesteading off-grid in Alaska. https://www.youtube.com/@HoldfastAlaska

- New York Post. (2023, October). Off-grid couple survives winter emergency in Alaska [Event summary cited].

- Dr. David M. (n.d.). Quote attributed in-text: Wilderness Medicine Specialist and Survival Trainer.

- Trevor (n.d.). Golden Hour quote from off-grid trauma recovery experience [Survival testimony, in-text].

- Modern Off-Grid DIY. (n.d.). My ham radio setup for off-grid communication [Video blog]. https://www.youtube.com/@ModernOffGridDIY

Supplementary Reading & Source Influence

These resources informed your herbal remedy lists, emergency medical protocol structure, wilderness first aid flow, and training guidance. They were not quoted directly but contributed to your off-grid survival health framework.

- Wilderness Medical Society. (2022). Practice guidelines for wilderness emergency care. https://wms.org
- Herbal Academy. (n.d.). Herbal materia medica and off-grid preparation. https://theherbalacademy.com
- North American Rescue. (n.d.). Bleeding control and trauma response kits. https://www.narescue.com
- The Provident Prepper. (n.d.). Medical readiness for off-grid survival. https://theprovidentprepper.org
- Red Cross. (n.d.). Wilderness and remote first aid training. https://www.redcross.org
- Herbal Prepper. (n.d.). Field-based herbal medicine and off-grid care. https://herbalprepper.com
- Grow Forage Cook Ferment. (n.d.). How to make herbal tinctures and salves. https://www.growforagecookferment.com
- FEMA. (2021). Community Emergency Response Team (CERT) – Medical operations. https://www.ready.gov/cert

Chapter 10: The Cost of Independence Is Planning Ahead

The following sources were directly quoted, QR-linked, or cited in this chapter:

- Burkinshaw, J., & Burkinshaw, R. (n.d.). Gridlessness: Homesteading off-grid with a large family in Canada [YouTube channel]. https://www.youtube.com/@Gridlessness
- Cummings, S. (n.d.). Alaska's Off-Grid Mommy: Starting an Amazon product business off-grid [Video & brand reference]. https://www.youtube.com/@OffGridMommy
- The Guardian. (2024, June 3). The best neighbor you ever had: How a tool library transformed a community. https://www.theguardian.com
- YouTube. (2024). Bartering in the Desert: How We Trade for Off-Grid Living [Video]. https://youtu.be/AcJT7Tkb_Co?si=HKzUzddvmi3bMx9l
- BerkShares Inc. (n.d.). Local currency for the Berkshire region of Massachusetts. https://www.berkshares.org
- Leafe Christian, D. (2003). Creating a Life Together: Practical Tools to Grow Ecovillages and Intentional Communities. New Society Publishers.

Supplementary Reading & Source Influence

These sources shaped the financial models, remote income strategies, barter system design, and practical minimalism discussed in this chapter. While not quoted directly, they helped ensure the frameworks' realism and resilience.

- The Provident Prepper. (n.d.). How to live debt-free off-grid and start bartering. https://theprovidentprepper.org

- Financial Independence Forum. (n.d.). Frugality, alternative currencies, and self-reliant budgeting. https://www.choosefi.com

- FEMA. (2020). Disaster Financial Preparedness Toolkit. https://www.ready.gov/financial-preparedness

- Homestead Survival Site. (n.d.). How to barter effectively for survival. https://homesteadsurvivalsite.com

- Off Grid World. (n.d.). How much does it cost to go off-grid? https://offgridworld.com

- Tuttle Twins. (n.d.). The Tuttle Twins Guide to Logical Economic Thinking. Libertas Institute.

Chapter 11: Technology Won't Save You – But It Can Strengthen You

The following sources were directly quoted, QR-linked, or named in this chapter:

- DSIRE (Database of State Incentives for Renewables & Efficiency). (n.d.). Federal and state solar energy rebates and tax credits. https://www.dsireusa.org

- Low-Tech Magazine. (n.d.). Sustainable technologies that work. https://www.lowtechmagazine.com

- TEDx. (n.d.). Talks and demonstrations of sustainable innovation. https://www.ted.com/tedx

- NASA Tech Briefs. (n.d.). Engineering innovations and applied science for sustainability. https://www.techbriefs.com

- Gridlessness. (n.d.). Off-grid Canadian homestead with hybrid energy and barter systems [YouTube channel]. https://www.youtube.com/@Gridlessness

- YouTube. (2023). How I Built my Off-Grid Tiny House: Solar Panels, LiFePO4 Batteries & Smart-Home Controls [Video]. https://www.youtube.com/watch?v=8InYOnjWnGY

Supplementary Reading & Source Influence

These sources informed hybrid energy, DIY water systems, biogas construction, solar dehydration, off-grid gardening, and future tech covered in the chapter. They were not quoted directly but helped shape the practical frameworks and project guidance.

- National Renewable Energy Laboratory (NREL). (2023). Home solar and battery storage for off-grid living. https://www.nrel.gov
- The Humanure Handbook (Jenkins, J., 2019). A guide to composting human waste for soil health. Chelsea Green Publishing.
- Solar Cooking International. (n.d.). DIY solar dehydrators and cookers. https://www.solarcookers.org
- Practical Self Reliance. (n.d.). Biogas, greywater systems, and passive solar builds. https://www.practicalselfreliance.com
- Oasis Design. (n.d.). Water reuse and greywater system designs. https://www.oasisdesign.net
- The Provident Prepper. (n.d.). How to build and use emergency water filters. https://theprovidentprepper.org
- Mother Earth News. (n.d.). Homestead technology hacks and sustainable projects. https://www.motherearthnews.com
- Off Grid World. (n.d.). Hybrid solar/wind setups and off-grid innovation. https://offgridworld.com

Conclusion: You Can

The following source was directly quoted in the conclusion:

- Wildcraft, M. (n.d.). The Grow Network: Self-reliance, herbal medicine, and off-grid preparedness. https://thegrownetwork.com

Supplementary Reading & Source Influence

These sources were not quoted directly but informed the final chapter's structure for layered planning, resilience rhythms, and interconnected systems across water, energy, food, and community strategies.

- FEMA. (2021). 30 Days to Preparedness: Family emergency planning calendar. https://www.ready.gov
- The Provident Prepper. (n.d.). How to build a practical emergency preparedness plan. https://theprovidentprepper.org
- Practical Self Reliance. (n.d.). Sustainable system stacking: Linking off-grid water, energy, and food. https://www.practicalselfreliance.com
- Mother Earth News. (n.d.). Year-round homestead planning: Seasonal resilience and preparedness. https://www.motherearthnews.com
- Off Grid World. (n.d.). How to build redundancy in off-grid systems. https://offgridworld.com

- Grow Forage Cook Ferment. (n.d.). Starting with herbal resilience and backyard preparedness. https://www.growforagecookferment.com
- Low-Tech Magazine. (n.d.). Stacking simple systems for sustainable living. https://www.lowtechmagazine.com

Before You Go—Let's Keep Building Together

You've just walked through one of the most practical, complete guides to off-grid resilience. Now it's time to bring it to life.

SCAN ME

Ready to turn knowledge into action?

The **Off-Grid Survival Companion** is your next step—featuring printable checklists, system planners, troubleshooting charts, and decision tools built directly from this book. Access the full digital toolkit to start building your off-grid setup with clarity, confidence, and fewer costly mistakes.

And if you're ready to go beyond survival, **Book 2: Practical Projects for Off-Grid Homesteading** is coming in late 2025 or early 2026. It's your next-level guide to building a self-reliant homestead from the ground up—covering year-round food production, livestock and poultry care, preservation and fermentation, root cellars, low-labor land management, and long-term infrastructure that supports a sustainable off-grid life.

Just like Book 1, it will include step-by-step projects, printable checklists, troubleshooting guides, and practical systems you can build, adapt, and improve over time. Whether you're working with five acres or a backyard plot, this next book will help you create not just a setup that works, but a life that lasts.

This journey doesn't end here—it grows with you.

Keep building systems that serve you. Keep adapting as life shifts. You don't need perfection to move forward—just the next clear step. And you've already taken it.

Printed in Dunstable, United Kingdom

66046287R00165